PENGUIN HANDBOOKS

THE PATIENT'S ADVOCATE

Barbara Huttmann embarked on a nursing career at the age of forty-one, after having suffered through several horrifying hospital experiences, both as patient and as parent. The more she became involved in hospital work, the more dedicated she became to the concept of patient advocacy, on which she has lectured widely and to which she has devoted her expertise as Clinical Coordinator of Nursing Services in a major hospital in California. She has recently formed a professional health-care consultant service to hospitals, as well as a medical claims filing service to aid patients who find the business of filing medical claims an overwhelming task. She is currently continuing her graduate studies in nursing administration.

The
[Patient's Advocate]

Barbara Huttmann, R. N.

PENGUIN BOOKS

Penguin Books Ltd, Harmondsworth,
Middlesex, England
Penguin Books, 625 Madison Avenue,
New York, New York 10022, U.S.A.
Penguin Books Australia Ltd, Ringwood,
Victoria, Australia
Penguin Books Canada Limited, 2801 John Street,
Markham, Ontario, Canada L3R 1B4
Penguin Books (N.Z.) Ltd, 182–190 Wairau Road,
Auckland 10, New Zealand

First published in the United States of America in
simultaneous hardcover and paperback editions by
The Viking Press and Penguin Books 1981

LIBRARY OF CONGRESS CATALOGING IN PUBLICATION DATA
Huttmann, Barbara
The patient's advocate.
Includes index.
1. Hospitals. 2. Hospital care. 3. Hospital patients—
Legal status, laws, etc.—United States.
I. Title.
RA963.H87   1981b   362.1'1   80-26432
ISBN 0 14 046.492 1

Printed in the United States of America by
Fairfield Graphics, Fairfield, Pennsylvania
Set in CRT Century Schoolbook

Grateful acknowledgment is made to the California Hospital Association,
Sacramento, California, for permission to reprint medical forms from
the *California Hospital Association Consent Manual*, 10th Edition.
Copyright © California Hospital Association, 1978.

advocate, ˊad və kət, *n.* One who pleads
the cause of another; one who defends,
vindicates, or espouses a cause; a
pleader in favor of something; an
upholder; a defender; one who intercedes
on another's behalf.

Preface

Thirty-five years have passed since the day Mrs. Spoon, R.N., told me she would have the doctor cut my whole hand off if I didn't stop crying over the pain from my mangled thumb, but I remember her still. She was gone the next day. "She doesn't deserve to be a nurse," my mother said, and I was too young to realize that my mother had just played the patient's advocate and seen to it that Mrs. Spoon no longer haunted the pediatric ward of that hospital.

Future hospitalizations were no less traumatizing, filled with lurking shadows, clattering equipment, frightening sounds of pain through the halls, and a sense of impending doom heightened by wafts of ether and alcohol. Whether the hospital was in California or New York or anywhere in between, the sights, sounds, and smells were all the same—*menacing!* And they were no less menacing when *I* was the patient's advocate rather than the patient. I had a chronic case of hospitalphobia that grew worse every time I walked into one, even if I was only visiting a friend having a baby.

At the same time, I devoured books and films that had anything to do with medicine, and when I returned to college in middle age I found myself taking all the courses medical students take without even consciously thinking I was interested in medicine. I was "just having fun" with the chemistry, physics, microbiology, anatomy, and pathophysiology, hoping no one ever asked me to declare a major and become serious about being something other than a professional student.

When I wasn't in the lab mixing chemicals or dissecting animals, I was sitting at the bedside of one of my children, trying to help them survive the many hospitalizations it took to get them through childhood. On one such occasion it occurred to me that I was at a great disadvantage trying to calm the fears of a child when I was more terrified of the hospital than the child was.

Besides being terrified (of the unknown, I suspected), I was also angered by the horror tales I was adding to my hospital file. To each of the seventeen hospitalizations I had been involved in, I could attach two or three stories that would convince anyone a hospital is no place to go if you're sick. The turning point came when I sat beside my son's bed watching the nurses come and go while he told me about the dogs that were flying by his window. He was hallucinating, the foot of his casted leg was turning black, it was Thanksgiving Day, and the doctor was unavailable. At that moment I decided I would become a nurse so I would know how to get Alan out of such a situation if there ever was a next time.

I reasoned that I would get over my fears if I knew what was going on; I could reassure other people with hospitalphobia. In my fantasy I was going to don a white uniform and cap and float through the wards offering peace, protection, comfort, and compassion to the ill and frightened patients of the world.

"You are the patient's advocate," every nursing lecture had begun, but as it turned out there were a few major obstacles to that notion once I got out of school and into the unreal world of the hospital. To begin with I needed to do my job as a nurse. I could be a patient's advocate when I had time, but only on a limited basis, within the constraints of a busy bureaucratic institution governed by the elite medical community.

The more I talked with other nurses and with my friends about patient advocacy the bigger the problem grew. The nation is full of patients who have been denied their rights primarily because the public is victim to the mystique that surrounds the medical profession. Hospitalization is a game, of sorts, with its own set of rules and high stakes, and if you don't know the rules by which the game is played, you stand a good chance of losing. "It's really very elementary," I told my friends, "you just have to know who holds the trump card, how to play the tricks to your own advantage, and when to slap your trump card down on the table to win. The only problem is that there are no rule books for playing that game."

"So write one," my friends told me, "what are you waiting

for?" Within an hour we had thirty chapters of a book outlined, destined to answer all the questions they had wanted to ask on occasions when they had been patients. Not surprisingly, the questions they had were the same ones I had encountered as a patient, as the mother of patients, and as a nurse. In attempting to answer those questions while writing this book, I found myself reexamining all of my early fears as well as all of my hard-won experience and education.

Briefly, my position is that every patient is in a disadvantaged state caused by illness or accident but compounded by hospitalization, and that his or her ignorance regarding the rules of the hospital game can serve to enhance the disease process and retard healing. Cardiac arrests have even been precipitated by the fear and anger incited by hospitalization, and I look back on my own days as a hospital patient, and on those of my children, and I think "If I knew then what I know now...." If we *all* had known how to play the game, we could have spent our energy getting well.

Contrary to the opinion of many health-care professionals, "a little bit of knowledge" can actually decrease the risk in the game, and coincidentally decrease the escalating costs of hospitalization, yet another source of fear and worry to patients. This then is "a little bit of knowledge," an outline of the most important rules you need to know to play the game to your advantage. Here is the information that I as a nurse and patient's advocate would want to provide for all patients, the tools that could have kept those menacing shadows from my room when I was an uninformed hospital patient. Along with these bits of advice, I hope I can also pass along a sense of the peace, protection, comfort, and compassion that I try to give to every patient I meet—for these qualities can be as important as competent medical care when you or someone you love is ill.

Acknowledgments

For inspiration, aspiration, and dedication I am grateful to Kip and Lee; Jim; Peter Hein, M.D.; Lani Sward, R.N.; Faith Mahan, R.N.; Barbara Talento, R.N.; Penny Holland, R.N.; Katinka Matson; John Brockman; Amy Pershing; Barbara Burn; Dr. Andrew Montana; Dr. Pat Wegner; my mother, Audrey; my husband, Dean; and our children, Alan, Laurie, and Kim. Without their contributions to life and consequently to this book—"patient advocacy" would still be little more than buzzwords.

"All the genuine, deep delight of life is in showing people the mud-pies you have made; and life is at its best when we confidingly recommend our mud-pies to each other's sympathetic consideration."
—J. M. THORBURN

Contents

The Patient's Advocate

1

Who Shall Be
The Patient's Advocate?

Four of us waited: the surgeon, his partner, Kevin, and I. Only Kevin had no idea what we were all waiting for. His was the abdomen with the small stab wound about an inch below his navel, and the surgeon's stethoscope rested there now, listening. Two minutes of listening made the decision that would change Kevin's immediate future, if not his life.

Dr. Major shook his head and handed the stethoscope to his partner, Dr. Ryan, and he too listened, then shook his head. They gave each other knowing glances. "We'll go talk to your parents now," Dr. Major told Kevin. I followed them into the hall.

"Prepare him for surgery," Dr. Major ordered. "Can you do it within an hour?"

"What kind of surgery?"

"Open heart, of course," and they both laughed at their own joke. A benevolent look crossed Dr. Major's face and he held my arm as we walked down the hall together, his apology for having mocked me. "He has a perforated bowel. We'll have to repair it."

"But I heard bowel sounds just an hour ago," I protested. The doctors stepped into the elevator and Dr. Major repeated, "Just get things rolling for surgery."

They had both borrowed my stethoscope. We had all listened to the same abdomen. The stab wound was closed, at least from what I could see, and the laboratory reports were good—no indication that Kevin was bleeding internally. How did they know his bowel was perforated?

"How would you decide whether or not a quarter-inch stab in the abdomen with a pencil would have perforated the bowel?" I asked a surgeon who happened to be writing orders at the nurses' station.

"Simple. Look at his blood work, listen for bowel sounds." He was too busy to question why I asked, and I would not have wanted him to know I was doubting another surgeon's decision.

My supervisor listened to the story, looked annoyed and frustrated. "What do you want me to do?" she asked, and I had no idea what she *could* do, or what I could do. We stood in silence and then she challenged me, "Are you a doctor? What gives you the right to challenge a doctor? Would you like to go to the chief of staff and tell him your story? Do you like your job?"

The thought of challenging a doctor was *almost* as sobering as the thought of a fourteen-year-old boy, victim of a schoolyard fracas, going to surgery needlessly. "I was a mother before I was a nurse," I told her. "I have a fourteen-year-old son, and I wouldn't want him to go through the trauma of surgery if there were any way out."

"I repeat. Do you like your job? Only the parents can stop the surgery."

"I'll talk to the parents then." But I knew I would find them sitting in the lobby drowning in fear, without the slightest clue that they had any choice in the matter. The doctors were too busy to answer their questions, they told me, and they had no idea what kind of surgery Kevin would have, but: "The doctor says he needs it, so he needs it."

Their conversation made it obvious that anything I might say would only increase their fear. Surgery would indeed take place within the hour, with their sanction.

DR. "GOD"

How do you play patient's advocate to people who don't want an advocate or don't even know they need an advocate? I wondered. Silently I cursed whatever forces have us all believing that "doctor" and "God" are synonymous terms for someone who may or may not answer you, at his own leisure and discretion, in his own way. And if you don't get an answer, or if you don't understand the answer, you think it's something you probably didn't need to know anyway. He'll watch over you, and "all things work together for good."

Such is the nature of the medical profession that we mystify the art and walk the hallowed halls of hospitals speaking in hushed tones. Is it the fear of awakening to the inevitable truth, the knowledge that physical life is finite? Is it that same fear that causes us all to become so vulnerable before the medical profession, that turns us into little children who approach the medical community in blind faith? Is it that same fear that forces us to bend over, lie flat, hold still, say "ahh," stop crying, take a deep breath, drink this, remove your clothes, sign here, hold your tongue out, raise your left foot, ask your doctor, void in the cup, and pay before you leave, please?

The patient role is one of submission and obedience. "Trust the doctors and nurses, dear, they know what they're doing. Just do what they tell you." And he who for twenty-five years has controlled a major conglomerate rolls over, scrunches his body into a fetal position—"See no evil, hear no evil, think no evil, say no evil"—and becomes a child in the face of the medical community.

THE FUTURE OF MEDICINE

"The worm has turned," or at least is *beginning* to turn. No longer does the health-care consumer accept the traditional role of "good patient," the one who does as he's told, asks no awkward questions, and doesn't make waves. The frequent denial of fundamental rights to courtesy, privacy, and, most of all, information has brought the ultimate form of consumer rebellion—malpractice suits.

The large-scale survival of people into mature years has given us a population prone to the difficult illnesses of aging, but the medical advances that treat these illnesses also prolong life and expose the affected patients to increased amounts of medical care, some of which will be legally negligent. Just as an increase of cars on the highway increases your chances of being involved in an accident, your chances of receiving legally negligent care increase with more frequent use of health-care services.

Increasing confrontations between consumer and health-care provider are barely the tip of the iceberg of a major change in American society. The social revolution of consumer action, which stretches from air conditioners to tax reform, may, in the long run, have a much more dramatic impact on health care than would any series of exotic scientific discoveries.

As many physicians are quick to point out, the growth in malpractice suits also can be seen as the result of medical progress. The amount of medical care offered has grown in both complexity and size, with medical error the unfortunate by-product.

In 1977 well over forty thousand doctors (or about one of every nine in active practice) were named in malpractice claims. Health, Education and Welfare (which is now called Health and Human Services) investigators claimed that more than seven out of every one hundred persons who were admitted to a hospital could expect to be injured by the treatment they received while patients. Upward of two million injuries occur in hospitals annually, with about four hundred thousand of them caused by negligence.

There definitely are flaws in the medical system, which increases the probability of medical injury, but there are also flaws in the patients' perception of the services they can expect to receive for their health-care dollars.

Mr. Clarence Cowan was one example of false expectations and he wound up as an HEW statistic, a "hospital injury." Clarence was admitted for injuries suffered in an auto accident. He *loved* hospitalization and the constant attention of the nurses around the clock, but he particularly loved the nighttime because most other patients slept and he had the whole staff to himself.

One night, when several of the patients on the same ward as Clarence were in precarious condition, the lack of personal attention bothered him until he could stand it no longer. He didn't care that of all the patients he was the most nearly "well." Attention was what he demanded—and got! He set fire to his bedspread with a cigarette. The next day while completing the incident report for the hospital's insurance carriers I asked him if he had fallen asleep with the lit cigarette in his hand, and he blithely replied, "No, I was awake. I know it was a really dumb thing to do. I tried to put the fire out with my water cup, but that didn't work. Listen, damn it, I pay $265 a day in this place and I deserve some attention when I want it."

The incident report became one of HEW's statistics as do all unusual occurrences in hospitals, but the fault cannot always be laid at the doorstep of the hospital or the doctor.

THE PATIENT'S ROLE

Probably a majority of patients still enter treatment and undergo a variety of tests and surgery without a clear understanding of the nature of their condition, what can be done about it, and what their role in a cure might be. They "trust the doctor." Patients should know one very important fact—the doctor does hold the winning card, at least right now.

The current trend is for the courts to view the doctor-patient relationship as a partnership in decision-making, rather than a medical monopoly. This means you will not be allowed to holler "Foul, I've been injured" without the physician and the judge saying, "But, you were a partner in this decision. If the doctor has been wrong, you also have been wrong." You had better have a clear understanding of what's involved if you are going to be considered a "partner."

You'll be forced to weigh alternatives, you'll have to compare physicians' opinions, you might even have to decide between quality and quantity of life. Only you can decide how much is too much pain or how much is too much stress. Your uterus sags, says the doctor, do you want a hysterectomy? Actually, he won't say "sags," he'll say, "Well, Mrs. Jones, you've got a prolapsed uterus and eventually it will have to come out or it'll start bothering you. You've had your family, what do you need a uterus for? I recommend we remove it."

Unless you know that a "prolapsed" uterus is a "sagging" uterus, and that uteruses, and also faces, arches, breasts, and derrieres, all sag with age, you might be very tempted to "trust the doctor" and have your uterus removed, which is what thousands have done in what is now referred to as "the hysterectomy craze." Only you can decide how much sag is too much. Only you can weigh the sag against the potential problems of estrogen depletion and the expense of estrogen-replacement therapy. (This is covered more thoroughly in Chapter 7—Surgery.) You must know all your options before you can make an intelligent decision.

There was a time when health care had more charitable ingredients than it has now. In fact, most hospitals were run by religious organizations and were considered charitable institutions. However, those days have long since passed; health care is now the second largest industry in the nation. It is a business similar to any other and the rules by which one plays are no different from those in any other business. Only the stakes are higher—and your life is one of those stakes.

Suppose you are left a $100,000 inheritance and decide to invest it in real estate. Your friendly real-estate broker tells you the best hedge against inflation is commercial property and, besides, it helps beat Uncle Sam's April 15 tax bite. "Sounds like a good idea," you say, "let me talk it over with my wife." Your wife says, "Well, Harry's been in the real-estate business for years. He knows what he's doing. Why don't you trust him? Go ahead, buy the piece of property he tells you to." But you, being like most people, are not comfortable placing $100,000 in one man's hands and telling him, "I trust you, Harry, go ahead and buy a piece of property for me."

You wouldn't place $100,000 in one man's hands to do with as he saw fit, yet if you are the average American, you place your life in the hands of one man, your physician, and tell him, "I'll do whatever you think best." This is grossly unfair to him—you might later sue for malpractice—and no less unfair to you since many injuries are permanent. Ignorance is not bliss when dealing with the medical community and, increasingly, you will be expected to make decisions crucial to your health care.

THE INFORMATION YOU NEED

If you're going to be a participant, rather than a dependent bystander, you need just what's being produced for you in great quantity these days—volumes and volumes of literature designed to clue you in on how to protect and improve your health. Almost half the nation is jogging while the other half is dieting and those who aren't doing either are reading about it and feeling guilty because they're not.

You can read about how to protect yourself from heart attacks, how to keep from becoming a sugarholic, what to do if you have diabetes, how to learn to live with arthritis, what exercises to do to slim your hips, what to eat to keep your cholesterol count low, and how much vitamin E you might require to place your sexual potency at its peak. All this is fine so far as it goes. You need all the information you can get to help you stay well. If all these books could be counted on to keep you out of the hospital, you wouldn't need this one, but chances are that someday you will be a hospital patient, if only to give birth to a baby or have some wisdom teeth pulled. At the very least, you'll be a relative of, or visitor to, someone in the hospital and will need to know more than what these how-to books can give you.

You need to know which forms to sign and which ones might trap you. You need to know how to get a second opinion without angering your favorite doctor. You need to know who is the nurse and who the dietician. You need to know how to translate the "foreign language" of hospitalese.

You also need to know which tests you should endure and which you *must* reject. You need to know whether to tie that well-ventilated gown in the back or the front. You need to know how to find out what's on your chart. You need to know when to go to the emergency room and when to stay home. You need to know how to save money on your medical bills. You need to know how to avoid unnecessary diagnostics, lab tests, X rays, and surgery.

You should know what a "code blue" is, why you don't see more of your doctor, how to avoid swallowing other patients' pills, how to get a pill instead of a shot, what you have to pay and what the insurance carrier pays, what an IV is for, what it's like to be in intensive care, where to register a complaint, how to "fire" your doctor, why you don't have the right to die. Most of all you need to know how to approach the medical community and hospitalization as you would any other venture—as an informed, concerned consumer.

Since you are the "responsible" party when you're hospitalized, it follows that you can't afford to leave your options on the doorstep when you're admitted. You are obligated to understand what your responsibilities and rights are.

And that's a real toughy! How are you, already weakened and considerably compromised, supposed to shoulder all the responsibility that hospitalization demands? To begin with, you need to bring an advocate to the hospital with you; you'd better learn to be one for someone else too. This is the guidance you can expect in the next several pages. Then you need to learn how to conserve your energy so you can fend for yourself when your own advocate goes home.

How do you conserve energy? It takes a lot to deal with the "unknowns," all those silent fears that lurk like shadows waiting to inflict pain or humiliation. The fewer the "unknowns," the greater your energy, which you need to regain your health. "If I knew then what I know now" is said to me time and time again by patients who went through hospitalization scared out of their wits, shuddering from the "unknowns." I'll be telling you some of their tales throughout this book.

Basically, we'll be focusing on adult care in "acute" hospitals—"acute" as opposed to convalescent, mental, or rehabilitation hospitals, since the last three are deserving of a more in-depth study than space here will allow.

In addition, most of what is discussed will refer to fee-for-service hospitals, those in which you pay a separate charge for each service performed, as opposed to health-maintenance organizations or prepaid plans, in which you pay a flat monthly rate to cover any and all services whether you use them or not. Since 80 percent of your health-care dollars go toward hospitalization and the majority of Americans currently obtain fee-for-service care, you'll probably be seeing that term often in newspaper and magazine articles.

Chapter 2—Before You Enter the Hospital tells a little about the basics of a hospital, which should help you picture it as the ordinary business organization with which you are already familiar. Then you'll go on to the details that get you through the first day and on toward being a "professional" hospital patient.

Each chapter is intended to be independent, but don't miss the special section on how to read a prescription in Chapter 9—Hospitalese, because though you may never be a patient, you're bound to be a consumer of at least one prescription in your lifetime—you have rights, obligations, and responsibilities there, too.

By the time you finish the last chapter you should be prepared to approach the medical community as a well-informed consumer—an advocate for yourself or for someone else who is depending on you to see them through hospitalization.

YOU NEED AN ADVOCATE

There is one inescapable fact that I really want to impress upon you before you venture through the doors of the hospital. It is *your* body, *your* health, and *your* responsibility that is of primary importance during hospitalization. If you are very ill, which you are likely to be if you are a patient these days, you owe it to yourself to choose an advocate to see you through hospitalization. Not everyone is the appropriate choice. The primary characteristic of an advocate is that your well-being is crucial to that individual, which means your advocate should probably be your spouse, lover, and/or very best friend. If this person to whom you are crucial faints at the sight of blood, can't stand conflict, would rather switch than fight, and is totally intimidated by doctors and nurses, then choose someone else. How about that aggressive relative who picks a fight at every family gathering because he stands on principle and never backs down! Maybe he would be a good choice.

Perhaps you have a supersalesman among your bevy of friends. He's a good choice because he can joke his way through a crisis and come out winning, most of the time. Any sort of diplomat is perfect as an advocate and someone among your acquaintances probably stands out in your mind right now.

If your choice is narrowed down to one, who meets none of the above criteria, that's okay, *any* advocate is better than none. If you go into the hospital without an advocate it would be like going on a safari without a guide.

Now you have the message: When the doctor says, "You must be hospitalized," your first thought should be whom to enlist as your advocate.

CHAPTER

2

Before You Enter
the Hospital

More often than not you'll have some advance notice that you are to be hospitalized, in which case there is some time to get organized.

Your first question will probably be "How long will I be there?" The doctor's reply will probably be "That depends...." While it may seem it is up to him and partially up to you, it is also up to hospital policy, your insurance company, and several regulating agencies. In every hospital there is a utilization review department that usually has the final say in determining your length of stay, based on national averages for your diagnosis, with some flexibility for unique circumstances. "Average" for most diagnoses is six days and you would probably be safe in planning on that length of stay as a rule of thumb.

More about your insurance policy in Chapter 13—The Patient's Paperwork, but for now find out what expenses will be covered and plan accordingly. Remember, a hospital is a business organization and wants to know how your bill will be paid before it even puts you in a bed. If your insurance does not cover you completely, call the hospital business office and discuss your options. They may offer you a number of alternatives or may insist on advance payment of several hundred dollars—you wouldn't like to be turned away on the day of admission.

SELECTING THE HOSPITAL

Most patients assume they have no choice in selecting a hospital, but this is not necessarily true. There are different kinds of hospitals and different types of needs that are served within them. In the hospital world we judge hospital size by the number of beds it contains, which can be very misleading, but as a rule of thumb it does define the terms "large" and "small." "Large" is anything over 500, "average" is 200 to 500, and "small" is anything under 200. To find out if you're dealing with a small or large hospital, call the admitting office and ask about the bed capacity. Size really matters when you have a complex disease or are contemplating having some very intricate surgery. As you read along, you'll be able to tell when a "large" hospital is imperative if you're to get the best care.

Most often the large hospitals are affiliated with medical schools, are tax-supported, and employ full-time physicians. How much you pay for care is dependent upon your financial status—you might be charged *more* than in a private hospital or you might be charged less. Large-scale research takes place in a large hospital, which is one reason it's a good place to be if your condition is comparatively rare.

Laurie was a four-year-old with gray-black teeth that had been examined by five pediatricians and six dentists, all in different cities, all saying the same thing: "Tsk, tsk. Such a pretty little girl. What a shame. I've never seen teeth like that before; can't tell you what the problem could be. Anyone else in the family have black teeth? That's really interesting."

Eventually one doctor referred Laurie to a major medical center, a huge teaching facility for "last resort," "no hope" type problems. Nine physicians gathered and looked at her teeth under ultraviolet lights. "Hey, I know what that is!" exclaimed one of the doctors. "How about that! I've only seen it once before. It comes from the mother having taken tetracycline during pregnancy, it happens in utero first trimester. How about that!" The nine strode out, all of them looking very solemn except the one who had just won the game of one-upmanship. Obviously, they had forgotten that Laurie and her mom were there for some purpose other than to see which doctor would "win" the game that morning. This is why you may feel that care in a large medical center is usually very impersonal, although it does have the distinct advantage of great amounts of diagnostic skill, brilliance, and experience gathered under one roof.

In a thousand-bed teaching hospital the complexity of producing the meals is enormous, so gourmet food is low on the priority list. Furnishings aren't usually planned by a decorator, the halls are likely to be narrow and cluttered, each room houses a large number of patients, and the bathroom might be quite far from your bed. You might be a bank president in bed next to a skid-row indigent—the care for both will be the same. Research, diagnosis, and treatment are the large hospital's business—all else is superfluous.

The smaller hospitals vary considerably. You might know them by such terms as proprietary or community hospitals. They may be owned by a religious organization, a group of physicians, stockholders, a corporation, or a community district. Some are nonprofit, and others are profit-making.

While their profit structure is of little apparent consequence to you, there is one item I would like to bring to your attention. In a hospital run for profit on a fee-for-service basis, profiteering has been known to occur. For instance, the respiratory-therapy department in some (if not all) hospitals offers one of the largest returns on investment. The more frequently doctors order respiratory treatments, the greater the profit. In fact, I've been told of a doctor-owned hospital where *every* postoperative patient is given respiratory treatments routinely, though it is a well-known fact that not all postoperative patients *need* respiratory therapy. In Chapter 13 you'll read more about such "backward incentives," those practices which increase the bank accounts of the medical community.

Your choice of a hospital isn't so easy—that is most often dictated by your choice of a physician. He must have staff privileges at a hospital in order to admit his patients there. While some doctors have privileges at many hospitals, others are allowed to admit their patients in only one or two. This says less about the physician's quality of practice than about how he cares to define the scope of his practice. For instance, a southern California cardiologist specializing in coronary-artery–bypass surgery is on the staff of only three of the seventeen hospitals within a fifty-mile radius of his office. Those three are the ones with the sophisticated equipment for his specialty and the only ones in which he chooses to practice.

A gynecologist in the same area is on the staff of only two of the hospitals, both within walking distance of his office. At the larger one, he performs most of his surgery, while he does therapeutic abortions at the smaller since the larger one is Catholic and does not allow abortions. He does not want to spend all his time driving to visit his hospital patients, so he has asked for staff privileges at only two hospitals. If you are his patient you will be limited to one of the two.

If your doctor has staff privileges at several hospitals, it might help you to "shop" for a hospital since there can be a considerable difference in rates as well as services. Some hospitals allow fathers in the delivery room and others don't. Some might have special wards for stroke rehabilitation, alcohol rehabilitation, oncology (cancer), and burns, while others may have none of these but instead may specialize in psychiatric, neurologic, or metabolic disorders. If a hospital has a special program, you can be certain the care is more sophisticated for that particular specialty, a fact that can be very important to your recovery.

Standards for hospitals are rigid, as you might expect, but "rigid" is relative if you are the patient. The "Big Daddy" of regulators is the Joint Commission on Accreditation of Hospitals (JCAH) and a hospital covets its approval, especially if it intends to be reimbursed for Medicare patients. The scope of its accreditation extends to such matters as the hospital's relationship to the community it serves, personnel policies and practices, sanitation, ventilation, storage, methods of record-keeping, peer-review policies, patients' rights, standards for nutritional care, standards for nursing care, library services as well as the preparing, labeling, and sterilizing of drugs, just to name a few.

An inspection team of physicians and registered nurses tours the hospital, writes its recommendations for changes, and then approves (or disapproves) the hospital for accreditation for a period of either one or two years.

If a hospital is not JCAH approved, I would be hesitant about being a patient there. Look for the framed seal of approval displayed in the lobby or call and ask, "Is this hospital JCAH approved?"

In addition to JCAH inspection, there are agencies concerned with particular aspects of the hospital, such as safety, infection control, utilization review, pharmacy, etc., who also exert control. This is not to say that all hospitals are kept flawless by regulating agencies—you know how the speed limit doesn't always keep us moving slowly on the highways—but to let you know that many agencies are keeping their eyes on hospitals. At least 25 percent of your hospital dollar is spent on paperwork demanded by these regulating agencies.

MAKING "RESERVATIONS"

If the hospital offers private, semiprivate, or ward accommodations, call the admitting office ahead of time to ask what the difference is in the rates. You'll probably be surprised at how little it will cost you personally to have a private room if your insurance will only pay for semiprivate. It is often as little as $5 a day, and well worth it if you covet privacy. While you may have a choice, and should certainly advise the admitting office of that choice in advance, the hospital, like a hotel, has only so many of each type of room and you may not get what you prefer. There have been some very ugly scenes when the admitting person has brought a patient to a room and the patient immediately decides the view, the roommate, or the location is not suitable and declares: "If I have to have this room, I'm leaving."

A typical day in the life of those who assign rooms in the hospital might give you the best picture of how you end up in a room that seems intolerable to you: the admitting office has a "chessboard" of sorts that shows who is in which bed and what beds are empty. They also have a list of who will be admitted that day, what the diagnoses are, whether the patients are male or female, smokers or nonsmokers, and their ages. Suppose there are ten beds empty in the hospital and eight patients to be admitted. Eight of the beds are semiprivate and two are private. Six of the patients have requested private rooms.

The first consideration will be to isolate any patients who might have something contagious and they will be given the private rooms. Unique needs will be considered next. For example, if one of the patients is to have a wired jaw and will be unable to speak, that patient will be placed with one able to summon help or perhaps assist in other ways. Next, males will be placed with males, and smokers will be placed with smokers. There will also be an effort to separate like kinds of surgery—patients recover at different speeds and often become upset if their roommate who had the same surgery appears to be recovering faster.

Patients with certain problems have a very low tolerance to infection; thus they will be placed at the greatest distance from those who could be suspected to be harboring contaminating organisms. In a "bed crunch," however, all the rules are broken and patients are placed wherever there's an empty bed. The problem is that you have no way of knowing whether or not a "bed crunch" exists before you arrive, because the room assignment you receive may be arbitrary. For satisfaction, your best insurance is to call the admitting office the day before you go to the hospital, tell them your circumstances, and place your room request. If at all possible, they will honor that request.

Like hotels, the checkout time in most hospitals is around 11:00 a.m. Housekeeping takes over when the patient is discharged and the bed is made ready for the next patient. You will probably be told to present yourself for admission between 1:00 and 3:00 p.m., but no matter what time you arrive, in most hospitals the "day" begins at noon on your bill. In many cases, arrival from 1:00 to 3:00 p.m. is a perfect example of "nursing the system" rather than "nursing the patient." You may not be scheduled to have surgery until 3:00 p.m. the following day, but you will still be admitted at the same time as the patient who is having surgery at 6:30 a.m. the next morning. You will be told that this is for time for lab tests and "etceteras."

Actually, there are many situations when you can save a whole hospital "day" or at least several hours of jangled nerves by arriving for admission much later than you were scheduled. You just need to know what the "etceteras" are and act accordingly. One of those "etceteras" might be the preoperative physical exam that could be done in the doctor's office a few days before surgery if you insist. Each hospital has its own list of "routine" lab tests before surgery (watch for insurance rules to

abolish this policy; to cut costs, the government is going to prohibit routine tests), but these could also be done on an outpatient basis before you're admitted.

If you plan a late arrival, inform the admitting office of your
arrival time, and be sure you arrive when you say you will.
Don't ask for a meal after you get there. The kitchen is probably
the department least able to deal with inconvenience, and a late-
meal request involves many more people than only those in the
kitchen.

WHAT TO BRING

The single most important item to bring to the hospital is your
insurance card. Don't bring just the numbers; the admitting
clerk will want a photocopy of the whole card.

You'll also need to bring the name and address of someone
close to you who can be notified about changes in your condition.
The business office will probably want the name and address of
your employer, your social security number, and/or advance
payment of your bill. Remember, the hospital is a business first
and foremost. It uses the same means of checking your credit
status and collecting accounts receivable as any of your other
creditors.

As for what to put in your suitcase, pack what you think you
might need. All of it will be available at the hospital anyhow, so
if you've arrived under emergency conditions, don't worry, the
hospital will provide—but at a fee. Creature comforts such as
toothpaste, comb and brush, shampoo, lotion, razors, deodorant,
and slippers are your own expense when purchased through the
hospital, so don't expect your insurance policy to pay for them.
The cost for these items will be triple what you would pay at
your own corner drugstore.

In intensive care units only the most basic items are allowed,
while in other areas nothing more than a bathrobe should be
added to your list of essentials.

Don't bring your wedding ring, watch, or cash over $3. Statis-
tics indicate there will be fifty-six different people in and out of
your room in an average day. Your room assignment could be
changed any number of times, to say nothing of the fact that

closet and drawer space in hospitals is severely limited. So do yourself and the hospital a favor by leaving home anything you don't feel you can afford to lose.

Fire-safety rules, pacemakers, and monitoring equipment prohibit the use of most electrical appliances in hospitals. In addition, can you imagine what would happen to the hospital's electricity bill if every patient brought the assortment of electrical grooming appliances we are accustomed to using these days?

Shaving can be a problem. In fact, I shaved off the first three layers of a patient's chin when I was a neophyte nurse, using a hospital safety razor designed for shaving areas other than the face. To avoid similar mishaps, bring your own safety razor or preferably a battery-operated shaver and shave yourself if at all possible—only you instinctively know all the nooks and crannies of your face. Next best choice is to have your wife shave you since a really good shave takes more time than most nurses have.

Hospital pillows are usually filled with a crunchy material that can be either sterilized or discarded, so don't expect a comfortable one unless you bring your own—and don't bring your own unless you're sure you'll be alert enough to keep track of it throughout your stay. There won't be anyone to separate yours from the hospital's if yours should happen to get into the laundry. The same is true of blankets, since most hospitals contract with a linen-rental company, and the linen brought into the hospital today may be carted off in a truck tomorrow, never to return.

Most patients bring along magazines, books, puzzles, newspapers, needlework, or any number of diversionary items, but one of the most peculiar characteristics of hospitalization is the inability to concentrate. There is a certain amount of disorientation that accompanies hospitalization for anyone, and it is very difficult to attend to anything other than the constant interruptions by the staff. Gone are the days when one goes to the hospital "for a rest"; it is unlikely that you will be kept hospitalized if you are well enough to need entertainment. Of course, if you are one of the few who requires a lengthy hospitalization for something such as traction, your friends and family will no doubt use a great deal of imagination in providing entertainment. But if you intended to finish an afghan, write a book, or prepare the year-end report while hospitalized, forget it—it probably won't get done.

Most hospitals provide televisions, so a tv schedule would be nice to have. Often it is available through the ward clerk, so ask for one if you forget to bring it with you. It's also nice to have your friends' telephone numbers (though you pay for every call) and to take along your address book, writing paper, and postage stamps if you intend to write to anyone.

MEDICATIONS

Andy was a patient with a pages-long list of ailments that he had tended over a long period of time. When he was admitted the doctor ordered no medications for him because it was obvious his system had become confused with reactions to this and counterreactions to that. As the days went by, he confounded the medical and nursing staff with symptoms that seemed totally unrelated to this list of ailments. He slept for hours upon hours, stumbled when he walked, slurred his speech most of the time, and generally acted confused.

Though he answered negatively to the routine admitting question, "Have you brought any medications from home?" it turned out he had pills of every color and description buried away under his pillow, in his drawers, and in every pocket of the clothes he had brought with him. He was afraid to be without the medications he had been taking at home and so had been subjected to many diagnostic tests that could have been avoided had the doctor known Andy was producing his symptoms by medicating himself.

On the other hand, there is no automatic communication system that tells your doctor or the nurses that you have been taking a birth-control pill every day and need to continue, or that the digitalis that you take daily is the only reason your heart still beats strongly. You must tell your doctor exactly what you take at home as a routine. The chart in his office is not sent to the hospital and, contrary to popular opinion, there is no magic little black book in his pocket that tells him the medications you routinely need or the ones that are known to cause adverse reactions for you.

To be sure you get what you need, take a list with you to the hospital and read it to the nurse who admits you and again to the doctor on his first visit. Tell them the drug name, strength, and how often you take it. The doctor may want to alter your routine medications, but insist on clarification if your pill cup arrives with drugs unfamiliar to you. This is *your* responsibility and one that is far too often neglected in the hospital. Patients assume the doctor has ordered everything needed, the nurse assumes the patient and doctor have worked it all out, and the doctor assumes the patient has worked it out with the nurse—but it's not so!

FOR ADVOCATES

If the patient has a chronic disease controlled by medications (diabetes, seizures, hypertension, or estrogen deficiency), it's a good idea for the advocate to ask the nurse in charge if the patient will be taking the same drugs he was taking at home. This is just reinforcement to insure that this often neglected matter is resolved before trouble occurs.

YOUR MEDICAL HISTORY

A large part of medical practice is sleuthing and you'd probably be surprised to learn the number of unanswered questions that abound in the biological sciences. For instance, did you know that you could eat a diet that is completely cholesterol-free and still end up with an abnormally high cholesterol level in your blood? Why? Who knows? The doctor is a sophisticated detective of sorts. He gathers all the facts, shuffles them around a bit, and hopes to arrive at a conclusion that fits.

Some of the most important facts he will use are generated from your history and physical (H&P). Have you had previous surgery, headaches, major illnesses, joint pains, fainting spells, visual difficulties, muscle weakness? When, for how long, and how often? When did your periods start, are they regular, how old are your children, what major diseases have your parents and grandparents had, how much alcohol do you consume a day, how many cigarettes, what kind of work do you do, have you been dependent upon drugs, do you have bowel or bladder problems?

Most patients become annoyed when they're asked the same questions over and over again, yet each question provides one more piece to the jigsaw puzzle that is you, and the same question asked a third time might trigger your memory to provide the most important clue of all. Arrive at the hospital with a written list of the most important facts and dates pertaining to your medical history, and you can save yourself the agitation of racking your brains when you're already not feeling your best.

ALLERGIES

We had given Linda all the medication at our disposal for pain relief and she continued to moan and groan, pleading for more medication. Finally, we got her doctor to change the order to a more powerful pain reliever and we shot it into her with a sigh of anticipated relief. The syringe was just emptied when she asked what the medication was; we told her, and she flew into a rage. "Why in the hell would you give me that? Dr. Agros knows I'm allergic to it. He didn't order that. He wouldn't order something I'm allergic to. Are you trying to kill me?"

Every patient's medication card has any allergies written in red and Linda's indicated no such allergies. In fact, she had forgotten she was allergic to that particular drug. She was also allergic to iodine dyes, which are often used in diagnostic tests, and several foods, but she assumed her doctor knew her allergies because she had considered him her personal physician for many years. This is an unrealistic assumption if one considers that the practice of the average physician includes hundreds of patients. And when we page him to ask for a change in medication he may answer us from a booth in a restaurant, a gas station, or a phone on the freeway. He relies on you to tell us your allergies when you're admitted.

Somewhere in your home you should keep a health file on all members of your family. It should include the dates of major illnesses and what medications were taken during these illnesses, the names of any pain relievers taken and how effective they were, the dates of any surgery and the effects of anesthesia, the dates of any diagnostic tests and the reactions to them, and the names of any foods which have caused problems. Your own list *must* go to the hospital with you or be available to those who might be responsible for you if you go to the hospital in an emergency situation. Such a list could save your life, since there are drugs which may cause you slight problems in one dosage and prove lethal in slightly higher dosages. This is your responsibility and yours alone!

ENTERING THE HOSPITAL—A CHECKLIST

1. Ask your doctor to tell you the approximate length of your stay.
2. Contact the hospital business office regarding your financial obligations.
3. Advise the hospital admitting office of your room preference; be prepared to tell them your diagnosis, physician's name, date of admittance, date of surgery, your age, and whether or not you're a smoker.
4. Ask the admitting office what time you are scheduled for surgery and what time it expects you to arrive; if that time is not convenient for you, ask when and where you should appear for lab tests the day before your admittance. If you plan a late arrival, advise the office accordingly.
5. Gather your pertinent papers:
   a. Insurance card and forms
   b. Social Security number
   c. Driver's license
   d. Name, address, and phone number of your spouse or a friend who will be available in emergency
   e. Name, address, and phone number of a credit reference (a relative who lives locally is a good choice)
   f. Name, address, and phone number of your employer
   g. List of allergies

   h. Medical history
   i. List of medications you are currently taking
6. Pack a small suitcase including:
   a. Toothbrush and paste
   b. Deodorant
   c. Comb and brush
   d. Slippers
   e. Bathrobe
   f. Shaving gear
   g. Friends' phone numbers and addresses
   h. Note pad and pencil
   i. Paper bag to send your clothes home in
7. Don't bring jewelry or more than $3 in cash.

CHAPTER
3
Day One

ADMISSION TIME

If the smell of crisis assaults your nose as you make your feeble entrance into the hospital and paste on your best "I'm not scared" look, you're already one step ahead of many who enter—your sense of smell is at least intact.

Actually, the smell is of alcohol, which is to the hospital what the scent of yeast is to the bakery. *Every* hospital worker totes a pocket full of crisis scents (alcohol swabs) and you'll find they're used for everything from polishing the entry-door handle to cushioning an abrasive finger splint.

You need to look for the information desk, which is not too unlike the registration desk in a hotel. Chances are your body will be sending out the most common distress signal found in people about to become patients—your bladder is screaming to be emptied. You're normal! Hospital architects are sharp, they've placed the bathrooms right near the information desk.

The clerk at the information desk is usually a volunteer in a pink or yellow uniform, and she and her cohorts are your number one friends, ordinary people like you and me, devoted to making you happy, the unofficial public relations people of the hospital, the mascots and darlings of the staff. Even if it's an off day and your clerk is crabby, the volunteer is your friend, one who will not poke, probe, sting or stick you. She'll show you to the admitting office, where you'll fill out all the legal forms, and

FOR ADVOCATES

This is a good time for you to take note of the comforts you'll need later: public bathrooms, phones, newsstand, gift and flower shop, visiting hours, and the cafeteria. The lobby is where you will wait while your patient is in surgery, and the clerk at the information desk is the one you want to sign in with when you're awaiting a call from the patient's doctor.

then she'll take you to your room. Later she'll deliver your flowers and mail, direct visitors to your room, and perhaps wheel a cart down the halls each day with books, magazines, snacks, and cigarettes for sale. If ever you decide to write a note of praise to a hospital, I hope you'll include the volunteers, the unsung heroes of the hospital.

While you're in the admitting office, there are a few things you should remember. The clerks there probably have no idea what's in store for you; they are the business end of the hospital; and their job is to insure that your admission is legal, financially sound, and voluntary. Of all the forms you'll sign in this office, the most important is the Consent for Treatment, which gives the hospital the right to photograph your body parts and covers the hospital in the event that your treatment fails to meet your expectations. As you will see in Chapter 10, there is more to this form than meets the eye; it is your responsibility and right to sign the form as an *informed* participant in a legal contract. *Don't sign blindly!* Read it, every last word of it, have your advocate read it, write amendments to it if you like, question the clerk if you must, and be positive you agree to everything you are signing. If there are left- or right-body parts mentioned on the form (most of your body comes in pairs), check and recheck to be sure the correct side is indicated.

By now your heart will be racing, your fingers tingling, your mouth will be desert dry, and your body the receptacle of a thousand tiny jolts of electricity. The plastic band, which now identifies you as a computer number and your doctor as an accomplice, is snapped on your wrist to accompany you through-out your stay—you're officially admitted. Nervous? Good! That means you're normal and in good shape for the next event.

THE LAB

If you have not already completed your lab tests, you'll probably be sent to the lab before you go to your room. Your advocate may accompany you and you may have to wait in line. This might be your first encounter with the word "void," which means urinate, and you'll be asked to do it in a cup which seems too small to hold anything, let alone the urine it's intended for. Ironically, most patients have stopped by the bathroom shortly before they are sent to the lab and find themselves without much urine to contribute for a specimen. Not to worry! All you need is a little, about half an ounce, and then you return the container to the technician.

The components of the urine tell a great deal about your body and how it uses or abuses chemicals and fluids. Often, diseases which have not exhibited symptoms may be detected by a simple urinalysis; thus every patient contributes a specimen at least once during hospitalization.

Likewise, a blood sample gives the physician another set of in-formation about what's going on inside you, so count on at least one blood test. Make a fist, grit your teeth, and get prepared for the needle that looks like a bayonet but feels no different from the self-inflicted razor nicks you give yourself each time you shave. With one prick, the lab technician can gather several tubes of blood and your body will never know the difference. If you don't watch, there's a chance you won't even feel the prick.

How much "routine" lab work is ordered often depends upon which hospital you go to. Some hospitals do an extensive chem-istry workup, to the tune of around $100, on *every* patient ad-mitted, but the government is beginning to clamp down on such flagrant abuse of health-care dollars.

YOUR ROOM

Next you will be whisked to your assigned room. Once you do get there, if you don't like your room assignment or if it is not what you specifically requested of the admitting office, speak up or have your advocate speak up before you even sit on the bed! Ask if there is a "bed crunch" or if your assignment could be changed, and if you don't like the answer you get, sit in a chair until the admitting nurse arrives and ask her if a change could be arranged. But whatever you do, don't get testy. A change of assignment involves the business office, the kitchen, the house-keepers, the pharmacy, the linen room, the laboratory, the mail-room, the switchboard operator, the admitting office, the nursing office, and your doctor. In fact, statistics have indicated that the cost of changing a patient from one assigned bed to an-other is approximately $100, so naturally you are bound to run into resistance from the staff if you request a change, even if it is from one bed to another in the same room.

How persistent you or your advocate might want to be in this matter should depend on how long you suspect you'll be in the hospital. If you're in for minor surgery and expect to be dis-charged in two days, take the room you're assigned. On the oth-er hand, if you're in for a total hip replacement and will be confined for a few weeks, there is no point in being unhappy with your room for that length of time, if there are options open to you. Speak up!

Now that you are settled, more or less, another wait is in store. The person who brought you to the room will deliver the admitting papers to the desk at the nurses' station. How long it will be before a nurse visits you depends on many factors. If it's 7:00 a.m., 3:00 p.m., or 11:00 p.m., you're in for a long wait—it's shift-change time and illness takes a coffee break while one group of workers sheds responsibility and the other picks it up. This may take up to an hour.

If there is an emergency of any kind in progress, the nurses responsible for you may be involved elsewhere for up to half an hour. And there is the very real possibility that notice of your admission escaped those responsible for your care, in which case you'll wait until someone recognizes there's a new body on board. There is also the happy but unlikely prospect that the nurse assigned to you will arrive in the room the same time you do

---

FOR ADVOCATES

If at all possible, stay with the patient until the admission process is complete. This is a very lonely time, one when the patient most needs a familiar person around.

Those patients with painful conditions, such as a kidney stone or broken limb, find waiting intolerable. If that's you, then the most valuable lesson on how to be a patient follows.

Whether you call it assertive, aggressive, nasty, demanding, antsy, or picky, that's what you have to be in a hospital. Remember, "the squeaky wheel gets the grease," "no one looks after you but yourself," "a stitch in time saves nine," and "the early bird catches the worm." While it would be nice to leave the hospital with a flock of new friends waving good-bye, put "new friends" at the bottom of your priority list and "improved health" at the top. Anger does not improve your health, waiting produces anger, and there are times when assertive behavior is the only way to reduce a needlessly long wait.

THE CONTROL PANEL

There's a little button that summons assistance, if you can find it. The control panel might be on the wall at the head of the bed, in a console as part of the bedside stand, or in a little device that looks just like the remote-control boxes for tv. All buttons are labeled and you could push them all without doing any harm, except the one labeled "code" or "emergency." If you push that one you're likely to have a room full of nurses, doctors, and technicians within seconds—which may be exactly what you want! I'll never forget crafty little Mr. Peters. His biggest problem was senility, and his mind was in faraway places most of the time. He claimed to be unable to feed himself, but if we took too long to get to him he always managed to eat everything on his tray by himself. He also claimed to be unable to see and we were forever drumming up people to read to him, or find his Kleenex for him, or puff his pillows. Actually, he was simply very lonely and would have been most content if one of us sat at his bedside around the clock and listened to his tales of days gone by.

In the bathroom of every hospital room there is an emergency button. When it's pushed, a red light in the hall over the door of the room flashes and a buzzer or bell insistently sounds at the nurses' station. It can only be turned off in the bathroom where it was pushed, so there is no way it can be ignored. One morning Mr. Peters' bathroom light flashed and the bell clanged, which was very alarming since we knew he was bedridden. The rule is that *every* nurse responds to an emergency call since no one knows what sort of trouble it signals, and we all ran in to find Mr. Peters standing in the bathroom with a sly grin on his face. "Well," he said, "I finally figured out a way to get someone in here when I want. When's someone going to feed me my breakfast?" As an inveterate patient's advocate, I couldn't help but laugh—a patient had finally beat the system! I wouldn't advise pushing that button if breakfast is all you want, but I *would* advise pushing it if you're desperate for pain medication, so keep that trick under your hat as your final trump card.

The ordinary call button, from either the panel on the wall, console by the bed, or hand-held little box attached to your bed, signals the ward clerk at the nurses' station. She pushes a button that activates an intercom system and you and she can talk to each other. "I want a nurse" may get you one eventually, but you'll get one faster if you state *why* you want a nurse, because there are nursing systems which confine certain tasks to certain nurses. For instance, there might be only one nurse who has the keys to the medication drawer and she'll be the first to get the message if you tell the ward clerk you want pain medication. Obviously, "I want a *TV Guide*" doesn't summon action as quickly as "I need a bedpan," and "I'm in *terrible* pain" works faster than "Is it time for my pain shot yet?"

If you're in pain (the volunteer has just brought you to your room and you haven't yet seen a nurse), push your call button and say, "This is Mr. Whatever. A nurse hasn't had a chance to get in here yet, but I'm really in excruciating pain and wonder if someone could bring relief in a hurry." Chances are your doctor has not yet been informed of your arrival, so the nurse assigned to your room will have to call him and get orders for your medication before she can do anything. Then she may have to send the order to the pharmacy and wait for return of the medication to the ward. Then she must fill out forms that record when and what you were given. Give her twenty minutes at least, then call again. In fact, no matter what you call a nurse for, twenty minutes should give her ample time to respond ... and then call again. The second call places you higher on the priority list, maybe even at the top.

Since you've found the control panel by now, take a look at the other buttons. There'll be one to control the tv and it's destined to frustrate you if you don't know that most hospital tv's are turned off by hitting the button that changes the channels. On some, one push past Channel 12 turns it off, on others it's one push after Channel G, so you'll have to "play" with your controls to see where yours turns off.

Another set of buttons controls your bed, raising and lowering it in relation to the floor, raising and lowering the head only, and raising and lowering the foot only. "Head up" and "Head down" are the only ones you should ever touch; try them out now so you won't have problems when you really need them. Many hospital beds are afflicted with slow motion, and others jump into action the second you touch the button, so it helps to practice before you have a tray full of food in front of you that could be dumped by a fast-moving bed.

Now that you can call a nurse, turn on the tv, and activate your bed, you're in business and have only to learn to work the tray table that rolls across your bed. Look for a lever underneath the tray portion at the end that extends to the floor. If you squeeze that lever while pushing or pulling on the tray, the table will go up or down.

FOR ADVOCATES

Your patient might be too ill to manipulate the call bell easily, in which case request that the nurse bring a "pillow call bell," which has an extra long cord and can be placed in the patient's hand. Because it's activated by minimal pressure, your patient is never without a means of summoning help.

TELEPHONES

Unless your doctor has ordered otherwise, you must be provided with a telephone. Some hospitals charge a small daily fee for incoming calls, others provide only a pay telephone in the hall; but more often than not you'll have a telephone of your own and need to know the ground rules. If the instructions are not on the phone, call the operator and ask the charge for outgoing calls, the number to dial for an outside line (usually 9), and the number to dial if you wish to make a long-distance call (usually 6). Remember that *all* calls you make from your room are considered "operator-assisted," which means they can cost as much as triple what you would pay if you dialed direct from your own phone at home.

In observance of your rights, you may make outgoing calls twenty-four hours a day, but many hospitals close the switchboard to incoming calls at a certain hour, usually 10:00 p.m., so inform your callers accordingly.

Nurses and doctors will gnash their teeth when I tell you this, but I *am* the patient's advocate and cannot resist the temptation. You have no obligation whatsoever to submit to total control in a hospital, and the rights that were yours outside the hospital are still yours inside. This includes the right to use the telephone for any purpose you deem appropriate. There is no law which says you cannot phone your doctor yourself, though there does seem to be an unwritten one to that effect. You can avoid calling him by using these magic words, "Are you going to phone the doctor or shall I?" Addressed to a nurse, these words prompt instant action.

Under most circumstances, the nurses are more likely to be able to reach the doctor than you, but they may delay calling the doctor much longer than you would like to delay having your pain relieved. Use the magic words first, and if that doesn't work call him yourself or have your advocate do it.

Speaking of advocates, friends and relatives have a proclivity to all get on the phone at eight in the morning and ask the nurse how you weathered the night. That's no big problem if you are the only patient, but most nursing units have about forty patients. There are few things more annoying to nurses than answering the queries of relatives at the same time that they are trying to bathe, feed, and medicate patients. Eight o'clock in the morning is the worst possible time for anyone to phone the nurse. Besides, she's only been on duty an hour at most and probably has very little idea how you weathered the night. She'll probably say your condition is unchanged, which is a neat way of getting out of making any commitments about a patient she doesn't know very well. And there are confidentiality laws; nurses aren't allowed to say very much about you on the phone. But if friends and family must call, ask them not to do so until after 11:00 a.m.

THE HISTORY AND PHYSICAL EXAM

Why do so many people ask you the same questions over and over? Well, each person's perspective differs, but sometimes the reason may be one caused simply by the profit motive. The average charge for a history and physical (H&P) is about $75, and I've seen as many as nine H&Ps on one chart because that's how many consultants saw the patient. But I've also seen the chart of a patient in a prepaid plan who had nine consultants, while there was only one H&P, the one developed by the admitting physician. (See Chapter 13 for more information on prepaid plans.) If the medical students' assignment for the week is to gather three H&Ps, you might be poked, probed, and questioned by any number of student doctors—but at least you don't have to pay for these.

You have the right to refuse more than one history and physical examination and should feel free to do so, though there are times when one examiner will see or feel something another examiner overlooked. In addition, some physicians have "special" examinations. For instance, a neurologist has a bag of tricks unique to his specialty and chances are other physicians wouldn't explore the areas important to him. Likewise, the gynecologist will be more thorough in areas that the ophthalmologist has no interest in, so it is difficult for you to judge when you should refuse an examination.

As a rule of thumb, if your diagnosis is already known, the treatment has already been planned, and you and your primary physician have a fairly good idea what the outcome will be, you can probably safely refuse another history and physical examination. Don't be shy! Challenge the next person who wants to poke, probe, and question you—and chances are you will be able to avoid the examination.

THE GOWN

"Slip this on, I'll be right back." A sacklike, square, one-size-fits-all, neutered, frayed white gown is thrust at you, slit open from top to bottom in the back (or is it the front), with two sets of strings to hold it closed, and one set is always knotted together. Put it on with the strings in the front, and the strings will be in the wrong places and *everything* will poke out. Quickly turn it around so the slit is in the back and again *everything* pokes out. Then join the 100 percent who opt to leave the opening in the back—you can cover what pokes out by sitting on the bed!

The white sterile walls of your room shout at you, "Naked body, frail body, ugly body, pierce, poke, probe, sting," and you are never so dramatically alone as when you shed your clothes and don the gown which forces you to relinquish control of your dignity, privacy, and individuality.

If your fear has been replaced by feelings of despair and depression, you're normal. You might think that bringing your own sleepwear from home could help you avoid the trauma of the gown, but the simple fact is that we do not normally appear before strangers in sleepwear and it doesn't matter what the color or fabric is, sleepwear makes us vulnerable.

You might as well be practical and resign yourself to the hospital gowns, because whatever you wear is likely to get spilled on with all sorts of liquids you never suspected. Besides, it is your body that is going to be treated and hospital gowns are designed to make every part of your body easily accessible. The short sleeves make it easy to put a blood-pressure cuff on you, the open back makes it easy to put a bedpan under you, and the shortness makes it easy to put a bandage on your leg. Glamour is wasted in a hospital, so save your beautiful sleepwear for when you're convalescing at home.

Sometimes you can delay the gown trauma by several hours. For instance, if you know you're having some uncomplicated surgery the next day, your lab work's been done, and the doctor has ordered no treatments to precede the surgery, there is no reason you can't keep your clothes on until bedtime. Just because there's a bed in the room doesn't mean you have to put on a gown and get in it. But you do have to have one arm accessible so the nurse can apply the blood-pressure cuff, which is one of the first things she'll do—this will be done more often than anything else during your stay.

YOUR VITAL SIGNS

Like the dials on the dashboard of your car, your vital signs (temperature, pulse, respirations, and blood pressure) indicate what's going on inside your body. In fact, they are one of the first indicators of trouble, which is why the nurses record them so frequently. The first three, TPR in medicalese, can be taken simultaneously and you've probably had it done several times before you arrived at the hospital. There are some professionals who still believe the results are confidential. However, the Patient's Bill of Rights obligates the nurse to tell you "the score." First, though, you must know your baseline in order for the numbers she tells you to be relevant. For instance, "normal" temperature is 98.6 degrees Fahrenheit. However, many people do not run a "normal" temperature. "Normal" blood pressure is 120/80, but normal for you could just as easily be 130/72. The average person breathes 12 to 20 times a minute, but your respiration might be 24 and normal for you. And most people have a pulse of 80, but yours could very normally be 72 or 88.

If you are at all anxious, as you're likely to be, your blood pressure will rise, you'll breathe faster, and your pulse will race. In fact, your vital signs change with weather, exercise, stress, illness, sleep, eating, and thought processes, so what the nurse is really looking for when she records your vital signs is a pattern that is obvious throughout a series of recordings, which is why she places them on a graph on your chart.

Of course, there are many other indicators that reveal what's going on inside your body, but the vital signs are the most accessible and are quite reliable over a period of time. As soon as you're admitted, the nurse will record your vital signs so there will be a starting point on your graph. Then she will take them with whatever frequency the doctor orders, probably four times a day. She may even awaken you during the night to take them, but only if the doctor so orders.

NURSING ASSESSMENT

Some time during your first twenty-four hours as a patient, someone will ask you a whole raft of questions you might feel are quite personal, but it's really because they want to give you the best, most comprehensive care possible and they need to know quite a bit about you to do that. Often they ask such things as who you live with, whether or not you live in a two-story house, and if you have dependents at home to take care of. What they really want to find out is if you need any help after you get home such as a Visiting Nurse, Meals on Wheels, a housekeeper or an aide. Obviously, if you live with an able-bodied adult you will need far less help than someone who lives alone and will not be able to get around unassisted.

This nursing assessment is really to discover clues about what makes you tick, what makes you happy, what kind of support systems you depend on in your own environment. Be honest with your answers, since honest answers could help you in a pinch. For instance, if you normally take Dilaudid (4 mg) for pain at home (a lot of narcotic, by the way), then she'll know right away that the Tylenol that's been ordered for you won't work at all and you're bound to be in pain unless she calls the doctor for an order change.

Well, you've now been through the admitting routine, you know how to work the controls of your ship, you're plopped into bed in the ugly nightgown . . . so what's next?

FOR ADVOCATES

You'll be tempted to answer questions when the patient seems too slow in providing the nurse with information, but don't. Part of her assessment involves the manner in which the patient responds, perceives the illness, and remembers past events. She needs to hear the patient say it, even if the patient is a small child.

THE DOCTOR'S ORDERS

Very little happens in a hospital without a doctor's written orders, and if it happens he isn't available to give orders, you may sit in that alien room for hours with nothing much happening. You can't have anything to eat or drink without an order. You can't get out of bed after surgery without an order. You can't have any medication without an order. And you can't have any treatments or tests without an order. In fact, you can't even have an aspirin without an order, under ordinary circumstances. The *unordinary* circumstances could cause you a great deal of confusion, so you should know the rules by which nurses play.

While nurses practice under your doctor's orders, they are also required to use their own judgment and do a fair amount of interpretation of your symptoms and of the doctor's orders. More often than not, they see the results of your tests in the hospital before the physician does, and they must respond to those results immediately if it is in your best interest. In addition, your condition could easily change within minutes after the doctor has written your orders and left the hospital, and nurses are obligated to respond to that change. The doctor may not be immediately available, in which case a nurse may proceed with some form of treatment not previously ordered and then obtain the order when the doctor is available.

For instance, you may be receiving therapy to thin your blood. If the results of a lab test show your blood is dangerously thin, she will probably discontinue therapy until she reaches the doctor. If you are on a regular diet and something happens which makes you unable to tolerate that diet, she will order a more appropriate diet for you and receive orders later. One nurse may know a doctor very well, have practiced with him for a long period of time, be well acquainted with his methods of treating patients, and proceed with something new, knowing he will cover the order, which is why you can sometimes obtain something you want from one nurse and not from another. Patients have said to me, "Well, the nurse last night gave it to me—why can't you?" Perhaps the nurse last night knew something I didn't know, and I can only do what my own conscience and knowledge allow me to do, so don't be surprised if you think you see inconsistencies among nurses.

Generally, the physician will give your admitting orders in response to a phone call from the nurse. This first set of orders will identify your diagnosis or at least what he expects your diagnosis to be, your diet, your medications, the tests he wants performed, the kind of activity you're allowed, the frequency with which your vital signs are to be recorded, and any special procedures he deems necessary.

Ideally, the nurse who admits you will tell you what the doctor has ordered so that you aren't left wondering what's coming next. I can remember, as a patient, dreading the sound of equipment rolling down the hall because I had no idea what gruesome treatment the doctor had in mind and what sadistic piece of equipment might be destined for my room. My fears were unfounded—nothing gruesome ever assaulted me, but knowing what was in store could have saved untold hours of worrying. If the nurse doesn't tell you, ask her what the admitting orders are. She'll tell you what's going to happen and when, and then you can sit back and relax the rest of the time. If nothing will take place until two days after you're admitted, there's no point lying there anticipating heaven knows what.

THE DOCTOR'S ROUNDS

The only sure thing about the doctor's rounds is that nurses have no idea when the doctor will make them, so if you're thinking a doctor visit in the hospital resembles an office visit where you have an appointment, you're in for a surprise. It may be a golf day, a weekend, a convention day, or a surgery day that interrupts a doctor's normal schedule. There is really no way of predicting when he will show up to see you, but Murphy's Law dictates he will show up when you are in the bathtub, off to a physical-therapy session, or sound asleep. For most patients, the whole focus of each day is the doctor's visit, yet when he arrives, if you do happen to be right where he expects to find you and are awake, you will have forgotten all the questions you wanted to ask him. He will tweak your toes, ask how you're feeling, and be with the next patient before you have a chance to answer that you really feel quite rotten.

Mass depression hits the wards after the doctor's rounds, since he rarely seems to say what patients want to hear, so you might as well get prepared for some hard truths right now. Many doctors could treat the patient very well by remote control. The test results, vital signs, history, nurses' notes, and graphic chart tell him just about all he needs to know, and seeing you is sometimes frosting on the cake. Whether he sees you or not, he will write a progress note on your chart which indicates any major change in your condition and what he intends to do next. In addition, he writes new orders to reflect any changes and the nurse will tell you what these are if you ask her. So don't despair if it appears you've received nothing for your doctor-visit dollar.

On the other hand, you do deserve some personal concern. You have paid a handsome sum for his visit, whether or not he saw *you* in the flesh, and you have the right to demand that you see *him* in the flesh *every* day that you are hospitalized. Some doctors wouldn't think of neglecting a daily visit to their hospitalized patients; then there are others who admit a patient and disappear for days on end. I would feel abused if I were a patient of the latter type and you should too. Here's another area where it pays to be aggressive. If you haven't seen him by 10:00 a.m., ask the nurse to find out what time he expects to see you so that you won't spend the entire day propping your eyes open in fear of sleeping through his visit. Give her an hour to get back to you with an answer, then call him yourself as a last alternative. Chances are his office secretary knows exactly when he intends to make rounds and will be happy to tell you.

FOR ADVOCATES

If your patient is a child, or in no condition to communicate effectively with the physician, don't frustrate yourself by attempting to be present for his rounds. Call him daily, around 2:00 p.m., and ask the same questions the patient would ask. Identifying yourself as the patient's advocate from the start of hospitalization insures that the doctor knows someone is interested in what's happening. If he isn't able to speak with you when you first call, ask when you can expect a return call. If you don't get a call at the specified hour, call again and ask the secretary if there is some time that would be best for you to call each day. This lets everyone know that your patient's welfare is high priority and you intend to make your daily call a habit.

If you're mighty low on assertiveness one day and can't seem to work up the courage to inquire about his visit, your last chance is around 4:30 p.m. He'll probably leave the office around 5:00 and then you would have to cut through the red tape of his answering service to reach him, which is nearly impossible in some cases. If he's a true "night person," he may prefer to make rounds after dinner, but very few doctors fall into this category.

In the ideal situation, a nurse makes rounds with the doctor, listens to what the patient is told, and later can reinforce or interpret what was said, but the ideal situation is often impeded by the hospital routine that keeps nurses busy in too many places at once. If the medical jargon needs translation, you'll have to remind the doctor yourself. To compound your frustration, most doctors could well use thirty-six hours a day and have very little time to spend with you, so be prepared for the visit. Have the questions you want to ask written down, and if the doctor still seems too busy to answer you, just remember this visit is costing you about $35 and you deserve a few answers in return.

In nursing school we learned right away not to place patients in pigeonholes, not to judge. However, there is a group of patients that does get judged, and Mrs. Watson is a prime example. Her doctor was a "night person," but she always began the day begging to see him, carrying on about all sorts of different aches and pains, moaning, crying, threatening to check out any second if he didn't appear. She didn't care that he made rounds at night, she wanted to see him "right now, and you'd better get him over here or I'll call him myself." We would call him, relay her complaints, receive orders, placate her for a while, tell her he would visit shortly, and then begin the routine again.

Finally he would appear at about 8:00 p.m. and ask her how she was. Every single time, she smiled sweetly, told him she was doing just fine, asked about his wife and kiddies, cooed how sweet he was to come visit her, and generally acted as if the day had been a happy social gathering. Her doctor would then come steaming out of her room, ready to string all the nurses from the rafters for bothering him so many times during the day to plead for help for Mrs. Watson, who was obviously in no distress at all. She made fools out of us every time and made sure that we all forgot that nurses are not supposed to judge patients.

When the doctor asks how you are, he doesn't want to hear you're "just fine" unless you really are. He wants to know concrete things: exactly where your pain is; if it has increased or decreased since the last time he saw you; if you have any new symptoms such as nausea, vomiting, diarrhea, headache, shortness of breath, or dizziness. He's sleuthing much of the time. He's trying to put together pieces of a puzzle which will identify your exact diagnosis. Any one of fifty-two diseases can have the same symptoms with only one small deviation and it's everyone's job to provide the deviation that will clinch it. The final clue could be provided by tests, X rays, side effects from medications, specimens, a graphic of your vital signs, observations by your nurses, or a change in your condition that you've noticed yourself.

If it's your own doctor's day off, he'll send an associate. You'll have to remember this is a "pinch hitter" who won't know everything about your case, so fill him in with a brief sketch of your symptoms and why you're in the hospital. His real job is to maintain your comfort and safety while your doctor is away, so don't expect much more than that. If he prescribes a medication or treatment you've had without success before, don't be afraid to tell him you've tried it and it didn't work. He feels the same way about filling in for your doctor as you feel about filling in for someone who works with you—you can prevent a crisis, but you can't solve any big problems.

VISITORS

We once had a gypsy queen as a patient in our intensive care unit and, though we thought we would never survive, the experience has provided us with a trunkful of fun memories for times when the doldrums set in. We all knew next to nothing about the customs of gypsies, but we soon found out that no patient has as many visitors as a gypsy queen and there was no room except the auditorium big enough to hold the whole clan who attended her day and night. They arrived in droves with the ambulance that brought her and they literally took over the hospital for the week she was there. This was all fine except that they insisted on performing their candlelighting pageantry in the ICU, which with all its gases is no place for any kind of open flame. In addition, they all brought their children along and children are the prime carriers of communicable diseases. (Now you know why children and open flames are frowned upon in a hospital.)

If you're a smoker, you'd better make sure the room you're in doesn't have oxygen in use, because oxygen is an inflammable gas. If you must smoke under these circumstances, ask to be taken to the patient day lounge where there is no gas, and don't let your visitors smoke in your room.

Children are a health hazard to very frail, ill people, but some units of the hospital, such as orthopedics, pediatrics, and geriatrics, encourage young visitors if the patient will be confined for a long period of time. Ask the rules for your area and, if you want very much to see a child when you are in a prohibited area, ask for "lobby privileges." Your doctor will write an order for you to be taken to the lobby. Sometimes it will be a nurse who has to take you to the lounge though, and that means time away from patient care. Remember her priority list; taking you to the lounge may be very low on her list unless your case is unique.

When patients go into crisis it's obvious, so nurses do count on visitors to announce a crisis if it happens while they're there. If you have visitors all day, you'll probably see very little of nurses "just checking up on you." Visitors can empty your bedpan, get you a glass of water, rub your back, hold your hand, sit on your bed, answer your telephone, give you a bath, bring you a Coke, water your flowers, take you for a walk in the hall, feed you, read to you, help you turn over, empty your ashtray, and any other little creature comfort thing—as long as they use *caution!* All a visitor needs is common sense and a tiny bit of knowledge about your diagnosis. Obviously, if you have a broken hip, only trained hands should turn you and, if you're on a fluid-restricted diet, no one should bring you a Coke, but there are many other things visitors can do if you want them to.

Your visitors may be tempted to play messenger between you and the nurses, which is a very big no-no unless the visitor is also your advocate and then you should only have one. The quickest route to a nurse is through the intercom system at your bedside. The visitor who decides to save the nurse a trip and goes to the station with a request is destined to end up in a chaotic area that has no room for visitors. Most activity that takes place at the nurses' station requires uninterrupted concentration; doctors dictate orders and progress notes, nurses draw up medications, secretaries transcribe orders, and all departments communicate with one another at the station. Interruption only increases the chance for error—and error is what we all avoid like the plague. You can be sure your visitors will not be welcomed at the nurses' station!

FOR ADVOCATES

Amelia came to us on Thanksgiving Day, lapsed into a coma shortly thereafter, and died in the middle of January. She was relatively young, in her early fifties, and had sons and a husband who had no intention of "letting Amelia go." They took turns sitting with her around the clock, coming and going like smiling shadows, growing years older as each day passed. Each time they came out of her room they smiled at us as though life were going on as usual, and it appeared they must have stuffed their grief into the Thermos bottle they carried with them as they closed her door behind them.

They were typical of a dying patient's relatives: tiptoeing, requesting nothing, scurrying out of everyone's way, disappearing into the woodwork whenever possible, afraid to touch, afraid to cry, afraid to ask, afraid to tell, whispering as though noise might startle old man death into action. Far, far sadder than the sight of a dying patient is the pathos which shrouds the family of the dying. We nurses shed tears when a patient dies, not for the patient, who has been released from disease, but for the family who have buried their grief in their exhausting efforts to play "the good visitors" in hopes of insuring tender loving care for their family member.

Please, please, don't waste your efforts playing good visitor. Sit on the bed, cry if you feel sad, ask the nurses anything you like, laugh out loud, if you're afraid say so, don't hesitate to stay all night, ask for a blanket, ask where you can get coffee, use the bathroom, take a stroll through the halls when your bottom gets tired, ask for a guest tray for the next meal (it costs, but it's worth it), and don't scurry out of our way when we walk into the room. You belong there as much as we do and most of us love to have you there to comfort the patient.

It's a fact that there are some nasty "Nurse Ratcheds" in this world. "Visiting hours are *over*," they say, and they do indeed make you feel as though you're an intruder out to make the sick patient even sicker. But if you're a true patient's advocate you'll stand up to Nurse Ratched. Tell her you'll leave the room so she can carry out any treatments she has in mind but you intend to return in an hour and remain with the patient. If she continues to press you to leave, ask for the supervisor. And if the supervisor presses you, stand your ground and simply refuse to leave.

The nursing schools are finally getting around to teaching that visitors are a crucial part of the patient's recovery and even more crucial if the patient is not expected to recover. But if you as a visitor feel uncomfortable because of an inhospitable nurse, stick by your guns and by your patient.

In defense of the Nurse Ratcheds, there are some obnoxious visitors. They gather in groups at the patient's bedside as though at a cocktail party, carrying on conversations that totally exclude the patient, wander in and out of the hospital kitchen and help themselves to anything that suits their fancy, stand at the nurses' station and tell their latest bawdy jokes, turn the volume of the tv up loud enough for patients five doors down the hall to hear, bring their children and turn them loose to make a playground out of the lobby, strew their orange peels around the room for the nurses to clean up, and sprawl all over any empty surface. Bring on the supervisor with the hospital visiting-hours policy! The entire staff turns into a group of Nurse Ratcheds.

It only takes common sense to be a good patient's advocate and a visitor the nurses will go out of their way to please. Your role is far more difficult than the patient's, simply because it is true suffering to watch someone you love in the throes of illness while you stand by helplessly.

You don't have to be a good-time Charlie to the patient you're visiting; you don't have to tell tales of some other person you know who "has it much worse"; you don't have to say "You're looking much better today" if that is not the case; and you don't have to say "Oh, you'll be much better tomorrow" if you know there's no hope of such a miracle. Patients want to tell you how rotten they feel; they want to feel that they are unique in their illness; they want to be able to tell someone how frightening it is to be in such danger; and they want someone to cry with them over the hopelessness of their disease. Most of all, they *need someone to talk to,* someone to help them feel less isolated and helpless, someone who really cares that they are in a strange world, surrounded by strange people and equipment. They need you more than ever before just to listen and sympathize.

If you haven't been intimately involved with the patient before hospitalization, then chances are it will be work for the patient if you come to visit. Our socialization has taught us certain rules when acquaintances visit, in the hospital or out, and such visits require more of us than illness allows. You'll be doing the patient a favor by staying away; send a card, or some posies, or a box of candy, or a few magazines, or a softly scented soap. Duty visits are just added work for the patient and difficult for the visitor. Old-home-week at the patient's bedside is an exhausting ordeal that can easily be avoided if only those people closest to the patient come to visit. Gone are the days when people languished in the hospital for weeks on end after a minor operation, enjoying the visits of their fellow workers, neighbors, distant cousins, old school chums, and once-a-year cocktail friends. Hospitalized people are *really* sick patients, in no shape to carry on lighthearted conversations.

So that's it—all you need to know to get you started as a hospital patient or as the patient's advocate.

CHAPTER
4
Common Nuisances

FOOD

In one hospital the food is tepid, tasteless, and gruesome to look at, served on a Styrofoam tray with plastic utensils and paper plates, cooked in some faraway kitchen, and heated in a microwave oven by the nurse. In another hospital the food is still tepid, but garnished beautifully, and served on a metal tray with china dishes and stainless steel utensils. It's cooked in the hospital kitchen and wheeled to the nursing unit on giant carts—that hospital is known in the trade as the Hilton, the cooks are truly chefs, and the daily room rate is $25 higher than other hospitals.

If you're to survive hospitalization with any sort of equanimity, you will have to understand what goes on in the kitchen. In the first place, it's usually the farthest place from the nursing unit. It may be serving three thousand patients at one time. The task of preparing twenty different types of diets from a menu offering about four choices for each meal is monumental.

Your doctor orders the type of diet that you should have. It may be one high in protein, low in sodium, free from purine, limited to a certain number of calories, without caffeine, sugar-free, bland, pureed, liquid, low-alkaline, acid-producing, or one eliminating a certain set of foods such as nuts, tea, peas, and lamb for a particular test taking place three days later.

What goes into your mouth travels through your whole system and affects surgery, diagnostic examinations, X rays, lab tests, your mental capacity, and your vital signs. For a diet that has been ordered as 2 grams of sodium, low-residue, bland, soft, and diabetic with fluid restriction of 24 ounces a day, one would have to eliminate most fruits and vegetables, most salty foods, all breads, sweets, and pastas, most meat, all fats, anything not easily digestible, and most fluids. On top of all this the calories would be strictly calculated. This means that when your tray is served in the hospital what is on it is not through any haphazard guessing.

Even if you can't stand to see food wasted, squelch your desire to let your visitors eat your leftovers. The nurses must keep track of what you eat and how much. Almost all hospitals will supply guest trays if you place the order a day in advance, but don't expect the contents of the tray to be reflected in the price. There's usually no choice offered and the cost is the same for all meals.

The nurse has little if anything to say about what you get and the menu you filled out the day before may in no way resemble what you see on your tray. Your very best bet is to eat what you can, leave the rest, and look forward to some good home cooking after you're discharged. A hospital is simply no place to look forward to a meal!

Ask your nurse what your diet order is. Chances are there are few, if any, restrictions, and your visitors can bring in what you crave the most. One patient who was with us for two weeks dreamed of oysters Rockefeller until he had us all craving the delicacy. His wife called up the nearest swanky restaurant and had two dozen incredibly delicious oysters delivered. Our teenage patients often have hamburgers, fries, and milk shakes brought in, and our Oriental patients sometimes have their meals delivered.

But there is one thing you must watch out for. For certain tests, X rays, and surgery, your stomach must be empty. Somewhere around your room there will be an NPO sign (short for the Latin phrase meaning "nothing by mouth"), your water pitcher will be turned upside down, and you'll be expected to not eat or drink anything. Unfortunately, sometimes the nurses forget to explain this to you and think nothing about it until you've arrived in some other area of the hospital. Then they get an outraged call from a doctor or technician asking why it is that your stomach is not empty.

If you're having surgery, you can be sure that you cannot have food or fluid for at least twelve hours before. The same applies if you're having X rays of anything from your chest down (except bones). Accept this as your responsibility if the nurse forgets to tell you or you may find yourself staying hospitalized a day longer than you expected. Surgery will be canceled, and in hospitals with full schedules you could wait as long as a week to get on the schedule again. This may sound impossible but I've seen it happen. It doesn't matter that your surgery is to be on your left toe; what matters is that you will be having anesthesia, your gag reflex may be impaired, you may become nauseated, and the contents of your stomach could empty into your lungs. That is why even emergency surgery is often delayed for a few hours if you've eaten shortly before arriving in the emergency room with a raging appendix awaiting removal. The anesthesiologist wants nothing to do with a patient with a full stomach; the average stomach takes about two hours to empty. If the surgery is on the intestines, they must be empty too and that takes a good deal longer.

After anesthesia it may take several hours to several days for your digestive system to return to the point where it can accept food, so don't be surprised if you're on a clear-liquid diet of tea, broth, and Jell-O for a while. On the other hand, the doctor could easily forget that you are sitting there craving just one sip of coffee.

If you are to have a special diet after you leave the hospital, ask to speak with the dietitian. She has all sorts of charts, lists, and educational materials for you, and the most interesting part of her job is teaching you how to get along with your new diet. To be sure you fit into her busy schedule, ask to see her the day before you expect to be discharged.

Many hospitals have no cooking facilities of any kind, only a roomful of giant refrigerators. The orders are placed a day in advance, the food is delivered by truck to the hospital and goes to the nursing unit about two hours before mealtime to be heated in a microwave oven. There's no one to cook a steak for you if you suddenly decide that's what you want the most. In addition, the companies that supply these precooked meals offer a certain selection of food on a set rotation. If you want bacon on a day when sausage is the fare, it won't be available.

ACTIVITY

Your doctor also orders what kind of activity you'll be allowed. If you've just had surgery you may be surprised that he expects you to get out of that bed and get moving four hours later. Under most circumstances, the worst possible thing you can do after surgery is lie like a mummy on your bed to avoid the pain of moving. Your lungs will fill up with fluid and you'll develop a raging case of pneumonia. *You must get up and move around!* When the nurse refuses to give you a bath, or hand you the magazine from across the room, or reach the Kleenex for you, it's because the best therapy for you is movement.

On the other hand, you may have a condition which requires constant bed rest, or bed rest with bathroom privileges only, and as much as you might hate using a bedpan, there are times when you have no choice if those are the doctor's orders.

Ask what your activity order is so you'll know what you can and can't do. Often the order reads "Ambulate BID," which means you are to walk in the hall twice a day, no matter how rotten you feel. If the doctor has left orders for you to sit in a chair a certain length of time each day, you'll be put in a chair, even if it takes four people to lift you into it from the bed. This keeps unused muscles from deteriorating.

FOR ADVOCATES

You can help by encouraging walks during your visit, with your strong arm to assist, or by helping the patient to turn from side to side at least every two hours if he is confined to bed. Of course in some cases, such as bone surgery, you should not do the turning, but the nurse will appreciate it if you remind her when two hours have passed and it's time for her to turn the patient again.

For many people it's very difficult to allow someone else to bathe them when they feel perfectly capable of doing it themselves—bathing is a private affair! But if the nurse has received orders from the doctor, she must bathe you. She's been taught to do it with a bath sheet covering you, exposing only a small portion of your body at a time, and leaving the middle for you to bathe while she leaves the room to get clean linen. However, there are many nurses who have no sense of modesty at all and even forget that they are washing a human body and not their little red sports car. If your nurse is that type and just whips the covers off to leave you stark naked, tell her you're cold and wish to remain covered. If you're really sensitive about the whole subject, which many people are, you have every right to refuse to be bathed by anyone other than yourself or a family member, despite your doctor's orders. The stress caused by invasion of privacy is often much greater than the stress of giving yourself a bath and stress might just be what you need to avoid the most.

INTRAVENOUS (IV) THERAPY

In days gone by, the public measured the severity of one's illness by the presence or absence of an IV. "They're feeding him intravenously" was to say, "Tsk, tsk, he's really in terrible shape, almost dead"—which is really not the case today.

When the body is healthy, it keeps a perfect balance of fluid and electrolytes, calcium, magnesium, sodium, potassium, etc., all by itself. This is homeostasis in medicalese, a steady state of balance. But when the body has been insulted by disease or injury it's not always able to maintain this homeostasis by itself and intravenous therapy is indicated.

IV insertion is fairly simple and straightforward: a vein in the arm is selected, the skin that covers it is cleansed, a tourniquet is placed above the site to promote the expansion of the vein by blood, a needle is pushed through the skin into the vein, and fluid or medication is delivered through tubing and the hole in the tip of the needle straight into your bloodstream. The idea is to get fluid into you by the fastest route possible.

Most patients dread the starting of an IV. "Have you done this a lot before?" or "My God, that's a big needle," or "Wait just a minute, I have to go to the bathroom," or "Let me out of here" are the usual responses when the nurse approaches a patient with IV equipment in hand. Actually the whole thing looks more wicked than it is. The only pain comes when the top layers of your skin are pierced because that's where your pain receptors are. Once the initial jab is over, you're home free—but the nurse isn't.

With advancing age, the connective tissue that holds your veins in one place disappears and the veins have a tendency to roll from side to side. This places the nurse in the position of chasing your vein with the needle underneath the skin, which is much like chasing a lively eel with a spear in dark, muddy water. To complicate matters, in some diseases the veins are very fragile; the needle may get into the vein only to scoot out the other side. So you see that getting an IV started can be complicated for the nurse, but it shouldn't be for you.

You can help the nurse by holding your arm absolutely still so that she has a better chance of getting the needle in the right place; you also can help by relaxing as much as possible because anxiety tends to constrict the vessels.

If you are hospitalized without having an IV, you're fairly rare, since it is used for a number of reasons. If you have surgery, the IV will replace the fluids you lose during even the simplest surgery. In addition, anesthesia induction is easier if the medication to put you to sleep is sent into your bloodstream through the IV. You might also have blood replaced by IV, or you might receive pain medication through your IV if there are some contraindications to giving it to you by mouth or injection. If you're a cardiac patient, often there is an IV inserted allowing a very slow drip of fluid; this is to keep one of your veins open in case you need emergency drugs immediately. For any number of reasons, your body might be short on some essential nutrient, electrolyte, or fluid and the IV will replace it. This is not to say you don't need to eat. You can go for a certain length of time without solid food, but each quart of IV fluid only gives you about 250 calories, so you're destined to lose weight if you're not eating solid food as well.

In certain diseases the body fails to absorb nutrients properly, in which case you'll be fed with a very thick solution through the veins, usually a large blood vessel near your collarbone. This is called total parental nutrition or hyperalimentation ("TPN" or "hyperal" in medicalese) and is used when all other methods of providing food are contraindicated.

The drugs injected through IV tubing work the fastest. If a very small bottle of fluid is hanging next to the larger one on your IV pole, chances are the small bottle is delivering a drug that is most effective by this means, usually an antibiotic. When the little bottle empties, the large one starts running again, so don't worry when you see the fluid dwindling. In medicalese, the small bottles are "piggybacks" and are hung at set intervals.

Those bubbles you see floating down the tubing of your IV are dangerous only on tv shows where the writers want to create drama. Your body can tolerate at least 55 cc of air in a vein, and the IV tubing holds only about 14 cc. Empty IV bottles are nothing to be afraid of either: the pressure in your veins is higher than the pressure of air in the bottle, so the most that can happen is that a bit of your blood will back up into the tubing, which is not dangerous at all. It's a good idea to tell your nurse when the bottle has only about an inch more fluid in it so she can change it, but this is not essential.

If the insertion site of your IV is over a joint or in a place that might make the needle vulnerable to excessive movement, an arm board will be tied to your arm to keep the site still, although you can still use your hand for eating, bathing, dressing, and most other activities. Do take care that you don't wrap the tubing around anything that would tend to pull the needle out.

Jennifer was a "pro" at dislodging needles. Somehow she managed to get the tubing through the sleeve of her gown, wrapped around the pole that held the bottle above her bed, looped under the sheet and over the bedspread, and tangled in the telephone cord. Over the intercom she'd say, "I can't move my arm and there's something wet all over my bed," and two or three nurses would go running. After a time or two we started calling her Houdini, knowing her distress call meant the IV needle had been pulled out again and the solution was spraying her bed linen.

Once every day or so the tubing on the IV will be changed to avoid infections. This simply entails dislodging the old tubing from the hub of the needle, leaving the needle in place in your arm, and attaching a new tubing. Bottles of fluid are changed more often, at the other end of the tubing, and often various syringes of medications might be injected into little rubber "ports" that you'll see at intervals along the tubing. None of these procedures should cause you any pain, but if you should happen to feel discomfort, tell the nurse so that she can correct the situation. Some IV fluids are more caustic to veins than others and she might only have to slow the rate at which the solution flows into your arm in order to eliminate pain.

Speaking of slowing the rate, there is a little thumbscrew device on IV tubing that is used to adjust the rate of flow. You should *never, never touch it* since the infusion rate is very specific and important. Some solutions must be delivered in haste, while others have toxic effects unless they are delivered slowly, so leave the rate adjustment to the nurse. If the fluid is dripping in very slowly, only enough to keep your vein open, you might notice some blood in the tubing near the needle insertion site: this indicates that your blood is pushing up the tubing faster than the fluid is dripping down the tubing and there is no need for alarm. Tell the nurse if you like, although she might decide not to speed the rate of flow if she's concerned about giving you too much fluid.

When it comes time to discontinue the IV, you'll be just as nervous as you were when it was time to put it in, despite the fact that it never hurts to take the needle out. It really doesn't! What might be disconcerting is that the doctor may tell you at 8:00 a.m. it's going to come out, but may forget to write the order or the nurse may not see the written order for a couple of hours. Taking an IV out is fairly low on the priority list, so if you're anxious to get it over with, remind the nurse that it's your turn to have free use of your arm again.

Once the needle is out, take a look at it. Like surgical wounds, the *thought* is far more wicked than the actual sight and, once you've looked at it, you probably won't be half as frightened of it anymore.

After your IV is discontinued, you must drink enough fluids, especially, as is often the case, if the IV was to replace lost fluids. Dehydration is a very real problem in many diseases, so ask the nurse exactly how much fluid you should drink each day in order to keep the IV out.

INTAKE AND OUTPUT (I&O)

"You're on I&O now," says the nurse. "Here's a hat for you," and she disappears into the bathroom, leaving you to wonder if the hat is a prize and I&O is something good or if I&O is a disease that requires you to cover your head. Actually, I&O is medicalese for "intake and output," a recording of the quantity of fluids going in and out of your body. The "hat" is a plastic receptacle that is placed under the seat of the toilet to collect and measure the liquid body wastes you excrete.

Many bodies in a state of ill health seem unable to balance the fluids coming in and the fluids going out. Since this is crucial to your health, a chart for recording fluids is usually at your bedside and the amount is totaled at the end of each nurse's shift, with a grand total at the end of twenty-four hours, so the physician can prescribe the therapy necessary to keep your fluids in balance. For instance, there are some diseases in which the body accumulates excessive amounts of fluid. By looking at the difference between what you drank and the amount of urine produced, the doctor can predict your progress and perhaps increase or decrease your IV fluids, or encourage you to drink more or less.

FOR ADVOCATES

Never, never discard any body wastes or partially consumed fluids and *never, never* give your patient liquids to drink that have not been recorded if an I&O tally is being kept. This is one of the first commandments for good advocates.

If this is important to your care, a urinal dumped by a well-meaning relative can make your fluid-balance picture look worse than it really is. Anna was a favorite patient whose progress could best be monitored by the volume of urine she excreted each shift. We all had high hopes for remission of her disease until one day when eight hours went by with almost no urine output recorded. At report we all had very long faces when we told the next shift of nurses, "There's only been 125 cc output this shift. She must be in renal failure." This meant Anna's kidneys were beginning to shut down and the end might be near.

When the shift was over, I went in to spend a few minutes with Anna and her daughter, thinking I might never see them again. Anna looked better than ever and her spirits were high, which didn't fit with renal failure. "She's doing just great," her daughter told me, "ordering me around like a drill sergeant, even has me emptying the bedpan for her, turning me into a nurse." So much for Anna's renal failure.

There are some tests that require a collection of *all* the urine that's excreted by a patient over one twenty-four-hour period. It's amazing how many patients have spoiled that test by forgetting that we must *save all urine*. It's embarrassing to have nurses handle everything that comes out of your body, but you can be sure it means nothing to us; it's our job, we do it all the time. If you vomit we must measure it and if you bleed we must measure it, since the fluids you lose must be replaced by one means or another.

If you're well enough to keep your own I&O record, that's a great help to the nurses. Most hospital containers are measured in cubic centimeters (cc). Thirty cc equals one ounce, so if you drink an eight-ounce carton of milk, you must record 240 cc on your intake record.

If your body is retaining fluid for one reason or another you might have to be weighed daily. This seems a very big chore, especially if you are confined to bed and unable to help yourself at all, but there are bed scales onto which you will be lifted and the importance of the weighing is worth every bit of the effort.

BLADDER CATHETERS

Catheterization is a big bugaboo to the uninitiated patient, but firsthand experience has taught me that when you really need it, you couldn't care less how it's done, just so it's done in a hur-

ry. You know how it is to be on the highway, needing a bathroom like crazy, having no idea how far it is to the next gas
station—that's how it is to need catheterization, only worse. For
lots of reasons the muscles that work the "valve" that allows
your bladder to empty may be malfunctioning. Most often this
happens after anesthesia; there may be a temporary shutdown
of messages getting to the right place to start the muscles working. Your bladder fills up, is unable to empty, or empties in
small dribbles, and you become extremely uncomfortable.

Catheters are small, smooth plastic or rubber tubes, with a
few holes in one end, which are slipped into the urethra quite
painlessly. The urine escapes through the holes and drains into
a collection vessel. If it is thought that the malfunctioning may
continue awhile, a balloon is inflated through a tiny tube that
runs along the length of the catheter and the balloon holds the
catheter in place in your bladder. Imagine a lollipop on the end
of a stick: the lollipop is the bladder, the stick the urethra.

Urinary-tract infection is a common consequence of catheterization, since the catheter acts as a germ carrier from the most
germ-laden area of your body right into your bladder. You must
drink gallons of water to keep your urine dilute and the nasty
organisms flushed out before they get a chance to proliferate.
The drainage through the catheter is continuous, so drinking
lots of water (or any fluid, for that matter) is the best means of
avoiding a debilitating infection. The first sign of infection is a
sense of urgency, a feeling that you have to urinate even though
the catheter is keeping your bladder empty. You should be sure
to tell the nurse if this happens so that antibiotic therapy can
be initiated at once.

There are times when it might seem to you that there is no
indication for catheterization and that *may* be the case—you
should always ask *why* it is being done if the nurse approaches
you with all the equipment. If you have been unable to void
within twelve hours after surgery, the doctor may have left
"standing orders" for catheterization. You might be able to
avoid the situation if you tell the nurse to give you two hours to
drink a lot of fluids and see if you can get things working yourself. Or you might be too uncomfortable to wait.

On the other hand, if you had known you were supposed to

produce you might have gone on a drinking campaign. You should take advantage of the opportunity to solve the problem on your own by drinking perhaps a quart, relaxing, and listening to water run in the sink while you try to urinate. There are cases in which a very strict measurement of urinary drainage must be kept and continuous catheterization is the only accurate way to do it. In other cases, a sterile specimen of urine must be obtained, and a one-time-only catheterization is the only means. So be sure to ask the purpose. And don't be afraid, it really doesn't hurt!

MEDICATIONS

If I were to find one indictment against nurses it would be that far too many of them consider medications, especially pain medications, a tool of power. If you learn nothing else from this book, it is imperative that you learn how to insure that you get accurate, adequate medication with the least amount of conflict.

The first rule of the game is for males: *Pain does not build character,* nor is it good for the soul, nor is it "macho," nor does the tolerance of it get you into heaven faster. If you're sick, pain only makes you sicker!

Wards that house the open-heart-surgery patients are quite often filled with driven, goal-oriented, high-achieving, powerful, supermasculine men. The surgery creates a wound from the nose to the toes and such patients often look like a patchwork quilt gone awry. They have to hurt if they have any pain receptors at all, yet it's unbelievable how many reject pain medication. "Oh, I don't need anything ... I'm tough ... You're not going to make a junkie outta me ... I'm just not a pill-taker," they tell me as the sweat pours off their faces and their bodies are rigid as a board in their attempt to will away pain.

Then there are the women. Two-thirds of pill-popping abusers are women, which says a great deal about how most of them feel about taking medication. "If a little bit is good, a lot must be better," and they medicate themselves into a stupor.

For a little more stereotyping, males in their late teens and early twenties are a different breed; they have the lowest tolerance to pain imaginable, yet they are so terrified of injections it's amazing how so many of that age group could possibly become drug addicts.

DOSAGES

Much of medicine is practiced by the law of averages. The average appendectomy patient requires this much pain reliever, the average diabetic requires that much insulin, the average heart patient does great on this amount of digitalis, and the average arthritis patient gets by on that amount of prednisone—as long as you're "average," you're okay, but too many people aren't. The "average" dose of Seconal smoothes out the wrinkles in Betty's day, while the same dose zonks Phyllis clear out into left field for two days. Both weigh about the same and are about the same age, so rule out weight and age as deciding factors, as least in this case.

There are so many variables which figure into the action of most drugs that one can do nothing more than experiment with dosages until the perfect dose is found. This is why pain control is such a horrendous problem in hospitals, with diabetes control a close second.

Most physicians play it safe by ordering the minimum dose of a drug you will be receiving for the first time, or else they order a range within which the nurse may give the drug and she'll usually begin with the smallest amount. If you don't respond to that, the dose is increased and so it goes until the expected response is achieved. You can play a very big role in this experimenting by reporting your symptoms exactly. Some lab tests, such as for urine or blood, will do the reporting, but for many drugs the efficacy is purely subjective—do you *feel* better?

Hospitals have set times at which they give medications routinely. One nurse may be responsible for medicating all of the patients on a nursing unit—this could be as many as thirty to forty patients. Such was the case one day when I was operating by Murphy's Law. The morning had been such chaos that I was still working on passing out morning medications when it was almost time to begin passing out the afternoon doses. I had poured all the medications for each patient into little plastic cups that I carried on a tray from room to room and, as so often is the case, each patient had a list of requests that they'd been saving for the very next nurse who walked into the room. One wanted help to the bathroom, another wanted help into a wheelchair, another had an IV about to go dry, and on and on and on. I had three patients left to medicate when I handed Mr. Little his cup of pills, eleven in all shapes and colors. He swallowed them down in two huge gulps, handed me the cup and said, "Boy, that doctor must have really thought up new tricks this time. If he can't cure me I guess he must have decided to kill me with that whole cupful of horse pills."

I tried to keep the hysteria out of my voice as I said, "Is this the first time you've taken those pills?"

"Sure is. I usually take one little white one three times a day, same as I've been doing since my heart attack last year."

I looked at my tray and, sure enough, there was a cup with one little white pill in it. My mind went wild trying to think of how I could get those eleven pills back out of his stomach.

Then I wanted to lash out at him. "You dunce you! I might have handed you arsenic and you would have been dumb enough to swallow it without a question. How could you be so trusting?"

I flew back to my medication cart, made a list of those eleven pills, which actually should have been given to the patient in the next room, and riffled through the *Physician's Desk Reference,* which tells the actions and side effects of all drugs, to see what I could expect to happen to Mr. Little. I watched him like a hawk all day, with my heart in my throat, even though the drugs I had given him were fairly benign.

About six hours after the incident, Mr. Little came strolling down the hall to tell me, "Gee, I feel great! Whatever that doc's giving me in that cup, he's finally hit on the right stuff." I didn't have the energy to feel relieved.

Since then, I've never again given a wrong medication. You only have to live through that once to find out what your top priority is. But I *have* gone on a crusade to teach patients that they should never ever swallow a pill, accept an injection, or submit to a procedure without knowing exactly what they're getting and for what purpose. You should know the names of your medications, which is why most pharmacies now label all prescriptions, and you should certainly know what to expect from them. Ask what you're getting *every time* the nurse brings medication into your room. She'll love you for caring enough about what's going on to ask and she'll appreciate your shouldering one of the heaviest responsibilities that nurses carry.

Fortunately, more and more hospitals are realizing the dangers inherent in one nurse delivering the medication to a whole flock of patients. Now the best hospitals have the pharmacy deliver each patient's medication to the patient's bedside drawer until it is administered by the registered nurse who cares for only a small number of patients, perhaps five or six. If that's the situation you're in, you've hit upon a super hospital—but you *still* should know the names of what you're getting and keep a record of your reactions for the future. If your doctor should meet his untimely demise, it would help to be able to tell your next doctor what medications have worked best for you in the past.

MEDICATION TIMES

The time schedule for routine medications varies from hospital to hospital. The doctor usually orders how many times in one day the drug must be given to you but leaves the specific times to the nurses. Whatever the time, there's no guarantee that that is when you'll get it—you always have the nurse's priority list to deal with. For instance, if the patient down the hall has a respiratory arrest right at the time that you're expecting your medications, the nurses will be caring for him for as long as an hour—threat to life takes priority.

Sleeping pills are ordered for HS, which means "hour of sleep." In fact, the order might be HS, PRN, which means you can have it at the hour of sleep as needed (if you ask for it). You can choose the hour or leave it up to the nurses, but if you aren't nodding off within an hour after taking it, speak up! If the nurse doesn't have a repeat order, she can call the doctor, but neither of them will be very happy if you wait until 3:00 a.m. to tell them you're having trouble sleeping. By the way, most hospitals refuse to give any sleeping pills after 3:30 a.m.—they don't want you to sleep through the next day and miss all the activity they have planned for you.

Because you don't see the doctor's written order, medication times can be very confusing for you. You may get some medication on a routine schedule without asking, you may get some only once, and you may get some only if you ask for them—and there are variations on the theme. For instance, PRN (as needed) are left up to you and the nurse. One nurse might give you PRN medications only if you ask, while another might anticipate your need and bring the medication without your asking for it.

A laxative might be ordered as a routine medication, in which case it will be brought to you at the same time each day, or it might be ordered PRN and the nurse will bring it to you if she thinks you need it, or it might be PRN but you will have to ask for it. The same is true for sleeping pills.

As a rule of thumb, medication for pain relief is PRN and you must ask for it. You'll be further confused when the doctor changes orders (either time or type of drug) and no one bothers to tell you. Ask! Ask! Ask! It's the only way to know.

Legally, a nurse may give any medication a half hour before it's due; a pain medication ordered for every three to four hours can actually be given in two and a half hours after the previous dose. This means that a medication that only lasts a little while can be repeated; it will mean a lot to you if you're in pain.

HOW TO GET WHAT YOU NEED

It's a fact of life that one person cannot judge another person's pain, yet there are many doctors and nurses who do just that. "He doesn't need any more Demerol ... he only had an appendectomy," says the doctor who has never had one himself. "That kid's on the buzzer every three hours on the nose for that Demerol ... an addict, that's what he is," says the nurse who has no idea what it's like to be in constant pain from which there may be only minimal relief even after the Demerol.

Many surgeons have "standing orders" that are stamped on all their patients' charts after surgery, a recipe of sorts for the nurse to follow. Along with the diet, activity, and procedure orders will be medication orders for various phases of the recovery process. The usual order for pain control is 75 to 100 mg of Demerol every three or four hours. The same order is stamped on every chart, though one patient may be out on 25 mg of Demerol and another may feel nothing at all from 150 mg. If you're the kind of patient who lies there taking whatever is dished out to you, tolerating everything, then you'll be treated as the "average" patient. You'll always get the "average," whether it works for you or not, unless you advise the nurse otherwise.

It doesn't take long to figure out if "average" is not for you. If you are given a pain reliever and you don't feel markedly improved within forty-five minutes, then you can be sure "average" is not going to do the trick.

Demand a change in medication *now,* because pain that endures soon becomes an intractable pain that refuses to respond to any kind of medication. It's true that the nurse won't want to call the doctor in the middle of the night, but phone calls in the night are just one of the inconveniences for which doctors are so highly paid. Night calls, though, are usually rare, because most patients don't suddenly leap into pain in the wee small hours. The hour is irrelevant—remember, if you're in pain, something's not right!

One of the "tricks" to being a hospital patient is knowing how to play the game of getting your pain relievers. You'll get a lot more cooperation out of some nurses if you don't seem to be focusing all your attention on getting medication. Of course, if you're *constantly* in pain, then obviously the medication ordered for you is not correct and you should insist that the physician be called. If it is working and you just want to be sure it keeps you out of pain, vary the intervals at which you ask for it.

For instance, suppose you know your Demerol is ordered for every three to four hours PRN. Ask for it at two and a half hours one time, three and a quarter the next, three the next, and so on. If you ask for it at three hours every single time, a little red "dope addict" sign lights up in the nurse's brain and she'll tend to delay giving it to you—not that delay ever "broke" an addiction, but there are nurses who consider their ability to give or withhold medication their only power in life—subconsciously, of course.

FOR ADVOCATES

This is one time you might have to be the most aggressive if your patient is unable to speak for himself. You know the patient better than anyone else and you're in the best position to recognize when he's in pain. Don't be timid about asking for medication. And by the way, if *you* have a terrible headache, the nurses can't even give you an aspirin without a doctor's order. They can only medicate the patient—that of course might indirectly relieve your headache!

You are the very best judge of what you need, which is why you need to know what you're getting. On the eighth day of one of our patients' hospitalization he complained of having had diarrhea for the past three days. He had been receiving a laxative daily because one of the known side effects of one of his other medications was constipation. We could have stopped the laxative immediately if he had told us he was having diarrhea. *You* must report changes to the staff if you are to be appropriately medicated.

ROUTES OF MEDICATION

Some drugs are most readily absorbed if taken by mouth, while others would be of no value at all if sent to your stomach. Some must be injected just slightly under the skin, while others will do nothing but cause you more pain unless they are injected deeply into a very large muscle. Nitroglycerin acts within three minutes if placed under your tongue, but you could wait forever for a vitamin pill to do anything for you if placed in the same location.

Then there are those very convenient drugs that work well no matter what route is chosen; Compazine relieves nausea whether it's taken by mouth, injected into a muscle, inserted in the rectum, or injected into the bloodstream through an IV. This is where the patient comes into the picture. You probably won't know the preferred route of administration, so you'll have to ask a physician or nurse if you would like a change in the route prescribed for you.

For instance, you may be getting Tylenol with codeine as a pain reliever in pill form. If you've just had a tonsillectomy it can feel like murder swallowing that pill. Fortunately, the same medication comes in liquid form and goes down much more easily. I know you would think the doctor would anticipate that your throat will be very sore, and you'd expect him to order the liquid from the start, but it could be that the majority of his cases tolerate the pill very well. Remember, his practice is based on "averages," and if the "average" route of administration doesn't fit your needs, he wants you to speak up.

If the preferred route for a drug is by injection, the site and depth of injection can be very specific, which is why most medications are injected deeply into your biggest muscle (the upper, outer quadrant of your buttocks) rather than the arm, which is where most patients would prefer to get it; we'd all rather stick out our arm for the needle than our rear. You can minimize the "flashing," since the nurse only needs about an inch-square area of your buttocks exposed in order to inject and that area is almost as high as your waist and as far to the side as your hip bone. "Drop your drawers" is only a figure of speech!

The skill of the nurse has very little, if anything, to do with how much an injection hurts you. If you're tense, your muscles tighten up and the drug has difficulty fighting its way in. If your nerves are frazzled, you'll jump at the slightest pinch. If your skin is tough, the needle has more difficulty puncturing through to the muscle. Penicillin is the most viscous injectable medication I give, yet some patients say they never felt the injection and others won't let me near them again after I've given the first dose. So if it hurts, don't necessarily blame it on the nurse! Compazine leaves a lump on your rear that may stay for weeks, while other injections leave a bruise. It depends on your body, not the skill of the nurse, so remember to squelch your desire to put her on the list of "bad guys" if you dislike the results of the injection.

FOR ADVOCATES

A very small child can be eased through an injection if you hold him in your arms with his head over your shoulder and his legs dangling down. Clutch him tightly against you, one of your arms across his upper back to restrain his arms, and another just below his seat to keep him from kicking. The idea is to convince him he's safe with you and to avoid dislodging the needle once it penetrates his skin.

More often than not, deep injections are not painful to any greater extent than giving yourself a quick stick with a pin, since most of your pain receptors are in the upper layers of the skin and are triggered only momentarily while the needle punctures through. Try to keep your muscles relaxed, take a deep breath, and whatever you do, don't jump—the needle will dislodge and will have to be sent through your skin again.

A few drugs are injected subcutaneously (just slightly under the skin), usually in your arm, and are expected to raise a wheal (a small lump). Some, such as insulin and Heparin, are injected a bit further under the skin and may be injected in many different sites, including your abdomen. The needle for these drugs is very short and of a very small gauge. Nurses used to place an ice pack on the injection site after administration of Heparin. In most cases, that's an obsolete practice so ask the nurse not to plop that hunk of ice on your nice warm abdomen.

SIDE EFFECTS

Your body is a chemical factory that manufactures powerful drugs such as hormones and enzymes. These regulate the rate at which your body operates, stimulate growth, and aid digestion. Introducing other drugs into this chemical factory is a complex business that can have serious consequences, but also may very well be lifesaving. Often the effects, aside from the original effect intended for the drug, can be as life-threatening as the condition which indicated use of the drug. This is the calculated risk we expect physicians to take.

The best example of drugs promoting life-threatening side effects are the antineoplastic agents, those drugs used to fight cancer. Use of these drugs is commonly called chemotherapy. Given in doses that inhibit the growth of malignant cells, they also affect other cells to such a degree that noticeable symptoms, such as loss of hair, nausea, mouth sores, and a depletion of the cells inhibiting infection in the body usually occur.

Almost all drugs have some side effects and any drug may be poisonous if misused. The effects must be weighed against the dangers and sometimes you are the only one who can do this. If pain relievers nauseate you, then decide which is worse, the pain or the nausea; or perhaps you can take some other medication to relieve the nausea along with the pain medication. Prednisone causes peptic ulcers, so it is usually prescribed to be taken with an antacid to retard the possibility of ulcers. Codeine often causes constipation, so a laxative will usually be prescribed for once a day. Valium relaxes muscle spasms (among its effects), but also might leave you feeling very depressed the next day, so you must weigh its benefits against its side effects and decide which is worse. Many of the medications that relieve depression don't work until you've been taking them steadily for at least two weeks.

MYTHS ABOUT MEDICATION

"You should never take medicine on an empty stomach." *Wrong,* in the case of some drugs! Almost all antibiotics must be taken on an empty stomach or they will not be absorbed. Other drugs are inactivated by milk or milk products. Still other drugs must be taken only when certain foods have been eliminated from your diet.

"Over-the-counter drugs are 'safe.'" Wrong again! Aspirin kills one hundred people a year and creates disastrous medical problems for many other people. Almost all drugs, whether over-the-counter or prescription, are potential poisons.

"The American diet suffers from a vitamin and mineral deficiency." That's more fad than fact! Excessive doses of certain vitamins have been known to do irreparable harm; eating a variety of proper foods will insure a full quota of the nutrients you need.

"You can reduce excess pounds by simply taking a pill." To reduce you must consume fewer calories than you use up in daily living—it's that simple! There is no other alternative for losing weight because calories not used by your body to produce heat or energy build fat. Millions of dollars have been spent on alternatives to eating less food, but the simple fact remains that the whole key is in the number of calories you eat versus the number of calories you "burn up" through activity or ordinary body processes.

"Pain relievers are addicting." True sometimes, false other times. Many drugs besides narcotics, barbiturates, and amphetamines are potentially habit-forming. In fact, I know a man who has taken two aspirins before going to bed each night for years. He *must* have them; he swears he cannot sleep without them. It would be convenient if we had some sort of scale to predict our addictive potential, but there is no such thing. It does not always depend on which drug we are taking, or on how often we take it, or on our personality or body chemistry. Rather, it is an unpredictable combination of all these factors.

Dalmane is an extremely effective sleeping pill and one of the few that seldom produce a "hangover" the next day. It has been advertised as one which has no addictive potential, but that is not to say it is not habit-forming. One of our patients took it for five nights in a row. On the sixth night when he decided to stop using it, he couldn't fall asleep at all. In fact, he was awake seventy-two hours straight before he finally slept. For him, the drug can be considered to be "habit-forming," although for you it may not be.

"Most drug addiction begins in the hospital." False again! It is estimated that only about 2 percent of the nation's drug addicts began their dependence in a hospital. In the majority of circumstances, the physical condition that warrants the use of addicting drugs will subside within a week. It's highly unlikely that you would become addicted to the ordinary drug in that time. Here we are speaking of drugs that are commonly "abused" and sold as "street drugs." Don't be afraid to take whatever medication is prescribed for you while hospitalized.

"When the symptoms are gone, stop the medication." Such a practice is good common sense in some cases and pure idiocy in others. If you stop taking barbiturates suddenly, you can go into devastating withdrawal. If you stop taking antibiotics when your symptoms are gone, chances are that the infection that was supposed to be wiped out by the drug will return immediately. If you stop applying ointment to a fungal condition when the itching stops, you're right back where you were before you started. On the other hand, you know what happens when you take laxatives that you don't need.

"Take four a day" does not always mean what it says. Some drugs only act when the blood level reaches a certain point; if you skip eight hours between doses, your blood may never have the right level of the drug in it to do any good. If you forget to take "the Pill" one day, how many hours can go by before you're unprotected for contraception? And if you take two one day, to make up for the one you forgot yesterday, are you still protected? Good questions!

If you're hopelessly confused, that's to be expected. Think how confusing it must be for the nurse who is giving you your medication. Remember that 90 percent of the drugs we use today were not even on the market twenty-five years ago, when many of the nurses finished their training. You can't be sure your nurse will know all she needs to know about the medications you are taking, but you *can* be sure she will look them up if you ask her about them. She has the resources at her fingertips; don't hesitate to ask her which drugs you are taking, whether they should be taken on a full or empty stomach, if the timing is crucial, what effects you can expect, if there is addictive potential, and if they are incompatible with any other medications you are taking.

Pharmacists, physicians, and registered nurses can be counted upon to know the really *dangerous* effects of all drugs, but they don't always remember to keep you informed when you continue taking the drugs after hospitalization. Also they don't always remember the characteristics of a drug that make it valuable to you under certain conditions and a waste of your money under others. *You must ask!* Asking doesn't imply that you are not a "good patient," or that you mistrust those who are caring for you. It simply means you care enough about the state of your health to shoulder some of the responsibility for it. And no one can fault you for that!

ISOLATION

In some diseases the patient must be separated from other patients. If this is to keep a germ from spreading, it's called "isolation," and if it's to keep the patient from coming in contact with other people's germs, it's called "reverse isolation" or "protective isolation."

Whatever it's called, if you're the patient it's no fun. You'll be in a room by yourself, you'll see a minimum of staff members, your visitors will be limited, and chances are that all persons entering your room will be swathed in caps, gowns, masks, gloves, paper booties, and all sorts of weird-looking garb.

FOR ADVOCATES

The sign on an isolation patient's door saying "Visitors see the nurse before entering" really means you are not to go into the room without being properly garbed. You don't have to seek out a nurse if there's another sign on the door listing the proper attire and you can find those things to put on nearby. If the isolation is to protect the other patients from germs, remove the garb just before you leave the room and place it in the red-lined trash bin, wash your hands at the patient's sink, and leave the room immediately. If the isolation is to protect the patient, remove the garb *after* you leave the room.

It sounds very complicated, but it's easy if you just stop and think who is being protected from what—you and the rest of the hospital from the patient's disease or the patient from your germs and those in the hospital.

Some types of isolation demand stricter precautions than others. A sign on your door will tell those entering what precautions they must take. In certain circumstances, these will vary. For instance, masks might not be required for your type of isolation, but a pregnant nurse would probably don one just to be on the safe side.

"Reverse isolation" means your ability to fight off infection is impaired and precautions must be taken to protect you from contracting anyone else's disease. *Everything* and *everyone* coming into your room must be covered in sterile wrapping. Even the sheets put on your bed will be sterilized before they are sent to your room. Obviously, food and medications will not be sterilized, but the whole point is to *minimize* your exposure to disease-producing elements. Even a newspaper brought into your room may have to be gas-sterilized, in which case it might be two days old before you get to read it. Your responsibility is to provide the conditions that minimize your exposure: keep a list of things you need and ask for them all at once to decrease the number of times a nurse goes in and out of your room. Remember, every time your door opens, some germs are brought in. For the same reason, keep your visitors to a minimum. If anyone walks into your room without being completely covered from head to toe, send him out.

Your susceptibility to germs will be monitored by blood tests. Too many white cells indicate you have an infection, and too few mean you are a likely target for an infection (chemotherapy patients often have too few). As your white blood cell count increases, within limits your susceptibility decreases.

In regular isolation, which protects others from your germs, anything brought into your room must be specially wrapped before it leaves. The cleaning equipment, such as mops and buckets, will be brought into your room and left there until you are discharged. This can cause a great deal of clutter, but there is no alternative. Each person who comes into your room risks catching your disease. You can minimize their exposure by doing the same as the person in protective isolation—store up your wants so that the nurse can bring many things in one trip and limit your visitors, especially those who might be more susceptible to disease: the very young, very old, or pregnant.

There are times when patients are isolated just as a precautionary measure while certain contagious diseases are being ruled out. When it turns out that you don't have anything contagious, it will have seemed like a lot of trouble for nothing, but better safe than sorry.

MISINTERPRETATIONS

When you arrive for your daily visit with the patient, chances are you'll hear some hair-raising tales of what's been going on since you were last there, especially if the patient is elderly. Perception is altered immeasurably during the night hours, and the sound of a utility cart being pushed through the quiet corridors becomes a gurney destined for the morgue in the minds of patients lying there slightly disoriented and frightened.

If the patient down the hall cries out in the midst of a nightmare, you might be told a story about the nurses harming one of the patients. You'd be amazed how often the clamor of an emergency is interpreted as "those nurses were all having a riotous party."

Misinterpretations occur during daylight too, usually related to IVs, injections, and catheters, the procedures that frighten patients the most. A ten-minute wait for a nurse becomes an "hour" in the minds of patients for whom each day seems an eternity. Your first half hour with the patient is likely to be spent listening to an exhausting tirade about the inequities of hospitalization—some of it might actually be true.

FOR ADVOCATES

Your job is to separate fact from misperception and act on the fact. A subtle way to accomplish this is to speak with the patient's nurse. Tell her you're wondering if your patient has become slightly disoriented. She'll ask what makes you think so and then you can relate the story as it was told to you. She'll tell you she'll "look into it," which she will, and you'll have accomplished your mission. If there has been some error or infraction of the rules by the staff, her investigation will prompt the responsible people to alter their actions. If, on the other hand, it was your patient's misperception, she'll probably be back to tell you what *really* happened.

If the incident was severe enough to warrant further action, you'll want to speak with the supervisor. To help you decide what is "severe" and what is not, you'll need to think about hospitals and what they really are like today as opposed to what we think they should be. They are businesses serving hundreds of patients including yours with treatment of each patient far less personal than we all would want it. If a patient becomes suddenly critically ill during the night, the majority of the staff may be coming and going to his room; peace and quiet for all the other patients will be low on the priority list. It probably *will* sound as if there's a party going on and your patient may indeed wait an hour for a nurse to respond. You must also remember that nurses have a "sixth sense" and can anticipate when their responses need to be quicker than an hour in order to avoid trouble.

Like other groups of employees in any business, nurses celebrate each other's birthdays, retirements, engagements, etc., so this is not to say a patient may never hear a party or may never have to wait for a nurse needlessly. Other groups of employees are able to leave their work area during business hours; nurses must be constantly available during their shift, which makes it more likely that the patients will hear a little of the tension-breaking activity or conversation that goes on among nurses.

CHAPTER
5
The Emergency Room

An emergency room can be expected to generate about 20 percent of a hospital's business. Wonderful statistic, isn't it? If you want to increase the profits in a department store, you might add on a tea room and, if you want to increase the profits in a hospital, you just open up an emergency room. That's the business end of it from the administrator's view.

For many doctors, an emergency room serves the same purpose—increased business. The patient is first seen by the physician who is a full-time employee of the hospital (and usually opts not to have a private practice) and is referred to the next physician on a rotation list for follow-up care. A patient with stomach cramps walks in, and she is referred to the doctor on rotation, who gets himself a brand-new patient. And if he has a polished bedside manner, he might get her friends and relatives for patients as well.

From the nurse's view, the emergency room is the best of all worlds. A little surgery, a little orthopedics, some obstetrics, urology, cardiology, and multiple trauma, and no long-term patients to sap emotional energy. To top it off, the pace is fast, the responsibility is high, and the opportunities for exchanges with the "outside world" (the police, firemen, paramedics, ambulance drivers, and street people) far exceed those offered to nurses in other units of a hospital.

THE PATIENT'S VIEW

There are three routes that might take you into an emergency room. You might get there under your own steam because you feel terrible and you don't know any doctor or it's a weekend or the middle of the night and you don't want to bother your own doctor. You may figure your insurance will pay for your illness only if you go to a hospital or claim an "industrial accident." You might get there in the car of a friend or relative who has run every stoplight along the way with his horn on constant "blast," determined to save your life, or you might arrive by ambulance. If you're conscious you might be dismayed that there are no screaming sirens to announce your private disaster. Sirens are reserved for the patient in crisis.

FOR ADVOCATES

You might be tempted to accompany your patient to the hospital in an ambulance, but remember that there will be no one to return you to your home. If you're not too distraught to drive, you might as well follow the ambulance because you will have to sit up front with the driver, not in the back with your patient.

The most important point to know about emergency rooms is that there is a distinct difference between what the medical profession considers an emergency and what the general public considers an emergency. Pain is not an emergency, a broken limb is not an emergency, a cut finger is not an emergency, vomiting is not an emergency. *Most* problems are not emergencies. Very rarely can you go into an ER and get immediate treatment, but you can be sure you will get it if you really need it. This is one time you have to leave the decision up to the doctors and nurses. If your life is threatened, they'll take care of you immediately. If it isn't, you'll just have to wait until they've taken care of everyone whose life *is* threatened and trust that they know the difference.

If you could be a fly on the wall of an emergency room for just one day, you would probably understand why so many dissatisfied patients leave the emergency room and go on to proclaim to the world how cold and heartless nurses and doctors are. In fact, the staff is constantly besieged and impeded in their work by those who cry wolf and use the ER as an outpatient clinic, which it is not. If you just feel "crummy," don't want to go to work, and your employer demands documentation from a physician that you are unable to work, don't be one of the hundreds who saunter into the ER every day with just such a goal in mind and expect concerned, kind treatment. The desk clerk will snap at you, the admitting nurse will snap at you, and the physician will show very little sympathy. You can expect them to act as if you're faking it, because to them you are faking a true emergency, a life-threatening situation.

As always, there's another side to the coin and doctors and nurses have been known to mistake a real emergency for a "fake" because all life-threatening conditions are not immediately visible. In their defense I must say that they see so many people each day who should have gone to a doctor's office rather than the ER that they approach each patient with a certain amount of skepticism. They are human, after all.

WHAT CONSTITUTES AN EMERGENCY?

As a public service, some telephone companies have published a "survival guide" in their directories. You should take a look at yours right now and become familiar with its contents. The guide will tell you what to do in an emergency and also help you decide whether or not you indeed have an emergency on your hands. The same information is available from the American Red Cross in a handy little booklet available to everyone.

Any survival guide will tell you that breathing is the most critical thing we must do to stay alive. Anyone who is not breathing is a definite case for the emergency room. Lack of oxygen is a 24-karat emergency.

Blood carries oxygen to all cells of the body. Lack of blood means lack of oxygen. The quantity of blood lost is the essential factor. Bleeding from the scalp can be very heavy, even when the wound is not serious, so it may be difficult to judge the extent of the injury just by observing the quantity of visible blood. On the other hand, traumatic injury to an organ, such as the spleen, may cause a tremendous blood loss internally that can't be seen.

How much blood loss is too much? The average adult has sixty thousand miles of blood vessels carrying five quarts or more of blood. Of course, when you're in a state of panic, it's difficult to tell the difference between a cup of blood and a pint, but heavy bleeding is also a true emergency. "Heavy" means a pint or more.

The American Heart Association offers free four-hour courses to teach you the lifesaving techniques of cardiopulmonary resuscitation (CPR), which everyone high-school age and over should learn. Besides being invaluable techniques for heart attack and drowning victims, CPR may reverse the effects of not breathing due to other causes, such as emotional shock, electric shock, traumatic injury, poisoning, and drug overdose.

THE PHYSICIAN

Whenever possible, the first thing you should do is contact your physician. He can smooth many troubled waters before you arrive in an emergency room. If you're in doubt as to whether or not you really have an emergency, he's the best one to tell you. If he's advised you to meet him at the emergency room, your arrival will be anticipated by the crew and it's likely you'll be seen long before those who arrive without the blessing of a physician in advance.

GETTING THERE

"Can you imagine? There he was, sprawled out on the highway, his car little more than a rubble heap, and that ambulance driver had the audacity to ask me how we intended to pay the sixty dollars it would cost us to have him taken to the hospital?" The cocktail-party crowd gasped in horror! Well, ambulance companies are not charitable organizations. They pay for their vehicles, equipment, office space, dispatchers, and technicians as any other private business and they don't want deadbeats on their books any more than the corner grocery store does. It would behoove you to be able to offer them some sort of security: an insurance card, a check, a health-plan membership card, or some cash.

FOR ADVOCATES

Don't panic. Your chances of encountering a truly life-threatening situation are rare. Most people can survive a major assault long enough for you to summon help easily, with time to spare.

Most true emergencies are obvious and you should call the rescue squad/paramedics immediately. When they arrive, the victim will be taken to the nearest emergency room available. The goal is to stabilize the patient as fast as possible. There is no point in being too concerned about which hospital and which doctor are involved. Both can be changed when the threat to life has passed.

If there isn't a rescue van in your area, call the fire or police department and they will send you assistance. Be sure to tell them your address over the telephone. You'd be amazed how simple it is to forget such information when you're in a panic.

WHICH HOSPITAL?

If you're given a choice of which hospital the ambulance should go to, you've got a tough problem on your hands. A children's hospital is the very best place for a child, obviously, but the choice is more difficult for an adult. If you belong to a health-maintenance organization, then you'll want to be taken there since the care is "free." Many ambulance companies have their favorite hospitals and that's where they'll suggest you go. In any case, one thing you should know is that a county hospital is not free unless you can prove you are unable to pay for your own care, so don't opt for transport to a county facility solely for financial reasons.

If I were in an unfamiliar community and needed hospital care, I would go to a university hospital—but that's personal bias! You might prefer a little community hospital's homey atmosphere. That's fine if your case is fairly routine, but for the rare or complicated case requiring sophisticated techniques and equipment, the largest hospital is usually the best bet.

ADMITTANCE

If you're in bad shape upon arrival, the admitting procedure seems ludicrous. All you want is fast help or relief from pain and here stands some clerk asking you silly questions while you're sure you're dying. Remember, unless your life is in immediate danger, you're going to have to show proof that someone will be paying for your care. A hospital is not a charity organization. You'll be asked to sign a Consent for Treatment form. *Don't sign anything unless you know what you're signing!*

Consent for Treatment forms are essential, especially if you have children who might need treatment when you are unavailable. Many local hospitals appreciate having such forms for your children on file in advance of need; it's a good idea to check with your closest emergency room and see if it has such files. These forms are particularly valuable because you can designate the physician of your choice, thus eliminating the element of chance from your child's treatment. Don't forget to include any allergies or special problems (such as diabetes, epilepsy, or congenital defects) that might affect treatment.

Once the admitting papers are completed, if you aren't in dire straits you'll be asked to wait in the lobby. Look around—if the room is filled wall to wall with people, you've a long wait ahead. Take a look in the Yellow Pages of the phone book and see if there's another hospital within driving distance, then phone ahead first and see if their waiting list is long. Have you ever gone into a restaurant, been seated, then decided you didn't want to eat there after all? Well, you can leave a hospital the same way you can leave a restaurant.

Once you've been seen by a doctor, it's not so easy to leave against medical advice (AMA). Most insurance companies won't pay your hospital bill if you leave under those conditions. Once you've been seen by a physician you'll probably be tempted to leave because you're tired of waiting around, but if you've had any lab work or X rays done you must wait for the results. This *could* take several hours.

PAIN

When you enter a hospital in pain, it's only logical for you to think that the first thing they should do is give you something to alleviate it, but they won't. In the first place, a nurse can do nothing without a physician's order and, in the second place, a physician will not order anything until he's sure what the next hour will be like for you. For instance, suppose you have fierce abdominal pain. You may need emergency surgery—in which case they're not about to give you any drug that would interfere with anesthesia. They must first determine from lab tests what will happen to you next. The same is true of a broken limb. Sometimes fractures can be treated without surgery, in which case you could be immediately medicated for pain, but not until the physician has been assured, usually by X rays, that you definitely won't be having surgery.

In any case, if you aren't medicated for pain as soon as you think you should be, speak up! When everyone is busy it's difficult to tell if they are neglecting you or if they are waiting for test results before medicating you.

FOR ADVOCATES

If you are an advocate sitting in the waiting room, ask the patient to have a nurse keep you informed of his progress so you don't sit outside wondering if he's dead or alive. If you feel you should accompany the patient "inside," insist—especially if the patient is a child. If you aren't "inside" with the patient, wait an hour and then ask the desk clerk to speak with the patient's nurse so you will know how things are progressing. You may be allowed to sit with the patient if there's a wait for test results.

The end result of an emergency room visit might be admission to a regular hospital room, in which case you need to return to Chapter 3—Day One to see what you should do next. Don't forget that the advocate should take the patient's money, jewelry, credit cards, and clothes home so they won't disappear in the shuffle.

6
Specialty Areas

Through the years, as physicians have become more specialized, certain areas of the hospital have catered to these specialties with certain equipment, supplies, routines, and trained staff unique to the specialty. Each has its own implications for patients and visitors.

INTENSIVE CARE UNIT

The intensive care unit (ICU) is definitely the ultimate in sensory assault areas. It is as if a recalcitrant child were standing on the street corner with the fire alarm permanently pulled into the panic position—pandemonium is persistent, both day and night.

Those who thrive on crisis situations collect ICU stays as badges of heroism. "Last winter when I spent five days in ICU ... " or "By the third day in ICU I was ... " For the surgery patient with a coronary-artery bypass, the shorter the stay, the higher the points in this game, but for everyone else, the longest stay wins.

View from an Intensive Care Unit Bed

Some would say that oblivion is the choice one's brain makes as defense against the poorly tuned orchestra of the beeping heart monitors, the clacking print-out machines, the whistling respirators, the gurgling chest tubes, the buzzing balloon pump, the shrieking IV alarms, the twanging intercom, and the rumbling X-ray machine—the continual cacophony of crisis.

The return of sound, the first sense to awaken after a major physical or emotional assault, is followed by the return of vision, in fleeting glimpses at first, as though the glaring lights and blazing machinery threaten to burn one's eye sockets. Most patients report the maze of tubes as their first touch with reality. One tube pushes fluid in, another delivers blood, the fat one carries urine out, and the smallest one drips antibiotic. The pleated one pumps oxygen in, the rubber one drains chest fluid out, the glass one measures pressure in the heart, and the inflated one measures pressure in an artery. And that's not all! There may be one of this type and three of another, with four slim wires tangling toward the heart monitor, all of them to measure body functions and become scribbles on a piece of paper that map out the patient's destiny for the physician.

Who Goes to ICU?

Certain surgery cases are routinely sent from the operating room to ICU, while other surgery cases are routinely sent there if the patient is in a certain age group. The major point to remember is that there are more nurses available to observe you in ICU than there are on the ward, about one nurse for two patients as opposed to one nurse to eight or ten patients on the ward. Sometimes that's the only criterion for sending you there. If your urine must be measured hourly, this obviously takes more time than a ward nurse has. Perhaps you've experienced a blow to the head—it may be nothing or may be a big problem—you need constant observation for a period of time to be sure of your condition. Sometimes your stay in ICU may be nothing more than a "wait and see" period.

On the other hand, you may need the very sophisticated equipment and technological skills available in ICU. Whether life hangs in the balance or not, the staff is prepared to retrieve life at a moment's notice.

The Routine

In ICU there is no day or night, there is no privacy, there is no shower, there is no toilet, there is no radio, there is no quiet. Don't look for anything familiar like your clothes, a newspaper, or the flowers your kids sent you yesterday. The entire unit is designed with one purpose in mind: physical crisis must be eliminated. You can be observed from any corner of the unit and it's the obligation of the nurses to make sure that you are. A bedside commode will be brought to you and your bath comes from a small plastic pail.

Fortunately, most ICU patients are fairly heavily medicated and much of your stay will take place in oblivion or at least through a sedated haze. The trade-off is intense observation and care—you can relax in the knowledge that the nurses won't miss even your softest cough and nothing could happen to you for which they are unprepared.

As hooked up to machinery as you are, it's easy to panic when you hear some sort of alarm ringing. After all, it may be that your heart has stopped beating! If you look up above your head and to the right or left, you'll see a screen similar to a tv screen but a little smaller. Wires go from that to little pads strategically placed on your upper torso so as to transmit the electrical activity of your heart to the screen. The etching on the screen can be interpreted by the staff and keeps it constantly informed as to what your heart is up to. If the machine constantly goes "bleep, bleep, bleep," it's "bleeping" every time your heart beats. On the average, it will bleep about eighty times a minute; but remember, "average" does not mean "normal"—sixty "bleeps" a minute may be normal for you. The machine will have alarms set a certain amount above and below your normal rate. If your heart rate violates these, the alarm goes off and the nurse reacts by giving you drugs to speed up your heart or slow it down. *You must remember this*—the alarm can be triggered by a sudden movement of your body, wires that have jiggled loose, or pads on your torso that have lost their sticking power. The alarms will ring because of loosened pads far more often than to signal a change in your heart condition.

The other alarm that rings quite often is the one on the machine attached to your IV tubing. These fancy little boxes on a pole measure the rate at which fluid goes into your veins. This is critical with some fluids. If the IV tubing gets a little kink, or a bubble, or the bottle is about to go dry, the alarm goes off to remind the nurse that your IV will soon need attention. Don't panic if she doesn't come running instantly—this alarm does *not* signal crisis.

If you or someone else in the unit needs the assistance of a respirator, there's a large boxlike machine beside the bed with an accordion-type device on top and pleated tubing stretching to the patient. The accordion pumps up and down rhythmically to deliver oxygen. The alarm on this machine is horrid. It "blats" incessantly when it's not puffing, so there is no danger that a defect in the amount of oxygen the patient gets could go undetected. Since mist is added to the oxygen, moisture tends to accumulate in the patient's lungs and is suctioned out quite frequently by nurses or respiratory technicians. During the short period of time the machine is disconnected for the suctioning, you'll hear the "blat" of the alarm. Don't panic, you're being carefully monitored. Also, don't panic if there's a power failure. The hospital's own generators take over where the power company leaves off; there are several other methods to keep patients breathing if the machines fail—nurses can puff air mouth-to-mouth or use a bag (Ambu bag) to puff air through a tube from the bag into the lungs.

Sobering Thoughts

There are some who disagree with the usage of such highly sophisticated care as is found in an ICU: " . . . the modern-day torture chamber. I'll never let this happen to me," writes Peter, my medical-student friend, which is what many nurses would say in circumstances that inappropriately catapult patients into ICU. For instance, there are doctors who practice as if the patient were *never* terminally ill, even when they are quite willing to *say* such is the case. A patient of theirs ends life in ICU after multiple attempts to retrieve it, away from his family and friends. Of no small consequence is the bill the family is left to pay, ICU care being the most costly of all care.

How does one circumvent such situations? Anyone can refuse a transfer to ICU. One bonus to such a refusal is the fact that in most hospitals respirators are not maintained outside ICU, thus refusal of a transfer to ICU is also refusal of the mechanical maintenance of life. Chapter 15—The Ultimate Crisis will help you with these decisions.

The Nurses

The only pace in ICU is "full tilt." This doesn't mean the nurses are always rushing to a crisis; it does mean they are like finely tuned machines ready to react to anything. A cancer patient I knew for two years would occasionally require the constant attention available only in ICU. He always hated it and the robot-like atmosphere and spoke very disparagingly of the impersonal nurses, but he couldn't deny that he got the ultimate in physical care; the ICU nurses were always ready to retrieve him from crisis.

The "burn-out" rate among ICU nurses is higher than in most jobs because the crisis atmosphere can be tolerated only for a certain length of time before the nerves become frazzled beyond repair.

If it seems that ICU is a mechanical world, run by mechanical nurses, and you wish just once someone would squeeze your hand or wipe your brow, be patient—"tender loving care" is much further down on the ICU priority list than it is in other areas of the hospital.

FOR ADVOCATES

The job of an advocate is tough under any circumstances, but the advocate of a patient in the special-care areas is most definitely working under the greatest sort of pressure. To begin with, your initial view of ICU is a monumental mindblower since you approach it with all senses alert (unlike the patient, who is usually pretty well "fogged") and the sight is generally not a pretty one. Stifle your initial urge to panic as you walk into the unit. Hold your eyes still for just a moment to focus on reality: you'll realize that almost everything you see is something you've seen before, it's just that there's so much more of it and all confined in a small space. Be prepared to hear all the bells and buzzers ringing and expect to see all the nurses rushing. It's a frantic, crazy, cluttered place, at least to the uninitiated. You can handle it if you just walk in fully expecting to see what appears to be mass confusion.

If you've brought along flowers, candy, or gifts of any sort, take them home with you and save them for a better day. The only items allowed in ICU are dentures, eyeglasses, and essential toiletries.

Most units have very strict visiting privileges usually limited to the closest relatives only (no children) and very short time spans, probably five minutes once every two hours. It's easy to be intimidated if you're a visitor to ICU, since the message put out by the nurses is that you are definitely an intruder in their world, but try to remember the stress they work under and forge ahead with understanding. To avoid potential conflict, agree with all members of the family on *one* person as the advocate. That person should introduce himself to the nurse in charge to identify himself as the liaison for all family and friends. He should be sure the nurses have his phone number since conditions in ICU are more flexible than in other hospital areas and the nurses appreciate knowing who they can call if the patient has a special request.

If your patient has difficulty communicating, ask questions that require a simple nod, a blink of an eyelid, or raising a finger and tell the nurse what system you are using so she can use it too. Ask, "Are you too cold? Are you hungry? Do you need to go to the bathroom? Are you in pain?"

It helps if you have spoken with the doctor recently and can offer your patient some reassuring words about his progress. It also helps if you do a lot of hand-holding. Just feeling the touch of someone familiar helps recovery, particularly if the patient appears unresponsive. Many comatose patients respond to touch, indicating they are not as "down under" as they look, and studies indicate that the patient in a coma often hears much that is said.

CORONARY CARE UNIT

The coronary care unit or coronary observation unit (CCU or COU) is much like ICU only there's far less machinery around and there is a day and a night. *Rest* is the biggy in this unit, because the heart patient needs relaxation in order to allow the body to promote alternate routes of circulation for increased heart function.

The heart-monitoring machines appear as they do in ICU, and can be observed at the desk where a duplicate screen is always in view of the nurses. If you see all the nurses sitting at the desk, appearing to be watching tv, they're actually watching the monitors of all the patients.

Most CCU rooms are private, with glass walls that can be covered with curtains for privacy, since peace and quiet are what you need. Because you'll be allowed very little activity, expect to be swathed in white elastic stockings from your toes to your upper thighs. These very snug hose compress the valves in the veins of your legs so that the blood flowing to your heart will not slip back into your leg veins and sit long enough to cause a clot. They're called antiembolism stockings and almost every CCU patient must wear them. They don't hurt!

If you're a smoker, you're in trouble in CCU or ICU—many patients will be assisted with oxygen, which is a gas waiting to explode. "No Smoking" is the rule but you can get around that if it really bothers you. The reduction of stress is the goal for heart patients, yet smokers who are denied cigarettes are under a stress that is sometimes unmatched by any other kind. If you *must* smoke, tell your doctor you need a cigarette and you want a nurse to wheel you out into the lobby away from the oxygen. He'll probably tell you it can't be done and so will the nurse; then ask him what he thinks the stress of a nicotine fit is doing to your poor heart. Be persistent—but if your doctor is as stubborn as you are, you might consider giving it up.

FOR ADVOCATES

This is a poor time to try to convince your patient to stop smoking, as much as you might be tempted to seize the opportunity to say "I told you so." He *knows* smoking is unhealthy but, until he really wants to stop, your nagging will only cause him more stress, which might be worse than the effects of a cigarette.

There will be no salt in the food and the coffee will be caffeine-free in CCU. Your fluids probably will also be restricted because a sick heart has difficulty pumping high volumes of fluid through the miles and miles of veins in your body. Ask how much fluid you can have and then ration it for yourself throughout the day.

The typical heart patient is called the "Type A" personality, characterized by a fast-paced life-style and a constant drive to "reach the top." This is a goal-oriented individual, often a "workaholic," usually a "high achiever," and the gregarious life-of-the-party type. Most Type As are males with high-pressure jobs. Work is their hobby, they have great difficulty relaxing, and the last place they want to be is in a CCU bed with no cigarettes, no coffee, no telephone, no martini for lunch, and a bunch of females in white telling them what to do, when to do it, and how to do it—to boot!

For all these reasons, there is great controversy over the efficacy of the CCU unit for the heart patient. To take away all that he holds dear is to create more stress than his heart can tolerate. This is why some physicians are very reluctant to place their patients in this special-care area.

CARDIAC REHABILITATION

Cardiac rehabilitation units are relatively new in hospitals. They are a product of the late 1970s in response to the massive increase in the latest vogue, coronary-artery–bypass surgery.

This area of the hospital resembles a gym more than anything else. In fact, the only difference is that there will be several heart-monitoring machines to measure the hearts' electrical activities of those participating in the "rehab" programs.

The value of such monitored exercise is controversial. You could look at it as a motivating device, if nothing else. Most people are likely to exercise as they should under supervision, which is probably why the health spas have had such commercial success in recent years. We would rather exercise with a group of people in pleasant surroundings with instructors telling us how to do it than exercise alone at home. The only problem is that monitored exercise is inordinately expensive.

Along with the exercise, the nurses who staff cardiac rehab units are trained to teach you everything you always wanted to know about your heart and how to make it well. You could save the expense by getting some books on the subject from your local library instead.

There is no proof that these rehabilitation units help you but there is no reason to suspect that they harm you—unless you worry about "harm" in relation to the escalating costs of health care.

BURN UNITS

Only certain large medical centers have burn units. Massive burns definitely require the highly specialized treatment available only there. The gravest danger for the burn patient is infection, so great care will be taken to adhere to strict isolation procedures.

The treatment unique to patients in the burn unit is called "débridement" and involves removing the necrotic (dead) material which accumulates on burns each day. This is usually accomplished by lifting the patient (often with the aid of a hammocklike hydraulic device) into a great vat of a warm, usually saline, solution. In addition to removal of the material by the jet action of water coming into the vat, special abrasive material is used by the nurses to "scrub" the necrosis from the body. Yes, it is painful, but it will be minimized if you request pain medication a half hour before your scheduled "tub time."

In fact, "request" is too mild a word if it appears you are to be taken to the tub without medication—"demand" is better.

KIDNEY DIALYSIS

If you have become a kidney-dialysis patient, the path to that unit has been long and arduous. The staff is specially trained in the intricacies of the equipment and in the psychological impact that dependency on mechanically regulated life has on you. Their goal is to assist you to live as normally as possible.

Some groups of physicians have concentrated on setting up equipment for home dialysis to cut the huge costs chronic-dialysis patients incur. Other groups have set up local dialysis units in all the major cities, as shown on the television show *Sixty Minutes*. Dialysis is a business, usually a "concession," in most hospitals and has the same moral and ethical dilemmas as other technologically sophisticated procedures. The patient whose life is saved because a poisonous overdose of narcotics has been dialyzed out of his blood might consider the procedure a modern miracle, while the patient whose natural death is prolonged by dialysis might consider it a violation of his right to die. It's a personal choice one should not make without becoming fully informed of the risks, benefits, and prognosis if you should choose to reject this treatment.

If you decide to proceed with dialysis, your first obligation is maintenance of your surgical shunt. Read everything you can get your hands on and listen carefully to the physician and staff when they teach you the techniques for keeping the shunt operating. Then teach your family members the same techniques so they can assist you when necessary. This is your responsibility and one most crucial to your health.

Continuous Ambulatory Peritoneal Dialysis (CAPD), developed in late 1980, frees 20 percent of dialysis patients from the machines. Ask your doctor if it would work for you.

PEDIATRICS

The bigger the pediatric unit, the more specialized the care. You should look for specially trained nurses, special equipment and supplies, special furniture, special decor, and special treatment for children and their parents. If there's a children's hospital nearby, that's usually your best option. Otherwise, call the hospitals listed in the Yellow Pages of the phone book and ask them the number of pediatric beds. Less than ten indicates it's safe to get care for minor things such as a broken limb, but for major diseases and injuries, seek more specialized care in a larger pediatric unit.

Few things are more traumatizing than hospitalization, especially for children under five years of age. Their fear of abandonment is exaggerated in any case and hospitalization only confirms their worst suspicions; Mom and Dad are going to walk out into the sunset never to return, and hordes of strangers will inflict all sorts of painful wounds. Indeed, in the eyes of a child the needle on a syringe is like a bayonet and no amount of reasoning can alter that perspective.

Pediatric nurses across the nation will wish this book had never been written, but personal bias obliges me to tell you that the best place for you is at your child's bedside around the clock, regardless of the posted visiting hours.

In the more progressive hospitals, parents are provided with a bed, free of charge, in the child's hospital room. While some would argue that tiny patients are much better off without parents around, it has been my experience that the only help absent parents give is to make the nurses more comfortable. When your child is old enough to have a bedside telephone and use it properly, he's probably old enough to be left alone more.

Literature regarding the effects of hospitalization on children suggests that the traumatization can be decreased through play. If you give the child a doll and some of the supplies used in his treatment, such as a syringe, tongue blade, Band-Aids, etc., the child will act out his fears on the doll. Sometimes the play appears violent and macabre, which gives you some idea of the child's perception of what is, or might be, happening to him and lets you know just how threatened he feels.

If you're in the midst of potty training just before hospitalization, forget it. The ill child naturally regresses to a more infantile state and you'll have to postpone such things as weaning, breaking the thumb-sucking habit, and decreasing dependency on favorite ragged blankets or disreputable teddy bears. Any behavior is socially acceptable behavior for a sick child.

Though most hospitals go out of their way to serve hot dogs, hamburgers, and tacos to little ones, chances are the child will reject far more food than he eats. Ask the nurse what you can bring from home.

In many hospitals, any patient under sixteen years of age is considered a "pediatric" patient. This is difficult on adolescents, who want nothing to do with childhood, and even more difficult on their parents. Children between the ages of twelve and sixteen can be unusually rebellious and abusive and you can expect them to embarrass you to tears. Nothing you say or do will be right.

The odds are that it would be a waste of time to seek understanding from the staff. You probably remember how you felt about the methods other people used with their teenagers before you had children of your own. "I'd never let my kids talk to me the way that mother lets her kids talk to her!" Many nurses have never had teenagers to contend with and, unless they have, it's doubtful they can understand the situation. So don't waste your time trying to make a "good patient" out of your teenager. He's terrified of losing control, of crying out in pain, of being dependent, of submitting to poking and probing, and, most of all, of the humiliation brought on by lack of privacy. He needs you to allow him to vent all this by being obnoxious. He also needs you to keep him informed about what's going to happen next. Surprises only make him more insecure, so be sure you speak with the doctor every day and know exactly what's in store.

For adults, visitors are tiring but this should be a minor concern when a teenager is the patient. The more visitors, the merrier (this does not make the nurses happy). Adolescence is a popularity contest of sorts and few things make a teenager more popular than being in the hospital. Chances are the most memorable events of hospitalization will be the visits of friends he didn't even know he had.

ALCOHOLIC REHABILITATION UNITS

The type of treatment program and the success rate mark the difference between one alcoholic unit and another. Some hospitals employ the aversion technique, which essentially is designed to make the patient "sick to death of alcohol." Others are based on Antabuse treatment; Antabuse is a drug that causes a violent reaction if alcohol is consumed while it is in one's system. Still others have very detailed programs with the focus on participation in group meetings led by Alcoholics Anonymous.

While the medical community has not reached agreement on the causes or treatment of alcoholism, all would agree that the physiological effects are serious, involving liver damage, electrolyte imbalance, audiovisual misperception, and disorders of the central nervous system. For this reason, withdrawal from alcohol should take place in a specialized unit of an acute (not a mental or convalescent) hospital, under the direction of a physician who specializes in this problem.

The best programs control withdrawal symptoms with large doses of medications in the beginning, then taper to maintenance doses. Rehabilitation of the psychosocial aspects of the patient's world is done through daily occupational-therapy programs, social-services counseling, and Alcoholics Anonymous programs.

As a patient on an alcoholic unit, you'll be expected to participate in your own care more than on other units. You should have comfortable street clothes with you because you'll probably be expected to dress and walk to the cafeteria for meals and you may go on outings with the group. Planned activities, such as card games, parties, and lectures, will keep you busy; the focus will be on returning your life to the level of functioning you enjoyed before alcohol took over.

For greatest success, you should participate in every opportunity presented, whether you feel like it or not, so that you develop a network of friends who will support you as you support them through the difficult period of "drying out" and retrieving your self-esteem.

The staff on an alcoholic unit is unique. They choose to work there and are among the most highly job-satisfied nurses in the profession. Expect more empathy and support from them on a consistent basis than you will find in any other area of a hospital. Some say it's because these nurses are recovered alcoholics, thus they understand the problem, but there are no statistics to support this notion. For whatever reason, they usually are a great group of nurses that you can depend on to give you gentle, concerned care.

FOR ADVOCATES

The alcoholic patient is someone you've loved or you wouldn't be the advocate. There's a high chance you feel as if you're sitting on the brink of an emotional disaster. This means you're normal, hanging in limbo, wondering if you really are going to get the "cured" alcoholic through this program and back to a normal life with you.

The first thing you should do is join the local Al-Anon group, which focuses on bringing people together to help one another deal with the problems of living with an alcoholic. This may seem a waste of time if you have high expectations of taking a "cured" alcoholic home with you, but "cure" doesn't happen in the two-week program of hospitalization. New patterns of living surround the cure and that takes time, patience, and more understanding than you'll probably have without the help of a group such as Al-Anon.

On the day your patient is to be discharged you're likely to feel that your world is caving in. You feel as if you're taking a stranger home with you and that really is frightening! You feel as if life hinges on your making all the right moves and there you are without a rule book. It's not easy. In fact, it might be the most difficult thing you'll ever have to do.

Rule number one is to change nothing since nothing you do will either keep the patient sober or catapult him back to alcoholism. Sobriety is a commitment that is his sole responsibility; your only obligation is to treat him as you would anyone else. His first priority is to retrieve the self-respect he lost when he admitted that he had given control of his life over to alcohol. You can help him best by treating him as a self-respecting adult.

OBSTETRICS

With organized medicine now in favor of humanizing maternity care, the revolution begun in a few hospitals throughout the country is certain to spread. The goal is a family-oriented childbirth that includes the father being present through labor and delivery, a homelike atmosphere, visits by the parents' other children, and the infant sleeping in the same room with the mother.

One reason for all this has been the growing rebellion among mothers and fathers against traditional hospital-delivery procedures. This has resulted in an increase in home deliveries and an attendant increase in risk to the infant. Which obstetrician you select is dependent upon whether or not you opt for home delivery, whether or not the father intends to participate in the process, and whether or not you feel strongly about "natural childbirth": settle these options and then choose a physician who shares your goals.

The Case for Hospital Delivery

Lani and I went through nursing school together and learned everything there was to learn about maternal and child care. She went on to become the perfect mother-to-be, sticking religiously to the twenty-five-pound–weight-gain limit, exercising daily, visiting the obstetrician regularly, and basing all her decisions on "what's good for the baby."

She and her husband, Lee, attended the childbirth classes that were designed to make both of them well-prepared participants in one of life's most poignant events. When it came time for delivery, Lee was well primed to don the surgical gown and play a part in the delivery of their child, but you know what happens to the best-laid plans. Lani labored for hours to no avail, the unborn child began to suffer respiratory problems, and the delivery was an emergency cesarean section under general anesthesia, with Lani fast asleep and Lee waiting in the lobby.

Lani was the perfect candidate for an at-home delivery, since her pregnancy had been flawless; but if she had not been in the hospital when she was, there would not have been the staff and equipment to rescue the infant and the nine months would have culminated in tragedy. There is no way to anticipate such circumstances.

Hospital Delivery

Given that you have made the decision to have a hospital delivery, you can make the whole event more pleasant by taking advantage of an orientation to the hospital about six weeks before your due date. Almost all hospitals offer a tour of the labor and delivery areas, so that there won't be any frightening surprises when you arrive as a patient.

Notice the small box at the head of the bed in the labor room. This is a fetal-monitoring device with sensors that are attached to the scalp of the baby so that distress during labor can be detected through interpretation of the waves projected onto the monitoring screen. In some hospitals, monitoring by this method is standard practice. However, the procedure is invasive (see Chapter 8—Diagnostic Exams), with maternal infection a common consequence, which is why this practice has become one of the big battlegrounds in American obstetrics. The approach to the infant's scalp through the birth canal often introduces bacteria into the uterus. In addition, the skin of the scalp is perforated, which also could introduce bacteria and subsequent infection.

The alternative method of fetal monitoring involves placing a special stethoscope on the mother's abdomen during contractions and listening for the relationship of the fetal heart tones to the mother's contractions. This is intermittent monitoring, as opposed to continuous monitoring discussed above.

It is said that the sophisticated machinery of continuous monitoring allows early recognition so that "high risk" babies can be anticipated and the necessary staff and equipment prepared for specialized care of the baby after delivery. If there were statistics to support the notion that continuous monitoring has been of significant advantage, it would be easy to advise you on the choice you should make. However, lack of proof that the advantages outweigh the disadvantages is precisely what has made the monitor the big obstetrical battleground that it is. Watch your newspaper for more information as the medical community attempts resolution and be sure to exercise your options when you enter the hospital as a patient. Though it may be hospital policy to use the fetal-monitoring device, you have the right to refuse the procedure.

During your tour of the labor and delivery suites, also notice the huge mirror at the foot of the table in the delivery room. It is placed there so that you can watch the birth and the anesthesiologist can monitor progress; however you can ask to have it partially turned away if you prefer not to watch.

Many hospitals encourage you to file preadmission forms so you won't have to contend with the admitting process when you arrive on the doorstep in labor. You should take advantage of this convenience because it's difficult to remember such simple things as your own birth date when you're having contractions and are excited about finally ending the nine months of pregnancy.

Once you're admitted as a patient, the preparation procedures are by the doctor's orders. Ask him in advance what his routine is. You can count on frequent pelvic examinations, which are not painful, for measurement of the dilatation of your cervix. Six is the magic number, the point at which the physician should be called. This should give him plenty of time to arrive for the birth, which occurs when the cervix is at ten centimeters. The time it takes to dilate to ten centimeters varies anywhere from one to twenty-four hours or more. The nurses can anticipate from your progress how long it's likely to take from the time they call the physician until delivery. You won't be disappointed if you just remember that they are making an educated guess, nothing more, and that babies tend to arrive exactly when they please.

Natural Childbirth

If the use of pain relievers seems like *un*natural childbirth, it may be some consolation to know that *very* few women complete the process without some assistance from medications. Labor is just what it implies, very hard physical work, stretching many muscles that protest loudly; it's no disgrace to need relief during the process. Despite the claims that medications are given only to cowards who couldn't care less about the consequences to the infant, your obstetrician knows all there is to know about the effects of drugs on babies and is not about to order any lethal dose of anything. It's wise to discover your physician's views on this subject during your very first visit—but remember, if he's a man, he's never been through labor and delivery himself.

After Delivery

Sanitary napkins are called "peri-pads" in hospitalese. These will be checked quite often in the hours after delivery to insure that you are not hemorrhaging. Don't be embarrassed; the nurses aren't.

If babies are brought from the nursery to their mothers at a certain time and yours is not—*don't panic*. Many infants, especially those of unusually high or low birth weights, need to stay in the nursery for a variety of reasons. By the time you ask why, your imagination will already have run wild. To make things worse, each nurse may give you a different answer. Ask to speak to the nurse in charge of the nursery. Large babies often need frequent suctioning of excess mucus from their lungs, while small babies may need more oxygen. It doesn't mean the baby is "in trouble."

If you have just had your first baby, ask for the equipment to bathe your baby under supervision. This one task seems to be the most stressful of all for new mothers. Placing a washcloth in the bottom of the basin makes the baby less slippery; you'll probably be surprised at how quickly you enjoy bath time much more than any other because the baby enjoys it so.

If your baby is doing well and you're not having excessive vaginal discharge, there's seldom any reason why you can't leave the hospital the day after delivery—as long as you have someone at home to help you. Rest is what you need the most and that's difficult to get in any hospital.

Cesarean Delivery

The surgical wound of a cesarean delivery, like all other surgical wounds, must heal. In addition, you've had general anesthesia. Read Chapter 7—Surgery so you know what to expect, how to speed your recovery, and how to minimize the discomforts. As with any major surgery, you can expect to be hospitalized longer than you would for the ordinary childbirth, probably about five days.

FOR ADVOCATE FATHERS-TO-BE

In some hospitals fathers are treated like intruders, while in others they have almost as much status as a doctor. Part of how you're treated depends upon the role you play. If you've been to childbirth classes and expect to be an active participant, you might have to assert yourself. Don't be intimidated by someone who says, "This is hospital policy." As in any other hospital area, you simply have to stand your ground and use common sense.

Fathers who decide to be present for delivery of the baby scrub and don the same surgical garb as the doctors, which is no problem except that the mask and gown can feel almost suffocating, especially under the hot, bright lights of the delivery room. The emotional impact of watching your baby's birth compounds the problem and it's not unusual to respond to such stress by feeling light-headed. The first rule for all observers in an operating or delivery room is "*fall away from the sterile field*," which means to move away from the delivery table and any equipment so that the dizzy feeling won't cause you to touch accidentally anything that is sterile. Sit down in a corner away from the action and put your head down between your knees. More oxygen will flow to your brain and keep you from feeling woozy. Don't be embarrassed; even professionals have been known to feel faint in the operating and delivery rooms.

Observing the Delivery

There is no rule that says a father-to-be must be present at the delivery. I remember one young man telling me, "I was sitting there, trying not to be nervous, acting as if I spent every night sitting in the fathers' waiting room, when this nurse walked in and asked me if I wanted to watch the birth. Now what was I supposed to say? She acted like it was some big privilege and if I was a very good boy she would grant me this favor. I didn't know what to do. How could I tell her I was scared to death?"

While watching surgery for the first time, as a nursing student, I wondered if the experience was analogous to a father watching a birth for the first time. I had seen surgery in movies, was thoroughly textbook prepared, and had listened to the tales of surgery told by instructors and scrub nurses, but nothing could have prepared me adequately for the impact of the first operation.

If you're an involved member of the team, it's one thing. You're caught up in the technological aspects, you see only the small undraped area you're working on, and the patient really ceases to be a human with a face and a name. If you're an observer though, the body on the table is definitely a human being and the whole procedure may be just too much to absorb.

People in the medical profession are not allowed to be members of the surgical team when one of their own family undergoes surgery because it's too difficult for them to remain objective. How much less objective could a father be when he's about to watch the birth of his child? Those who believe the father should be present for the delivery would say that objectivity is what should be avoided. However, the birth process is seldom, if ever, the romanticized event we would like to consider it, and a room full of doctors and nurses masked and swathed in gowns, with foreign sights, smells, and clanking sounds would tend to terrify anyone. Watching surgery is not for everyone and watching childbirth is not for everyone. Both have been dramatized out of all proportion to reality, yet we tend to condemn the father who makes the choice against watching the delivery.

To be a "good" father and advocate, you don't have to watch the birth, but you *should* be present during labor to offer reassurance. By the way, *don't* give the mother water, though she may be very thirsty. She should have an empty stomach in case she needs anesthesia.

As fragile as your new baby might look, there's no reason to be afraid that you will cause harm. Just remember that an infant's neck muscles are poorly developed so you must support the head with your hand for the first few weeks. You'll probably be more comfortable if you practice holding the baby a few times before you all leave the hospital.

PSYCHIATRY

A lady in her mid-forties stood like a soldier beneath the clock in the hospital lobby. She could have passed for any patient's visitor except that it was five in the morning, either much too early or much too late to be visiting patients.

"May I help you?" I asked her, thinking she probably was an early patient for the X-ray department.

"Help is *not* what I need. All I really want is a lawyer and a fair jury trial." It's not unusual to be confronted with odd requests in an inner-city hospital and even less unusual in a Catholic hospital noted as a refuge for those in need of care, so I invited her to join me in the cafeteria for a cup of coffee.

She went on to tell me that she lived in a hotel near the hospital but that she was without television or a radio because she lived in poverty. "The poverty I don't mind," she said, "but I have no access to what's going on in the world and that puts me at a disadvantage." The day before she had stood on a busy downtown corner and begged the people who passed by to converse with her. "Tell me what's happening. Discuss with me!" she shouted, but everyone ignored her.

"As I was crossing the street, I heard a young girl mention Pittsburgh and it came to me that I probably should go to Pittsburgh. Maybe that's where I belong. But how can I get there if I don't have any money?"

She wasn't really asking me and her monologue became more and more disjointed as time passed. Each time she changed the subject, I tried to think of some means of helping her solve her problems until it became clear that she indeed did not want help.

She demanded that I get her to Pittsburgh and assure her that she would have at least a half hour on tv and radio to discuss her views on the sorry state of the nation. She ended our time together—during which I had said nothing—by saying, "You are obviously a mental patient and unable to respond to my needs," and strode out of the hospital and onto a bus.

Not too many years ago anyone could have listened to her, decided she was mentally incompetent, called the police, and had her admitted to the psychiatric ward. But in recent years, investigation into what goes on in psychiatric wards, who is to be classified as a patient, and how one leaves such wards has caused significant changes in the criteria for admission. In addition, consumer consciousness has affected the field of psychotherapy almost as much as the other health-care fields, so that we are not allowed to judge anyone "mentally incompetent," "crazy," or "emotionally unstable" just because they do not fit our standards of "normal."

Basically, a person must be judged *dangerous* to himself or others in order to be involuntarily committed to a psychiatric ward. On the face of it this may seem very cut and dried—but it isn't. You may consider someone dangerous if he strolls naked across your front lawn. After all, he has violated the norms of society and heaven only knows what crazy act he might commit next. Actually he has done nothing life-threatening and thus he is not a case for the psychiatric ward. This is where most misconceptions about these wards begin.

The most striking difference between the psychiatric patient and people like you and me is the hospital identification band. The patient wears one, while you and I do not. His problems are probably very similar to ours, as are his life circumstances, but he has temporarily—sometimes permanently—lost the ability to cope. The loss may have been precipitated by physiological factors and may be easily exacerbated; the role of the hospital is to reduce the risks arising from the patient's inability to cope with these factors.

Most people are afraid to visit a psychiatric ward, assuming it is filled with "crazies," but its appearance is much like that of a social club. The patients wear street clothes, as do the staff, and the rooms are similar to motel rooms. Usually meals are served in an ordinary dining room; the "day" room has couches, a tv, perhaps a pool table; and the occupational-therapy room is outfitted for cooking, crafts, and various entertaining projects.

If you happen to be a patient there, the most important thing for you to know is that the Patient's Bill of Rights applies to you as well as to every other patient. In fact, there is an addendum to the Bill of Rights that applies specifically to psychiatric patients so that you won't be "locked up for life" or subjected to the treatment you saw in the motion picture *One Flew Over the Cuckoo's Nest*. A public telephone will always be available to you should you decide you no longer wish to be a patient. There are ordinary visiting hours so you won't feel isolated and each day you'll be visited by a physician.

Your time in a psychiatric unit will be relatively structured. You're expected to dress every day, appear for meals on time, participate in prescribed activities, and keep appointments with your doctor. Though you may have sought refuge in a psychiatric ward wanting to do nothing more than curl into a fetal position and wish the world away, therapy is designed to keep you oriented to reality while protecting you from some of the environmental stresses that have catapulted you there in the first place.

Why you have lost the ability to cope with your environment is of primary importance, so a thorough physical exam to eliminate or identify physiological causes will begin your stay. Chemical imbalances, drug reactions, brain tumors, circulatory disturbances, and a number of other problems can manifest in psychiatric disorders.

It's usually easier to "repair" a malfunctioning of the body; this is why it will be the first avenue explored. If biological disturbance has been eliminated, the focus will be on past and present life events that may have contributed to the loss of ability to cope. Exploration into psychological factors usually involves a few standard paper-and-pencil tests as well as sessions with a psychotherapist trained in diagnosis.

"Shock treatment," which is known medically as "electric convulsive therapy," has been the big bugaboo of psychiatric units for years. Still very controversial, it is illegal in some states one year, legal the next, and illegal the year after that. It may be legal when you read this book and illegal next year. Basically, it is an electrical shock of enough volts to produce a convulsion. Apparently the effect alters the patient's state of mind, so that profound depression is sometimes relieved. Why this happens is not clear, nor are the long-term effects; however, there are a number of psychiatrists who rely heavily on this treatment. Since you must sign a Consent for Treatment form, I would like to give you some expert advice, but all I can say is that it has been known to be effective in some cases, detrimental in others, and makes little difference in still others.

If you opt for this treatment, and that might be the case if you are severely incapacitated by depression, you should be aware that the treatment is almost always followed by a period of amnesia lasting as long as five days. While this is most often temporary, it can be very frightening if you haven't anticipated it.

FOR ADVOCATES

In some cases of mental illness, visitors are thought to inhibit recovery, while in others visitors may be crucial to the return of mental health, so the first thing you need to find out is what's best for your patient. If visitors are not allowed, you, as the patient's advocate, should identify yourself to the nurses and physician so that they know your role is not that of the ordinary visitor. The advocate should make a short visit daily, if only to insure that the patient does not feel abandoned. Because the hospital laundry is not equipped to handle street clothes, you should maintain a fresh supply for the patient. Hospital kitchens are not usually noted for their cooking. Perhaps you could bring some goodies from home.

You will probably be most uncomfortable around the patient. You don't know why it is that he lost control, you may feel you even had a hand in it, but none of us really "drives someone crazy." If you're scared to open your mouth for fear you might say something that will send the patient into an irretrievable psychotic state, that's normal—but incorrect. Naturally, you don't want to increase the anxiety of the patient; the best thing for you to do is to listen, which is mostly what the psychotherapist will do. We all feel a need to "do something" when a loved one is in distress, and listening is the very best thing you can do for a mentally distressed patient. He needs to sort things out, to hear himself say the things that are bothering him, to hash and rehash the thoughts and feelings that frighten him. The more he talks, the easier it is for him to sort things out.

If you find yourself weakening and feeling less and less able to cope yourself, keep in mind that this is not unusual and feel free to discuss your fears with the nurses and your patient's physician. They're highly skilled in interpreting the patient's behavior but, in the busy course of the day, it's easy for them to forget the impact the patient might be having on your life unless you too solicit some help.

Surgery

To have it or not to have it is often the question. Studies at home and abroad suggest that as the number of surgeons increases in an area, the number of operations also goes up, with no clear evidence that all this extra surgery is necessary. The United States has twice as many surgeons as England and Wales and twice the surgery rate per capita. Health-maintenance organization members undergo half as much surgery and demonstrate a 25 percent lower mortality rate than other patients. Some authorities contend that one out of every five operations is unnecessary.

Dr. Moyes walked by the nurses' station, greeting everyone with good humor: " 'Mornin', gals. Anyone got a gallbladder I can take out? I'm running low on surgery cases." Appalling? Well, think about it—if no one's house needs a new roof, how does the roofer pay the bills? And if no one wants a swimming pool, the swimming-pool company goes out of business. And if we all decide to go braless, the lingerie manufacturers will be in trouble. So how does the surgeon pay his mortgage if no one needs surgery?

ELECTIVE SURGERY

"Elective" means you have a choice whether to have surgery or not—but often it isn't very clear just when you have that choice. For example, during a routine examination my doctor felt a mass in my abdomen, ordered X rays and diagnostic tests, determined that the mass was on my kidney, and sent me to a urologist, a doctor specializing in kidney problems. The urologist ushered me into his office at 5:00 p.m., placed my X rays in front of the light, spent about two minutes scanning them and then said, "Well, you're a nurse so I'll give you the facts straight out. You have renal-cell carcinoma (cancer of the cells of the kidney) and should have a nephrectomy (removal of the kidney) immediately. Can you be in the hospital by eight o'clock tonight?"

It was a Friday night and I had no idea what I was going to do next, but I told him I would have to think about it, which I'm sure startled him since he had intended to make very clear the emergency nature of the problem.

For the first time in my life, I went to a second doctor for an opinion and it turned out that I not only did not need a nephrectomy, I did not have cancer.

To the physician, the surgery he recommended was "emergency," but to me it was "elective." How can you tell which is which? Sometimes you can't, but the first thing you want to ask is: What's the worst possible thing that can happen if I wait a day or two to have surgery? Many physicians will give you reasonable answers. For instance, if you present yourself to the doctor complaining of fierce abdominal pain and a blood test indicates your white-cell count has skyrocketed, your appendix is probably about to explode. The worst possible consequence if surgery is delayed is that your intestine will spill its contents into your abdomen and you will be filled with infection, which *can* be lethal. You are then a candidate for emergency surgery, no doubt about it.

On the other hand, suppose you unexpectedly begin vomiting large quantities of blood. You rush to the emergency room, some diagnostic tests are performed, and the conclusion is that you have a gigantic stomach ulcer. One way to cure it is to remove your stomach. Another way is to rinse your stomach with ice water passed through a tube inserted through your nose and on into your stomach until the bleeding stops, and then further resolve the problem with a regimen of a bland diet, antacids, and the newest wonder drug for ulcers, Tagamet.

On a routine physical examination, an eighty-two-year-old patient, Mr. Tomlinson, had an irregular EKG which indicated his arteries were cluttered with "sludge." He had no symptoms other than that of fatigue on exertion, which is a very common consequence of old age. His physician recommended that he have surgery to clean out the arteries (a Roto-Rooter job, we called it). We admitted him to the surgical ward the day before surgery and began the routine preparation—blood and urine tests, shaving of the operative site and so on. As the day wore on, he became more and more withdrawn, tears glistening in his eyes much of the time.

Sleep eluded him that night. I finally got a chance to go sit with him to try to make the night shorter. "You seem very sad tonight, are you worried?" He broke into sobs and went on to tell me about his life, saying "I had everything I really ever wanted." All he now wanted from the remainder of his life was to be comfortable and to sit back and watch his family enjoy life. It sounded reasonable to me.

It took him some time before he got around to the crux of the matter. He was convinced he would die if he had surgery in the morning. "If I had pain anywhere, or if I could count on living ten years longer after surgery, well maybe I could see it, but I feel fine right now, have for years. Why should I chance messing that up?"

FOR ADVOCATES

This is prime guilt time for you. If you press your patient to proceed with surgery and it is unsuccessful, you'll feel guilty. If you don't press him to proceed, you'll still feel guilty. Your best bet is to reject giving an opinion. Only the patient can make the choice, especially when it is one between the quantity and the quality of life.

There I was, wondering why indeed Mr. Tomlinson should submit to surgery, wishing I could tell him he'd be a damned fool to, knowing he had at least a 50 percent chance of not surviving the surgery, and wanting to know why any physician would subject an eighty-two-year-old man who was in no discomfort to the rigors of such a surgery.

All I could say to the patient was that he had the right to refuse surgery and that I could void the Consent he had signed the day before. I could not "bite the hand that feeds me," but I was obligated to inform the patient of his rights. I *wanted* to tell him that he should get his clothes on and go home and enjoy the rest of his life or, at the least, should consult a second physician for another opinion. However, my career was at stake and I had twenty-five more working years left of life that I really didn't want to spend at anything other than nursing.

When patients say they think they're going to die, I take it seriously, since authorities contend that many of us can indeed anticipate the moment of death, so I informed the physician of what Mr. Tomlinson had said. Then I phoned his daughter and told her he was apprehensive about surgery and would like to discuss it with her. His sons and daughters arrived in short order and convinced him it was his "obligation" to the family to have the surgery. His children cried, he cried, and the physician strode into the room in the middle of this drama.

"What in the hell's going on?" he asked. "I thought you and I had this all settled. They're waiting for you down in surgery, you're holding up the show. What's the problem?"

Mr. Tomlinson straightened up as if he had been scolded by the schoolteacher. "Nothing's going on, Doc. Guess I've just got the usual 'before surgery jitters.' Let's get on with it . . . wouldn't want to hold up the whole schedule." His sons and daughters let out great sighs of relief and off he went to surgery. From there he was taken to the intensive care unit; two days later his name appeared in the obituary column of the local newspaper. Later, thousands of dollars' worth of medical bills were paid, as they always are, whether the patient survives or not.

Mr. Tomlinson wasn't the only patient who first resisted surgery and then submitted, but there's a vast difference between the way he was handled and the way many other patients are handled. Often the physician gladly postpones surgery, knowing that the resistant patient is a poorer risk than the one who goes to surgery convinced of a positive outcome. Dr. Wineland is my idea of a supersurgeon. When one of his patients resisted surgery, he himself gathered the family together and calmly reiterated what he had previously told them. The atmosphere was unrushed and without threat; there was no sense of urgency or inconvenience to the rest of the hospital if his patient decided to "back out." He was happy that his patients went into surgery with some sense of responsibility for their own health; he actually found too trusting patients a threat to his profession.

SURGICAL RISK

Doctors are obligated to tell you the risks that attend any surgery they propose for you, which can be very frightening until they calm your fears with "... but that almost never happens. I've done hundreds of these operations over the years and never lost a patient yet." The risk is minimal for many surgeries, but the risk is there nonetheless; just the administration of anesthesia involves a risk that is compounded by the operation itself. This is not to say you should never have surgery, only that it is plain foolish to do so unless the need for it is 99 percent clear. Since you aren't a physician, it will be very difficult to tell when that's the case, so get a *second*, or even a *third* opinion. Read up on your medical problem, explore alternatives.

For example, in Chapter 1—Who Shall Be the Patient's Advocate?, I talked about the decision whether to have a hysterectomy, considering the potential problems of estrogen depletion. What is estrogen depletion? Well, it's the result of recalcitrant ovaries that refuse to function after a hysterectomy. Part of the decreased functioning can be attributed to the fact that removing the uterus also removes half the blood supply nourishing the ovaries, while the rest is probably still unexplained. The symptoms of estrogen deficiency include dry skin, changes in libido, depression, weight fluctuations, depleted muscle tone, premature wrinkling, emotional upheaval, "hot flashes," lusterless hair, migraine headaches, body-fluid imbalance, and general sagging tendencies. This does not *always* happen, but you must decide if you want to take the risk since you sign the Consent for Treatment form if you opt to have a hysterectomy. No ranting and raving or malpractice suit can stop the estrogen depletion if it happens to be a by-product of the surgery.

Estrogen-replacement therapy is the "cure" for estrogen depletion. For that you will be dependent upon the gynecologist, month in and month out for the rest of your life, at a cost of about $300 a year. This may seem like a minor inconvenience, but the medication that replaces your own estrogen also has its own serious side effects.

For many doctors across the nation, estrogen-replacement therapy is a lucrative business. Some can count on seeing their estrogen-depleted patients for injections every two weeks until death do them part, which *may* not have been the intent of the physicians who removed so many uteruses, but the financial impact is significant.

Also there are conditions that are exacerbated by the formation of scar tissue after a surgery intended to "cure" the condition. For instance, low back pain treated by a laminectomy may later reoccur as a result of scar tissue formation, requiring further surgery. Abdominal surgery is often followed by adhesions (scar tissue) requiring still more surgery. Surgery begets surgery—sometimes. There are many conditions that can be treated with medications rather than surgical intervention. You must know exactly what you're doing when you submit to surgery; never rush into it unless your life is in immediate danger.

Only you can make the decision whether or not to have surgery, but make that decision as a well-informed consumer of medical services. You owe yourself and your physician that much.

If you decide to proceed, read "Informed Consent" in Chapter 10—Your Legal Rights and Responsibilities, pp. 167–69, and sign nothing without being informed. Be sure "left" and "right" are labeled correctly. It's not always obvious to the operating team whether "left" or "right" should be removed, so make sure the Consent form has it spelled out correctly.

GENERAL ANESTHESIA

An anesthesiologist is an M.D. with special training in the use of gases and drugs to produce a sleep state so that you won't know what's going on during surgery. He sits at the head of the operating table with a "cockpit" of machinery, monitoring equipment for your circulatory system, and IV supplies. He will begin by giving you relaxing medications through your veins, and before you can count to three, you'll feel yourself drifting off.

Perhaps you've read that the anesthesiologist can be more important to your surgery than the surgeon, and you may have been led to believe that you have no choice in his selection, which is really not the case. Ask your physician and a few nurses whom they would want if they were going to have surgery. Ask your friends whom they have had and if they were pleased. Then insist on having the anesthesiologist of your choice, though this is not always easy as he might not be available at the same time as your surgeon.

A good anesthesiologist will visit you the night before surgery, inquire about previous experiences with anesthesia, want to know the date of your last surgery, list your drug allergies, tell you your options for your particular case (local, spinal, or general anesthesia), and will advise you of the pros and cons of each.

An anesthesiologist insures that you remember nothing from the time he begins the induction until the time you awaken in the recovery room. He also insures that the nurses have an order for an antiemetic to keep you from vomiting after surgery. The night after surgery, he will come around to check on you; you can thank him then for his work, while he can reassure himself that all is well and there are no aftereffects from the anesthesia.

When you've been pleased with an anesthesiologist, remember his name and tell your friends about him. You might also send him a thank-you note—many of us are in a fog during hospitalization and tend to forget those who were crucial to our care when we weren't quite "with it."

PREPARING FOR SURGERY

Before you ever go to surgery, you should be sure you know where the surgeon will make the incision—sometimes it's a matter of choice. For instance, there are two ways a cesarean section can be done: with a vertical cut or a "bikini cut." The vertical is easier for the surgeon, but the resulting scar can't be hidden under your bikini, so if it's important to you, speak up.

For other types of surgery, there may be no choice, but you should know where the incision will be, just so you won't be surprised later.

The preparation differs from operation to operation and surgeon to surgeon, but if an incision is going to be made, the site and a large area surrounding it will have to be shaved because hair harbors bacteria. Whether you can see it or not, all of the body is covered with hair. The goal is to present your body to the operating room in as germ-free a state as possible; especially if you're to have orthopedic surgery, you might be required to have several scrubs before you ever arrive in the OR.

The area you're required to have shaved or scrubbed should give you some clues: if you're going to have a knee operation and someone begins to shave your arm—watch out! They're working on the wrong patient. On the other hand, some surgeries involve grafts from other sites on your body which will also need to be "prepped," so ask just what's going on. Ideally, a nurse or doctor will have told you exactly what will be done before surgery and there will be no surprises in store for you, but the ideal is not always the reality. Always ask *why* something is going to be done. This insures that you're the correct patient, experiencing the correct procedure, and allays the jitters that always accompany the unknown.

For most operations you'll be medicated with something that makes you feel right with the world—it might even send you straight into dreamland—about an hour before the operation. If your surgery is for 9:00 a.m., don't plan anything for after 7:30 a.m. Once you've been given the preoperative medication, you won't be allowed to get out of your bed, so take a potty break about 7:25 a.m. The gurney (stretcher) from the operating room will probably arrive to transport you about fifteen minutes after you've been medicated.

Make sure you've given all your valuables, including your wedding ring, to your spouse or advocate. Also make sure you've removed your dentures or at least are carrying a denture cup labeled with your name. It's not practical to give you anesthesia while you have dentures in your mouth, so the ward nurse will most likely ask that you remove them and leave them in your room. If it makes no difference to you, fine; but if you abhor the thought of anyone seeing you toothless you can refuse to remove the dentures until you arrive in the operating room. You must be assertive if you want your wishes honored.

There's usually a holding area where you will wait with other patients while the operating room is prepared for your case. This wait might last up to an hour.

No doubt you'll be drowsy when you arrive in the OR, but anxiety may keep you from falling asleep. Don't be afraid to look around. Most of the people will be wearing wrinkled, sterile garb from nose to toes, all intended to help keep bacteria out of the operating area. The lights are bright, the machinery is glistening steel, the room temperature is freezing, and you're apt to feel more like a nonperson here than in any other area of the hospital. The operating room is filled with highly skilled, technologically oriented workers who must always function at top speed. Some TLC for you can easily be forgotten because they are accustomed to working with patients who are "zonked out" most of the time.

Once you've been transferred to the surgery table, if your surgery requires general anesthesia, you'll be put to sleep within a few minutes and you won't know a thing until you awaken in the recovery room when a nurse calls your name. If she asks for the name of your doctor, it's not because no one knows who he is—she's just checking to see how "with it" you are. Her job is to see that you come out of the anesthesia nicely, that your wound is not bleeding, and that your vital signs are stable, which means that she'll be checking you every few minutes for an hour or so. When she's sure you're doing fine, she'll transport you back to your room and give a report on your operation to your ward nurse.

Local and Spinal Anesthesia

For certain types of surgery, general anesthesia may be unnecessary and you will be offered the option of having a local—medication injected at the operative site or in the spine to produce numbness. In fact, for some types of plastic surgery and eye surgery, general anesthesia is contraindicated because your cooperation will be needed.

Though most people say, "Put me out. I don't want to know what's going on," you should always opt for local anesthesia because your risks are markedly decreased and the recovery period is shortened.

Before you're transported to the surgical suite, you'll be given drugs to produce a euphoric state so that you won't really care too much what's going on. Also, there are plenty of drapes and screens so you won't be able to see the operation.

Since spinal anesthesia alters the pressure in your spinal column, you must be careful to follow the postoperative directions for avoiding the headaches that might accompany the pressure changes. Usually this simply involves lying flat for a period of time, twelve hours or so.

Whether or not you spend any time in the recovery room depends upon your condition after surgery and/or the type of surgery you had. For instance, after a spinal your physician might want you to stay in the recovery room until feeling has returned to your legs.

RECOVERY

Much of your progress at this point is up to you. Pain is the most normal reaction. After all, you've been pushed, pulled, twisted, sliced, and stitched—your body is protesting! Ask for pain medication. If you don't get it, ask again in twenty minutes. If your blood pressure is still low from the anesthesia, the nurse might choose to delay medicating you, though your anger at having to wait will help raise your blood pressure. Don't give up asking.

Nausea and vomiting are common consequences of anesthesia. There are very effective medications to combat them, but you must ask for them. Don't wait until you've started vomiting as it is very painful to heave when you've had any kind of surgery on your torso.

Remember, most physicians write postoperative orders for the "average" patient. Those orders may not keep you comfortable, in which case it's up to you to see that they're changed. Suffering in silence won't do anything but retard your healing! Read Chapter 3—Day One for more about this.

Turn, Cough, Deep Breathe

Turn, cough, deep breathe (TCDB) are the most essential tasks after surgery, so essential that most doctors don't even write the orders, assuming that every nurse knows you must indeed turn, cough, and deep breathe. Anesthesia increases the secretions in your lungs and these must be coughed out so that you won't get pneumonia. Turning mobilizes the secretions, as does deep breathing, and the coughing brings them up. *You must TCDB no matter how much pain it causes you,* so learn some tricks to minimize the problem. Ask for a pain shot, then do your TCDB a half hour later when the medication effects have peaked. You can also minimize the pain of coughing by clutching a pillow to your abdomen (this is called "splinting").

If you're up walking a few hours after surgery, you won't have to worry about the TCDB. Just moving around does all that your lungs need. This is why you won't be pampered the way you think you should be by the nurses. They know that the very best therapy for you is to get you moving around and doing everything possible for yourself. Surgical nurses are often considered heartless drill sergeants, but their goal is to speed your recovery, not to play maid.

Certain surgeries require that you be placed on the operating table in very strenuous positions that use muscles you didn't even know you had, and these will scream in protest for days. In addition, there's always the incision that feels as if it's ripping open when you try to get out of bed. For minimum pain, do it this way: scoot your body to the side of the bed, roll on to your side, push the button that raises the bed into a sitting position, draw your knees toward your chest, and push your upper body up while you swing your legs over the edge of the bed. Do the last step quickly and then just let your feet dangle while you catch your breath.

The nurse will help you stand the first time. She's been trained to do this in a special way that should keep both of you from getting a hernia, so listen to her instructions and do it exactly the way she says. Once you're standing for a few seconds, you'll feel so much better you'll wish you had tried it sooner. Be sure to resist the temptation to stoop—straighten your back, take a big, deep breath, and congratulate yourself for taking the biggest step toward recovery.

If standing is contraindicated for the type of operation you've had, you'll probably be put in a chair for a while each day. I know it may seem silly to sit in a chair when you could sit in bed with a lot less effort, but the very act of getting into a chair uses all the muscles that would deteriorate if they didn't get any use.

Dressings and Drains

After surgery don't be surprised at the bulk of the dressing—sometimes they're out of all proportion to the size of the incision, especially if there are "drains" involved.

A "drain" may consist of a flat latex tube about a half-inch wide that protrudes from the wound or a stiffer plastic tube connected to a small hatbox-type container for collection of the fluid. There is no pain involved while the drain is removing the excess fluid from the surgical site and no pain involved when the drain is removed a day or so after surgery. The physician simply slips the drain out, places a bandage on the site, and goes on his way—you may not even know he's done it!

Incisions are closed from the inside out, layer by layer, with different sorts of stitches. Whether or not the sutures are to be removed later depends on the type your surgeon decided to use, based on the site of the incision, the stress likely to be put on the sutures, and his own personal preference. The portion visible to you may be closed with Steri-strips that look like tiny Band-Aids; with staples; with large clips; or with silk, synthetic, or catgut "thread."

A few days after surgery, the incision will have closed and the material holding it together will be removed. *Don't panic!* Removal is a painless procedure. I know; I've had sutures removed from an eight-inch incision and I was terrified, too. I'd probably be terrified the next time as well, just because it looks as if it must hurt. Chances are a nurse will remove your sutures and, if you're really frightened, you *can* insist that she give you a pain reliever before she begins.

Since most incisions close so quickly, the dressings over them are often nothing more than a covering to keep you from freaking out at the sight. Do take a look—you'll be surprised at how neat and clean such wounds really are.

Gas Pains

If you've had abdominal surgery of any sort, you will be plagued by gas pains about the third day after surgery. These are harmless but you'll be most anxious to get rid of them. Your best defense is to keep moving. Pace the halls, miles and miles of them, to mobilize the gas and get it moving on out. Ask the doctor for Mylicon or simethicone though their use is only for certain cases. You might also try my favorite home remedy: a glass of half 7-Up and half milk.

Casts

Orthopedic surgery is particularly painful, so don't be bashful about asking for pain medication. The day after surgery some nurse will come in and tell you to stand up; if you happen to be in a leg cast, you'll be tempted to tell her just where to go. Getting up will be exactly what you don't want to do but you *must* do it or you'll be sorry later. Just go slowly and remember: No gain without pain.

Almost every patient is convinced that his cast is too tight; that may well be the case as the surgeon is only guessing at how much your body might swell after he applies the cast. The nurses will constantly be checking the tightness and you can check too. If it's a leg or arm cast, your toes or fingers must be movable and pink. If they aren't, your circulation is impaired and your cast needs to be cut.

The saw that cuts a cast looks and sounds lethal, but is really only a vibrator that stops automatically when there's no more cast to cut through. Often the cast can be cut through and a small repair job done; this doesn't mean you are having the surgery done over again.

Some casts, especially those that cover your torso, are applied while you're asleep during surgery. This means you can't say "Hey, it's a little too snug here and too loose there." The next day you might find small areas that are very abrasive to your skin, but these can be fixed—don't hesitate to tell your nurse.

The newest cast is waterproof, allowing you to shower. Some hospitals have the equipment for application while others do not. Be sure to request it, in case you're where one is available. Otherwise, you'll have to be very resourceful with plastic bags or Saran Wrap if you're really anxious to take a shower.

SELECTING SURGEONS

You've probably noticed I've given no advice on how to choose a surgeon. That's because I'm really not sure there is a sound solution to the problem. I would want my surgeon to be able to demonstrate the lowest postoperative infection rate of any surgeon in the area, but how could you find that out? If I'm to have open-heart surgery, I would want the surgeon who has done that operation more times than anyone else, but how could you find that out?

On the one hand, I would want a surgeon who is fresh out of school because he knows all the latest techniques, but on the other hand, I also would want a surgeon who has practiced for many years because he has the greatest range of experience. You usually can't have both. I would want a surgeon who would operate only if there is no other alternative *and* only if the consequences of surgery are far less threatening than the condition that indicates the surgery. I would want a surgeon who would give me scientifically based statistics on the probable success of my surgery and valid statistics on the consequences if I chose to decline surgery.

If I were to have brain surgery, plastic surgery, neurosurgery, a kidney transplant, major lung surgery, a mastectomy, heart surgery, or a colostomy, I'd travel to a major metropolitan area where a medical center is well known for its progressive practice and I'd ask around to discover who the "big surgeon" is. These particular surgeries have massive impact on the quality of life and quality is what we are looking for.

Some surgeons seem to possess talent that's unrelated to all that I've just told you. For instance, we once received a patient through the emergency room who had been hit by a moving train. Dr. Okamoto, a very young ear, nose, and throat doctor, spent ten hours putting the patient's face back together again, like Humpty-Dumpty, with artistry that simply has to be attributed to inborn talent. Such remarkable results from surgery are not often achieved by even the most experienced surgeons.

You'd probably like some concrete advice, but the most I can tell you is that the selection of a surgeon is very, very difficult. Whatever you do, don't choose a surgeon based on personality or bedside manner; some of the most highly skilled surgeons do not pass out much tender loving care. Ask some hospital nurses whom they would have do their surgery. They have no vested interest in who does yours, so they'll be honest—as long as you ask them outside the hospital. If a surgeon's name is already on your chart, don't expect the nurse to recommend someone else.

ANXIETY

"Are you a night person, Max, or are you just jumpy about surgery tomorrow?" He sat there in his red silk pajamas, covers tossed to the foot of the bed, smoking one cigarette after another as fast as he could light them.

"Hell, no, I'm not jumpy! What's to be jumpy about?" He ran a hand through his hair for the thousandth time, crossed and uncrossed his feet, and stubbed another cigarette out. Nights before surgery are long and he hadn't even come close to shutting his eyes, despite the sleeping pill four hours earlier.

"I guess I'd be jumpy," I said, "though I'm not sure why. Maybe it's that I'd have to give up control. They wheel you into that operating room and you have nothing to say about anything. They can do whatever they want with you and you can't even say ouch."

He replied that he had the best surgeon in the country, knew there was no alternative to surgery, and he would be a whole lot better off having had it. He also had complete confidence in the anesthesiologist. But he couldn't help saying: "I sure have quitter's fever. I wanna walk on out of here right now in the worst way. Maybe that's it, maybe I can't let go of control. I've always controlled everything in my life."

When you sift out all the thoughts you have about surgery, the bottom line is that none of us wants to hand over the steering wheel to a roomful of strangers standing there with scalpels in their hands. If you feel terrified, you're normal; don't feel foolish if you can't talk yourself out of it.

You could be expected to be a lot less anxious about surgery if you weren't faced with a truckload of "unknowns." You don't know exactly how the shot before surgery will feel, what the anesthesiologist will do to you, what the surgeon will find when he cuts through the first layer of skin, what you might do or say to make a fool of yourself if or when you lose control, how much pain you'll have after surgery, if you're a real "baby" about pain, or if the surgery will affect your life-style a month from now. You probably saw the movie *Coma* and are not entirely convinced it doesn't really happen that way!

If you had taken a course in anatomy and physiology, many of your worries could be stripped away, because you'd find the whole thing is fairly straightforward and simple. Needles only hurt as they pass across the pain receptors of your skin—the injection an hour before surgery is *minimal,* no worse than pricking yourself with a pin. Anesthesia is not a "truth serum," so don't worry about making a fool of yourself. As for the surgical incision, you'd be surprised how very simple the structure of your body is.

Underneath the skin, there is no vast ocean of mystery. You've got the same bits and pieces as everyone else, in the same spots, down underneath the first few layers of skin and fat. When the surgeon is through, he sews each layer together again, one by one. You don't have to worry about the incision popping open; even if the first layer of stitches should pop, there are still all the other layers holding everything together. You won't bleed to death either, because your blood has natural clotting factors.

You won't wake up during surgery because the anesthesiologist has monitors taped to you in the right places; he can tell how asleep you are every second by watching your pulse and blood pressure. He has nothing else to do during surgery but watch to make sure you are breathing right, your heart's ticking away just fine, and your brain is filled with nothing but sweet dreams.

If an organ, such as the gallbladder or uterus, is being removed, your body couldn't care less. The rest of your organs just adjust a little to fill up the empty space. Your body will also find an alternate way to carry on the function of that organ if it happens to be one vital to your survival.

Did you know that if three-fourths of your stomach is removed, in a year's time the quarter left will have expanded to the size of the original one? And did you know that you have twenty-five feet of intestine, give or take a few feet, and that the removal of some will probably not be noticed by the rest of your body? And did you know that your body often makes new blood vessels to replace plugged up ones if you give it enough time and rest?

Did you know that there is no longer such a thing as a "partial hysterectomy"? If only the uterus is removed, it's a hysterectomy. If the ovaries are removed, it's an oophorectomy. If the uterus is removed via the vagina, the top of the vagina is closed, leaving a blind pouch with all sensation intact. Where do the eggs go that are matured by the ovaries? They wander out into the abdominal cavity, where they are absorbed. If anyone tells you that removal of the uterus does not alter the production of estrogen because your ovaries are still intact, that's not exactly a sure bet. *Often,* for unknown reasons that have nothing to do with your ovaries, production of estrogen slows or stops after a hysterectomy.

Since your gallbladder produces bile to help digest fats, you'd think you'd have a real problem if it was removed. Instead, your liver will send out enough bile to do the job.

If you're having a prostate gland removed, a fairly common surgery for men over fifty-five, there are three methods of performing the operation, depending on your particular problem. Impotence is often *not* a consequence; you should discuss this with your physician before you enter the hospital.

Mastectomies are certainly not pleasant to undergo, but do look into the latest in techniques and implants to simulate natural breasts. And, by all means, get in touch with a Reach for Recovery group for dozens of helpful hints.

Colostomy patients are helped immeasurably by others with the same set of annoyances who belong to the United Ostomy Association. All of the problems you could possibly encounter have been solved by them in various ways and you're sure to be given the assistance you need. You may be provided with only one type of appliance while you're hospitalized, but there is a variety of equipment to suit each person's need, so don't give up before you try them all.

There are dozens of surgical procedures, all with different implications for the future. I've told you only about the most common ones so that you won't worry needlessly if you're contemplating having one of them.

RETURNING TO NORMAL

Recovery is dependent upon many factors, including the prior emotional drain of anticipating the surgery. Expect to feel all dragged out and to feel quite blue on about the third day after surgery. By the third day, reality hits; life has become anticlimactic; the cards, gifts, flowers, and visitors have begun to dwindle; you're tired of all those strangers telling you what to do and how to do it; the hospital begins to seem like a clanking, bustling pain in the neck; and you've just plain run out of the strength it takes to "keep a stiff upper lip." Cry! It's okay, even if you're a male—you have a right to feel sorry for yourself.

After the third day, nothing ever seems quite so bad again, though you will have your ups and downs because it takes time to get your strength back and that is something that can't be pushed. You can't *will* it back, try as you might, so you might as well sit back and wait for it to reappear. Your very astute body knows just exactly how long it needs to repair and until the right time arrives there isn't a thing you can do.

For some people just out of surgery a very strange phenomenon occurs that may last for several weeks. Though it's difficult to describe and has not been studied enough to define how it happens, it is a feeling of disorientation, perhaps a result of the anesthesia. You might feel a floating-in-space sensation or sometimes you may reach out for an object and find it is not in exactly the spot you reached for. It's not painful, or frightening, or something to cure—it's just a *strange* feeling of not being quite "with it."

ABOUT YOUR SCAR

Scars are very interesting in that they're so unpredictable. Fortunately, they fade in color, width, and depth, but if you are a "keloid former," they may never disappear. "Keloid" means a thickening of scar tissue and on a long scar a keloid looks much like an earthworm. While it's thought that there may be a hereditary disposition to forming keloids, the exact cause is not known at this time.

Some people who have an exploratory laparotomy, usually involving an incision down the center of the abdomen, are left with only a hairline scar after about three months, while others may have a raised scar which is still fading three years later. If the scar persists, there is always the possibility of having plastic surgery performed to remove it.

And last, but not least, you should know that your belly button might be displaced during surgery. However, surgeons are marvelously creative and, since there is nothing on the underside of your navel but fat and muscle, they can fashion a belly button any place you want it, no doubt right back where it was to begin with.

FOR ADVOCATES

You can assist your patient through the surgical ordeal mainly by offering emotional support. He needs to tell someone his tales of woe and you're the most likely candidate. However, if you're like most people you'll try to cheer him up, take his mind off his problems, convince him there are others far worse off than he—but don't! Let him tell you how terrible it all is— he needs to get it off his chest; no matter how many people have had the very same surgery or surgery a lot more serious, this is a once-in-a-lifetime proposition for him and he needs to tell someone how frightened he is.

The sense of loss after surgery can be overwhelming and out of all proportion to the *actual* loss. There may be manifestations of the same reactions that accompany the death of a loved one: denial, disbelief, anger, pleading, and finally resignation. Your job is to listen and to provide support. You should do a lot of hand-holding. You can also help the patient by monitoring his visitors, steering their conversations, and prompting them to leave when you know the patient needs to be alone.

On the day of surgery you should arrive at the hospital about two hours before the scheduled time of the operation. The nurses may not be pleased to see you then, but surgery is so commonplace to some of them, they've forgotten how threatening it is to other people. Usually you may accompany the patient to the doors of the surgical suite, then you should ask the attendant where you should wait to hear from the doctor. You can count on having at least two hours before you will hear anything, so it's a good time to go do any errands or to have breakfast. If the patient waits an hour in the holding area, spends an hour in surgery, and then stays in the recovery room an hour, your wait might be extended—don't assume something has gone awry if your wait seems too long.

When the patient is returned to his room, the nursing staff should page you. That may not happen if they're very busy, so it's a good idea to check for yourself. You can ask a volunteer, the ward secretary, or simply take a look in the patient's room yourself. Don't panic if you go to the same room and find a stranger in the bed; sometimes patients are moved to another room after surgery to accommodate the needs of other patients. The ward secretary can direct you to the new room.

Some surgeries do not have happy endings; a simple breast biopsy may have turned into a radical mastectomy or a mass in the abdomen may have turned out to be malignant. Don't assume that the patient has been told by the physician. You need to meet with the physician and other significant people to decide how the subject will be handled. Read more about this in Chapter 15.

The patient will really need you most as an advocate during

the first several postoperative hours, because that's usually when it's most difficult for the patient to assert himself. You should be assertive, even aggressive if need be, and see that the patient is kept comfortable. The nurses will be happy that someone is looking after the patient; often they have several patients returning from surgery within a short timespan and are hard-pressed to care for them all at once.

By the second or third day after surgery, you can slack off and go have your private nervous breakdown. It is often more difficult to act as the patient's advocate than it is to be the patient.

CHAPTER
8
Diagnostic Exams

What you should know from the outset is that there are more questions unanswered in the world of medicine than there are answered, despite today's sophisticated technology and the hundreds of diagnostic tests available.

You should also know that very many diagnostic tests are subject to ambivalent conclusions. One drop too much of a certain reagent can skew the results of a test in the opposite direction. Six doctors can "read" the same set of X rays and come to six different conclusions. This doesn't mean that you should never trust any lab results, but if the treatment you receive, based on lab results, will have a great impact on your life, you might consider repeating the test—just to make sure the same conclusion is reached twice. Also, if you don't know *why* you are having a certain test, you have no way of knowing what the implications are for your future—be sure to ask.

THE BUSINESS END OF DIAGNOSTICS

You're probably aware that department stores often have several "concessions" within them. For instance, the shoe department is often owned by a company that leases the space from the department-store owners and pays a percentage of the profit to the store for the privilege of using the space.

Similarly, hospitals frequently give contracting physicians the sole right to perform certain designated functions under "exclusive" agreements. Not surprisingly, this sort of agreement is of-

ten attacked by other physicians in the same specialty who
complain that they are prevented from practicing their specialty
in that hospital; by still other physicians who complain that
they are barred from consulting with specialists of their own
choosing; and by patients who complain that their choice of a
doctor is unduly limited.

Radiology, pathology, nuclear medicine, chronic kidney dialysis, heart catheterization, and anesthesiology services are often
furnished through this type of arrangement in fee-for-service
hospitals.

One could argue that such "exclusive" agreements deny physicians their right to practice, that they illegally restrict the patient's freedom of choice, and that they constitute restraint of
trade in violation of antitrust laws. However, the implications
for you are not so complicated as long as you are aware of this
practice, if you ever decide to have some service repeated for
confirmation of a diagnosis. The physician who "read" your X
rays is very likely to be the same one who will read them the
next time *if* you have them done in the same hospital. Likewise,
if you have the results of your cardiac catheterization analyzed
twice in the same hospital, it's unlikely that a different conclusion will be reached the second time.

Shopping for Diagnostics

You should also be aware that charges for diagnostic tests vary
greatly from lab to lab; though you may consider the services
"free" if your insurance company picks up the tab, we all pay
in the end through higher insurance rates. Even if your employer pays the full cost of your insurance coverage directly, you pay
indirectly through decreased coverage of services or some other
alteration of your benefits package. Employers traditionally allow only a fixed percentage to be spent on your benefits.

If you are not a hospitalized patient, you should "shop" for
your diagnostic services. Besides influencing the cost, "shopping" may get you a completed test earlier or at a more convenient time in another lab. The requisition provided you by the
physician usually has the name and address of a lab at the top,
much the same way a mechanic gives you a slip of paper with

the name and address of a vendor of tires when your tire's tread is getting thin. Neither obligates you to seek service at that one location.

How do you shop? It's very simple. Look for Laboratory-Medical in the Yellow Pages. Select three or four in your area, call, and tell them the test you need. Ask them what they charge and how soon they can do it. It really is no different from calling around to determine where to have your brakes replaced.

Because I work in hospitals, it would not have occurred to me to have testing done elsewhere. However, for one test I was in a hurry and the hospital was not close to my home. Since I would be allowed a 25 percent employee discount at the hospital, I decided to find out just how much *more* it would cost if I went to a lab close to home. The shocking revelation was that the test would cost $16 at the local lab and $42 at the hospital, even with my discount! I called three labs and the prices for the same test varied just slightly, none of them even approximating the high price at the hospital. This may not be the case everywhere, but you should definitely check it out the next time the doctor gives you a requisition for a diagnostic test. *All* labs will give him what he wants, in either a phoned or mailed report.

Rush Diagnosis

It takes an assertive personality to orchestrate a "rush" diagnosis. There are situations that demand haste, although it is difficult to make busy health-care professionals aware of your particular situation.

Here's how to do it:

1. "Shop" for a lab until you get the first appointment the next morning for your test.
2. Tell them your physician requests the radiologist's written impression the same day and that you will pick up the results to take with you to your afternoon doctor's appointment.
3. Ask at what exact time you may pick them up.
4. Then call your physician's office and make an appointment shortly after the pickup time.

Certain results can be phoned in to your physician, but if X rays or sonograms are involved he might want to see them himself. In addition, if he sends you to another specialist because of the results, the other doctor would appreciate being able to see them too.

ABOUT INDIVIDUAL TESTS

Some patients want to know every last detail of a test from beginning to end before they will submit to it, while others want to know only one thing: "Will it hurt?" Still others simply want to know, "When can I eat?" If you want to know all about the most common tests, another nurse, Judith Nierenberg, has written an excellent book, *The Hospital Experience,* which will give you all the technical details. She tells you the preparation for each test, where it will take place, how long it will take, what the results are intended to reveal, and what it feels like. If there's any special care or problems expected after the test she tells you that too.

HOW DIAGNOSIS WORKS

Suppose you have a "mass" in the upper-right quadrant of your abdomen. Such a "mass" could be a benign tumor, a cyst, a malignant tumor, or a clump of residue in your intestine. The mass could be affecting your liver, pancreas, intestine, stomach, kidney, or just the lining of your abdomen.

The first task is to find out exactly *where* it is, then *what* it is, then *how* it should be treated. The doctor who discovers the mass may decide he's not the one to proceed and send you to a surgeon, since there's a high probability that the mass must be removed.

The surgeon probably will see you the next day, feel the mass, and decide to do some tests. The assortment of tests he has to choose from is mind-boggling; ideally he will move up the scale from the least expensive and traumatic to the most, ruling out possibilities until he arrives at a logical conclusion. By the time you arrive at his doorstep, the possibility of a "clump of residue

FOR ADVOCATES

Once a patient hears the word "mass," the brain tends to take a long coffee break in self-defense lest it conjure up visions of "terminal" illness. The result is that the patient hears and understands very little more of what the doctor says and becomes a compliant child willing to submit to anything. You can be a great help by listening carefully to the doctor and interpreting his advice to the patient several hours later, after the initial impact of the word "mass" has worn off. Crucial decisions regarding diagnostic tests and/or surgery might have to be made and the patient needs you to help him calm down, consider the alternatives, ask intelligent questions, and reach a logical conclusion.

in your intestine" has already been ruled out—it would have moved on through and out in the twenty-four hours since the first physician discovered the mass.

First he will order a barium swallow, the least expensive and traumatic test. You shop for the earliest appointment, and two days later you're back in his office. If the results are negative, a mass anywhere along the upper gastrointestinal tract is ruled out.

Then he will order a barium enema and an intravenous pyelogram (IVP)—the former to examine the lower intestinal tract and the latter to examine the kidneys and bladder. Both can be done on the same day, during the same appointment; however the IVP must be done *first* so that the barium from the enema does not appear in the X rays of the IVP.

"Shopping" will get you an 8:30 a.m. lab appointment, with the results ready at noon. You then take the results to the surgeon at 2:00 p.m. It is now his opinion that a mass is on the kidney; he calls a urologist and gets you an appointment that same day; and at 5:00 p.m. the urologist confirms that you should have surgery. You will be tied up for at least six weeks; career plans go out the window. At least you know where you stand. Your options have been narrowed considerably, *but not completely!* You have received one opinion and the big word here is *opinion.* No one actually *saw* the mass in your abdomen, remember; they only drew a conclusion from several tests.

The very best practitioners in the world are still subject to the risk in any *opinion.* Their opinion is simply an *estimate of probability.* They don't want to be held responsible for an error in judgment any more than you want to be the victim of an error. Rarely can the surgeon know positively what he will find inside you until he can see what's there with his own eyes. Diagnostic tests *suggest* and the physician arrives at an *opinion* based on the suggestions.

Getting a second opinion does not always involve the inconvenience and expense of going through the same tests all over again. Often a different physician can assess your symptoms and the already completed test results to arrive at a diagnosis that may conflict with that of the first physician. You should read Chapter 11—The Physicians to be sure you know how to go about getting a second opinion. What if you get conflicting opinions? If the prescribed therapy would significantly alter the quality or quantity of your life, choose the least invasive route.

There are cases when the diagnosis is cut and dried and the physicians would all agree on one diagnosis. But since you are not in a position to judge when that might be the case, your only alternative is to seek a second opinion.

"WASTE" IN DIAGNOSTIC TESTING

In an FDA-sponsored research project designed to reduce unnecessary skull X rays, it was found that emergency room and clinic personnel can safely eliminate 40 to 60 percent of all skull X rays currently performed on patients with head trauma, by using a specific rigorous set of criteria for selecting patients for X rays. In this particular study, the concern was not only for the welfare of the patient but also for the "waste" that proliferates in our health-care delivery system driving costs up.

The two most probable methods of curbing "waste" are through federal controls or through controls imposed by the public—and the public must be educated if it is to know how to impose safe controls.

What is "waste"? Well, it is waste when one physician performs an esophagogastroduodenoscopy on a patient who could as easily be diagnosed with a stool test. It is waste when another physician performs angiography on a patient who could as easily be diagnosed by a sonogram. It is waste when another physician performs cardiac catheterization on a patient who could as easily be diagnosed by a Bernstein test. It is waste when another physician performs esophageal manometry if the results will in no way alter the plan of treatment for the patient. And it is waste to do a bone-marrow biopsy when there's no hope of changing the patient's prognosis.

From a financial standpoint, the "waste" is clear. Angiography to diagnose a mass that appears to be on a kidney costs about $1600, including hospitalization. A sonogram, for the same purpose, done on an outpatient basis costs around $125. No dollars have been attached to the fact that the patient loses at least three days of work for the angiography. From the patient's standpoint, the waste is clear in several other ways. Hospitalization is traumatic, first and foremost! The cost in emotional energy is dramatic. And angiography itself is emotionally and physically trying. In addition, it carries high risk to the patient: risk of pulmonary embolus, anaphylactic shock, excess radiation, infection, paralysis—and the list could go on.

INVASIVE VERSUS NONINVASIVE TESTS

An angiogram is invasive, a sonogram is noninvasive. Esophagogastroduodenoscopy is invasive, a stool test is not. Cardiac catheterization is invasive, but not a Bernstein test. This is not to imply that both invasive tests and their counterpart, noninvasive tests, provide the exact same set of information in all cases, but only to point out that the physician is often able to obtain the information he needs without going to extremes. You, the patient, will be much better off if you can avoid them and we, the public, will have successfully curbed escalating health-care costs when the use of invasive diagnostic techniques has been minimized.

How will you know the difference between "invasive" and "noninvasive"? It's difficult for the layman, but first of all, you can simply ask, "Is this test considered invasive?" That at least sends up a little flag that tells the doctor you are concerned. He'll probably ask what you mean. Then you can ask, "Will it invade my pocketbook or my body more than some other test we could try first?" That's not exactly what a doctor means by "invasive," but at least it gives him some idea of what *your* concern is.

If you're too timid to ask, one way to tell how invasive the test is is by the papers you have to sign in advance. Invasive tests require signed and witnessed Consent for Treatment forms. Noninvasive tests do not require your witnessed signature.

If the doctor explains the test by saying, "We're going to put a scope in . . ." or "We're going to put a tiny catheter in . . ." or "We're going to put some dye in . . ."—that's invasive. As a rule of thumb, you can expect invasive tests to cost more than noninvasive ones.

PREPARATION

Much of the value of diagnostic tests lies in preparation and in you. If you are told "no food or fluid after midnight the night before the test," you must follow these instructions. The person who serves your breakfast tray in the hospital could easily have missed the message, so if she waltzes into your room with some bacon and eggs, do inform her that you are not supposed to eat. Each physician has his own favorite preparation regimen—don't be surprised if the instructions differ from one to another.

RADIOLOGY

Everything in our universe, including the human race, has been subjected to radiation since the universe was formed. Radiation is defined as energy moving through space as invisible waves. We can't taste it or touch it. We often can't see or hear it, but it does have some effect on us depending on the frequency of the waves. Heat and light, as examples of radiation, are beneficial, but the ability of some radiation to penetrate the body, to enter the molecular structure, and to cause damage can make it dangerous.

Ionizing radiation creates electrically charged ions that can disrupt body processes and cause death. Nuclear weapons, X rays, and some television sets produce ionizing radiation. Non-ionizing radiation—from microwaves, light, and sound—does not produce ions; however, it too can disrupt body processes and is lethal in massive doses. There is no way of determining how much radiation one has been exposed to.

Accordingly, precautions should be taken against unnecessary or excessive exposure to radiation and every available safeguard against radiation damage should be used. Say you've had diagnostic studies of your gastrointestinal tract, as ordered by your family physician. He then refers you to a gastroenterologist who sends you to the hospital. Once admitted to the hospital, your orders include the same diagnostic X rays you had done earlier in the week. "This is a different doctor," they say. "He wants to do his own studies."

That's a waste of money, as well as wasted exposure to radiation. What you need to do is pick up the phone, tell the lab where the first X rays were done and that they will be picked up by a taxi; then call a cab company and tell them what you want. Send some money down via a nurse to the emergency-room desk to pay the cab.

Technically, your X rays belong to the lab or hospital, but logically they should belong to you, especially if you've decided to switch doctors midstream and would like to reduce your radiation exposure.

In some instances, the physician may need repeat X-ray exams in order to follow your progress. For instance, a chest X ray each day during treatment for pleural effusion is common. The benefits in this case far outweigh the risks!

"Hold still!" the X-ray technician tells you. *"Don't move, take a deep breath. . . . Hold it!"* I don't know about you, but I'm usually shaking so from fright or the chilly table that I can't possibly hold still. It seems that all X-ray departments are stark

---

FOR ADVOCATES

When you are playing messenger to get X rays from a hospital, call first and tell them Dr. Whatever has asked you to transfer Mr. Doe's X rays. They will want to know the month the X rays were performed and what study you want (e.g., IVP, leg fracture, barium swallow). Go directly to the X-ray department, give the name, sign a "loan" slip (as in a library), and say that you will return them the next day. Don't be surprised if you never hear from the hospital again; they rarely have time to keep track of what films have been returned. Unless you know the name of the study (X ray) you are requesting, it will be obvious that you don't know what you are doing and any chance of getting fast possession of the X rays will decrease.

---

and cold. To add to the science-fiction atmosphere, the technicians wear lead vests and huge mitts, stand behind thick partitions with tiny viewing windows, then tell everyone *"Stand clear!"* and there you are—the vulnerable one, lying under a monstrous piece of machinery. You're not alone! No matter how much I know about the equipment and procedures and the fact that an X ray does not produce pain, I still feel frightened and so probably will you.

Because X rays are photographs of a sort, holding still insures a clearer picture—if you move, the picture is blurred. Why is the X-ray room so cold? It's said that the film used needs cool temperatures. And why does everyone wear *Star Wars* garb? Everything in the room is designed to minimize exposure to radiation. Usually this entails lead-lined aprons and mitts, since the technicians work with radiation all day every day.

As a hospitalized patient, you can expect to wait in the X-ray department, sometimes as long as an hour. Its schedule is arranged much as in an operating room, with cases slotted in a certain order, depending on the type and length of the procedure. When emergency cases come along, everyone is bumped to a later time on the schedule. If you have been NPO (nothing by mouth) since midnight, you're supposed to be among the first on the X-ray schedule and your tests should be completed by about 10:00 a.m. Don't suffer in silence waiting until 3:00 p.m. to announce "You know, I really am hungry and I'd sure like to get these X rays over with so I can eat." Schedules in any department can get mixed up. The order may never have reached the right department or someone may have skipped your name while making up the schedule. Whatever the reason, speak up. Tell the nurse you're still waiting and at 10:00 a.m. she will check to see what the delay is.

Angiographic Studies

Some areas of your body can only be visualized indirectly. For instance, since we know that a tumor will have increased the number of blood vessels, certain blood vessels can be filled with a dye to outline them. The radiologist can then look for abnormalities that would indicate the presence of a tumor. If he wants to "look at" the aorta, he can see it only if it's filled with a dye, and likewise for other vessels such as the heart, pancreas, or brain. Such studies are uncomfortable, expensive, and invasive and should be considered as a last resort.

Cardiac Catheterization

Cardiac catheterization is very similar to angiography in that it is also invasive and can be frightening. There's a great deal of equipment in the room, the technicians are gowned and masked to keep the area sterile, and everyone shouts and bustles. You, however, must stay calm because your cooperation is essential to the procedure. When you're told to cough, you need to give a hearty cough and when you're told to hold your breath, do so. Split-second timing is involved, which is what all the shouting is about, and everyone will almost forget that you are lying on the table. It's useless to try to tell you not to be frightened, but perhaps you'll be less so if you know that all the noise and banging around don't mean a crisis.

CAT SCANNING

CAT scanning (computerized axial tomography) is the most sophisticated new technology and has the potential to be the greatest gift ever developed for patients. Noninvasive and painless, the scanner moves along, taking many pictures of your body, and reads and interprets them via a computer. The machine is huge—in price and size—and you'll be tempted to shake with fear again, but relax! If I had my choice of any diagnostic test in the vast array of those available, this would be it! For detecting masses, tumors, or brain hemorrhages, the CAT scan cannot be bettered, and as the use of this tool becomes more common, it's likely that other more invasive tests will become obsolete. Your job is simply to lie *very still.*

NUCLEAR MEDICINE

Radioactive scanning involves a Geiger counter of sorts and is often done on an outpatient basis. Briefly, radioactivity-tagged chemicals are injected into your vein and then a scanning machine counts the radioactive particles that concentrate in specific organs. The degree of concentration provides valuable information to the diagnostician. Such testing is relatively harmless *so long as you are not pregnant.* The fetus *might* be affected, so such tests should be avoided except when the benefit would outweigh the risk. For some of these tests, the scanning is done in series, giving certain information which is multiplied at specific intervals—don't be surprised if you are returned to the nuclear medicine department some hours later. There will be no additional injections and you won't be subjected to any pain.

ULTRASOUND

This is a test based on sound waves that produce an echo when passed through the junction of tissues with differing densities. The echoes are converted into a visual pattern and the end result appears similar to Polaroid snapshots. Ultrasonography can often differentiate between a tumor and a cyst, as a tumor appears solid while a cyst appears translucent. The nicest part of this test is that you do nothing but lie still and it is totally painless. Some gel or oil will be applied to the area to be examined and then an ultrasonic transducer, which looks and feels somewhat like a Ping-Pong ball, will be rolled back and forth across this area. By the way, this test is noninvasive!

OSCOPY

Oscopy is a suffix meaning "looking into," which is exactly what the physician will do. If he looks into your lungs, it's a bronchoscopy; if in your stomach, it's a gastroscopy; and if in your bladder, it's a cystoscopy. The instrument is snakelike, with a small light on one end and a "steering wheel" at the other, which allows the physician to move it into the area he wants to see, while he looks through an eyepiece. Visualize a periscope, if you will, since the idea is similar. With some of the instruments a photograph can be taken or even a biopsy. The instruments are fascinating but also invasive.

Some physicians rarely use the "scope" as a diagnostic tool, while others abuse it. Cystoscopy is to the urologist what gastroduodenoscopy is to the gastroenterologist and cardiac catheterization to the cardiologist—a very direct albeit expensive and invasive route to diagnosis. However, the direct route is not always in your best interest, and control is in your hands since you must sign the Consent for Treatment form. Be sure invasive tests are the last resort; if an oscopy is the first diagnostic test ordered for you, I would be hesitant about proceeding without asking a few questions.

LABORATORY TESTS

Tests of stool, sputum, blood, perspiration, tissue, bone marrow, spinal fluid, gastric fluid, cervical secretions, amniotic fluid, pleural fluid, and urine all reveal invaluable information about what's going on at the cellular level of your body, which is where everything begins. However, they can be very annoying; more often than not a needle is involved in collecting the specimen—and we all hate needles.

One evening as a lab technician was drawing blood from a patient's arm the patient asked what the blood was for. "I'm not sure," the technician replied, "I guess you must have an infection somewhere." He drew it three times in a three-hour span, but the "good" patient kept quiet after the first time. The next morning, a physician strode into my office and threw an incident report on my desk: "Too damned bad I can't even get some blood cultures done around here," he barked. "Get on this and I want a report back."

It turned out that we had patients in adjacent rooms, one named Mrs. Gough and one named Mrs. Goff, both pronounced the same. The doctor had written the order on the wrong chart and, though Mrs. Goff had the infection, the blood for cultures was drawn from Mrs. Gough. Since blood cultures take forty-eight hours to provide the information the physician wants, time was lost. Also since the stab it takes to draw blood is not the most comfortable, the wrong patient was unhappy, though the error would have been far more consequential had it been a test involving spinal fluid. The lesson is obvious! Don't allow anyone to take any specimen from you without knowing *why* it's being taken. The lab technician will have the order in hand and will do as he's ordered unless the patient protests. It is not his obligation to know the patient's diagnosis or the indications for the test—*the patient* must accept the responsibility.

However, you shouldn't automatically assume that more than one blood test drawn in the same day indicates that the lab goofed up the first test. Actually, there are several tests that require serial specimens and there are other tests that must be drawn every day in order to chart your progress. If you've asked the nurse or physician, you'll know what to expect. The Band-Aid that's placed on the site is only for appearance most of the time, since the site closes almost immediately, unless blood has been drawn from an artery in which case the technician will apply pressure to the site for a couple of minutes.

STRESS TEST

The stress test is fun and a challenge of sorts; patients usually like to brag about how they did. It's similar to an electrocardiogram (EKG) in that small plastic discs are placed on your chest with adhesive and rubber bands are placed on your limbs, all with wires leading to a machine which will record the electrical activity of your heart. When you're lying down it's simply an EKG, but a stress test measures the electrical activity of your heart as you exercise. You walk on a treadmill that's gradually increased in speed and tilt as a technician measures your blood pressure and heart rate while the machine traces out the pattern that tells how your heart reacts under stress. If you aren't a chronic jogger, your leg muscles will protest and, if your heart is ill, it might protest—tell the technician if you become uncomfortable.

You will be told the day before if you're to have this test—there's usually a wait for an appointment—so you will have time to tell someone to bring your favorite jogging shoes to the hospital. Any hard-soled shoes or slippers will do, but it helps if you aren't bothered with mules or slippers that fall off easily.

By the way, the "average" result of the stress test is fifteen minutes walking on the treadmill with the heart rate up to 125 beats per minute. If you can walk longer, you have a right to brag!

A 1979 issue of *The New England Journal of Medicine* has concluded that the stress test has little value in predicting whether people have heart disease. In fact, test results in a research study indicating heart trouble turned out to be false alarms 54 percent of the time among women and 12 percent of the time among men. These statistics should influence your decision if you are considering coronary-bypass surgery based on results of the stress test. Seek a second opinion.

AWAITING TEST RESULTS

Often the most difficult part of a test is just waiting for it to be done—you're not sure what to expect and you won't believe there's no pain or embarrassment involved until it's over. The test itself is usually anticlimactic. Once completed, waiting for the result can be just as difficult, especially if the result will have an effect on your future.

In the majority of tests, the results are available within a few minutes, if not immediately. A physician will dictate his "impression" and the result will appear on your chart the next morning. You may have to wait until the next time your physician visits you in order to hear the result, but you might also ask the nurse what she knows. There is an unwritten law that nurses do not reveal test results to patients, but many of us are guilty of breaking the law if the patient is very worried, the physician is not available, and the results are good news. This *doesn't* mean the news is bad when you ask a nurse and she refuses to give you information. She may not have access to the test results or she may be one who *always* observes the unwritten law.

For nurses, the greatest word in the English vocabulary is "benign." If you're waiting to hear the same word, the wait can seem interminable, especially if there's a borderline test result involved. For instance, some lesions are so obviously malignant that one need never place the tissue under a microscope to verify the diagnosis. Other tissues, though, might exhibit questionable cells that place the diagnosis on the fence—it might be malignant, it might not. The pathologist may then send a sample to another laboratory for an opinion. There may be a distant laboratory with more sophisticated diagnostic equipment but the results might take days or even weeks to return. Some tests involve "growing" the suspected microorganisms in a medium for two or three days before a diagnosis can be made. In other cases one laboratory might not have all the equipment for the tests required. To compound the problem, the test might not have proved anything, a "false negative" or a "false positive" result might appear.

The problem then is knowing when you're waiting because there's no alternative and when you're waiting because you haven't been assertive enough to get the results.

Here's a mini-guideline for you: X-ray results are available as fast as a radiologist can find time to develop and interpret them. The same is true for angiography, ultrasonography, radioactive scanning, CAT scanning, EKG, the stress test, cardiac catheterization, and most oscopies. You might have to be more patient for other results.

DIFFERENTIAL DIAGNOSIS

While to most people a high blood sugar means diabetes, there are actually thirty different diseases that manifest themselves in a high blood sugar. "Differential diagnosis" is ascertaining which of the thirty you might have—is it this or is it that? It *might* be diabetes, but then again it could be something else. Nausea and vomiting could mean a brain tumor, an ulcer, pregnancy, an inner ear infection, or any number of things.

Herein lies the most difficult part of a physician's job—differential diagnosis—and herein lies the most frustrating situation for the patient. This is the reason you might sometimes feel like a pawn in a chess game as you get pushed from one diagnostic test to another while the physician strokes his beard and says, "Hmmm, very interesting, these results, but we still don't know what's wrong with you."

Those of you who have taken microbiology classes probably remember the search for the "unknown," the microorganism that it could possibly be. The testing might take several days and all the while you know that an incorrectly performed test would have sent you to a wrong conclusion. Those students who identified their "unknown" as anthrax (a dangerous microbe that never would have been in the lab) know the frustration of the physician who is searching for the correct diagnosis for you. When he pieces together all the clues, he may still be left with several possibilities. In fact, he may have *eliminated* every possibility and you end up with no disease and a case of disappearing symptoms.

When that happens, you have to remember that there is still much in medicine that is unexplained while every day brings new discoveries that change the list of clues the physician is gathering.

INTERVENTIONAL RADIOLOGY

While this is being written, the chances of a patient's encountering interventional radiology are small. However, it is almost certain that with new refinements in its technique and a growing corps of radiologists trained in its use, there will be great advances in this field. Along with the common tools of radiology, interventional radiology uses special new devices but goes beyond diagnosis to repair internal abnormalities.

For instance, the technique has been used to stop massive gastrointestinal hemorrhages, shrink selective brain tumors, clear artery blockages, plug bleeding points in internal hemorrhages, remove gallstones, clear obstructed bile ducts, drain obstructed urinary tracts, and destroy certain internal organs such as adrenal glands.

The process involves threading catheters through the body while following the progress on a television monitor, and then injecting drugs, pellets, balloons, clots of blood, or other devices into the target area—i.e., artery, bile duct, urinary tract—depending upon the goal to be achieved. There is reason to hope that the technique may replace coronary-artery–bypass surgery at one-tenth the cost. If this were the only hope it offered, it would be worthy of front-page news for a long time.

As there is very little information available right now, I can't offer you any tips on how to deal with it, but I would definitely ask your physician if it is an alternative for you should you be contemplating a surgical procedure of some sort. For many patients, it can provide treatment without surgery and greatly reduce hospital costs, the length of your stay, and risk.

FOR ADVOCATES

Diagnostic testing can be almost as trying for you as it is for the patient, because you can't plan any of your tomorrows. Testing can be finished in one day or go on for weeks.

Your job is to help the patient adhere to the preparation procedures and then to help with whatever follows the test. For instance, after some tests the patient must lie flat for twelve hours. "Flat" means the head may be elevated no more than twenty degrees, which could cause difficulty at mealtime. You could help by cutting food and placing it on the lowered tray table beside the bed.

Of course, you can always be the attentive listener. Some testing procedures seem as harrowing to the patient as surgery, and talking about them provides instant relief for the "victim."

CHAPTER
9
Hospitalese

In 1978 President Jimmy Carter directed that federal regulations be written in clear and simple language. "Everyone benefits," he proclaimed, "except the people who manufacture typewriter ribbons."

MEDICAL JARGON

As we all know, verbosity can be used to camouflage the cold, hard, miserable facts and Dr. Cutter was a past master at it. He was a gifted physician, brilliant in his particular field, but as a social animal he was a disaster. On a typical day he would walk into a patient's room and ask, "Martha, how are you feeling today?" Never once did I hear him wait for an answer before he launched into his speech for the day: "The primary site is of little concern, but the metastasis might respond to chemo or radiation and, if nothing else, we might be able to offer you palliation. Perhaps surgery might be a possibility, but right now we need to lower your calcium and magnesium levels and you could use some platelets too."

Martha looked up at him with an incredulous stare, hopelessness creasing her brow, then drooping her shoulders. "Who cares? I'm more dead than alive."

Her husband's reaction was not quite so complaisant. As the doctor spoke, Fred's neck became blotchy and his arteries bulged; he jangled the change in his pocket, edged toward the door, and his shoulders became set with resolve. As the doctor hurried down the hall, Fred pranced along beside him, fumbling with words. He couldn't bring himself to say, "When will she die? How long has she got? Will she ever get better? What are you doing for her?" These were all questions that he besieged the nurses with day after day after day. Instead, he asked apologetically, almost in a whisper, as though entreating God for a moment of his time, "Doctor, how is she doing?" All Dr. Cutter could say to Fred was, "She's doing as expected. Don't worry."

The signal Fred got was crystal clear—"busy." Dr. Cutter's steps quickened. He couldn't say: "Much too busy to tell you the truth in plain English . . . it's too harsh. We don't know where the cancer began, we're not even sure what we're dealing with. The drugs she's getting are investigational, ones we're not even sure about. We're trying to stop the growth of the tumors, keep her comfortable, anything we can, but the drugs have changed the electrolytes in her body, which makes her seem a little out of her head. As soon as we get her calcium level down, her mind will clear and she'll sound more rational to you. . . . Sorry, Fred, we're doing the best we can and all we can do is hope that this works."

Just a little bit of this simple, plain English would have been enough to satisfy Fred, to give him hope that he was not fighting for his wife's survival in an entirely uncontrollable world, to let him know that Dr. Cutter or someone cared that he was losing his mate of forty-two years to a fatal disease.

The truth was Dr. Cutter *did* care. In fact, he cared a great deal, but he had ceased to think in plain English and simply didn't know how to converse with his patients in terms they could understand.

President Carter may have banned legalese, but it is doubtful that medicalese will ever be abolished. It is the international language of medicine, but is also a language of protection for the entire medical profession. After all, who would want to admit that "iatrogenic" means the professional himself was to blame or that "idiopathic" really means "of unknown causes"?

The use of medical jargon is also a matter of convenience. For instance, "NPO" is much quicker to write than the plain English order "Nothing by mouth," and "Vitals QID" is far faster than "Take the temperature, pulse, respirations, and blood pressure four times a day." If you want a translation, you will have to ask.

Doctors aren't the only foreign-language speakers—the whole hospital staff uses medicalese—and the confused patient usually understands more from facial expressions than from the words used. I thought nothing of approaching my patients' bedsides every morning for two years and saying, "I'm going to take your vitals now," until I met up with little old Mr. Gibson. "You'll do no such thing," he exclaimed and drew away from me as though I were diseased. "If you're going to do anything with my vitals, you can very well get a man in here in the first place, then I'll talk to *him* about what's going to be done with them." I was so amazed that he would misinterpret my intent to simply measure his temperature and pulse that I headed for the door murmuring "Yes, sir, I'll get Bill in here right away, sir."

YOUR CHART

At the nursing station near your room a rack holds the charts of all the patients in that area, each in a separate binder labeled with the patient's name, room number, and physician's name. Each chart is divided into several sections; Doctor's Orders, Progress Notes, Lab results, Medications, X-ray results, Graphic Sheet, I&O (Intake and Output), History and Physical, Consultations, Respiratory Therapy, Discharge Summary, Surgery, Nurses' Progress Notes, and Admitting Forms, often in that order.

The chart is a legal document, above all else, but it is also the means by which staff from various departments communicate with each other regarding your care, as well as the doctor's major tool in deciding which route to take in your therapy.

Unfortunately for you, it is written in hospitalese. Fortunately for you, hospitalese is the same whether it appears on a prescription, chart forms, bedside signs, or doctor's orders. If you become familiar with the definitions and abbreviations and the forms in the Appendix, you've licked the "conspiracy of silence" that so often keeps patients in the submissive role.

It's your *body,* your *life,* your *health,* and your *responsibility.* You can't be expected to accept responsibility for something you know nothing about. In addition, you have a "right to know." You have a right to know what your vital signs are, what treatments you'll be having, the name of any person who is performing your care, your lab results—anything you want to know. Your chart should be readily available to you. In fact, part of your chart might be on a clipboard at the foot of the bed, partly to keep you informed and partly for the convenience of staff.

FOR ADVOCATES

If your patient is not alert and you have identified yourself as the patient's advocate, you are then acting on his behalf and should feel free to exercise his rights for him. This includes reading his bedside chart and asking questions that might help you understand his care.

Caution

Test results arrive in batches from several different departments of the hospital. Someone, usually a clerk, posts the results on the proper charts *sometimes*.

One day a clerk posted the results of a venereal disease test (which was positive for syphilis) on the chart for room 535. The next day Dr. Johnson, a consultant, visited the patient in room 535 and said, "Well part of your problem is the syphilis, you know." The patient was too stunned to reply "No, I didn't know," and it was several hours before the nurse could finally get to the bottom of the patient's hysteria—to a fifty-five-year-old lady, married to the same man and faithful for thirty-five years, a positive syphilis test meant only one thing, adultery.

As it turned out, the clerk had posted the test results on the correct chart number, but the results belonged to another patient who had been moved from the same room the day before. No one, even the doctor, had bothered to notice that the name on the lab slip was wrong, even though the room number was correct. The moral of the story is that you should always remember the high chance for clerical error when hundreds of forms are being transferred to charts daily. Question what seems unreasonable to you.

Bedside Charts

In hospitals where parts of the chart are kept at the bedside, you're most likely to find the Graphic, I&O, Medication, and Patient Care Plan.

The Graphic keeps a record of routine tasks performed by the nurses, as well as a serial recording of your vital signs. The top of the sheet gives the time of day, but don't be surprised if you find discrepancies. For instance, I wouldn't awaken you for midnight vitals, but I would take them whenever you happened to be awake and then record them in the midnight space. On the other hand, if timing is crucial to your care, the exact time of any procedure will be recorded. See Chapter 3—Day One for more information on vital signs.

As explained in Chapter 4—Common Nuisances the I&O sheet is a recording of all the fluids that go in and out of your body, but this sheet will be missing if this record is not essential to your care.

The Medication sheet is usually divided into three sections; Routine Medications (those that you get without asking), PRN (those you must ask for, such as pain medication), and One-time-only (preoperative injections, certain vitamins, hormones). Using the Appendix, you will be able to translate some of the Medication sheet into the intervals at which you're to receive the meds (hospitalese for medications) and the route of administration whether oral, injectable, rectal, or IV. See Chapter 4 for more information on your medications.

The Patient Care Plan indicates your therapy goals and should reflect what you have agreed to do to promote your recovery. For example, if you are dehydrated you and the nurse should agree on what kinds of fluid you would like to drink, when, and how much. If you're bedridden, you and she must agree on how often you will be turned and what positions you prefer. Essentially, the Care Plan is a contract between you and those who will provide for your care.

Charts as Legal Documents

Suppose you want to see the entire chart, for whatever reason. The policy on this varies from hospital to hospital, from physician to physician, and from state to state. Some nurses will hand you the entire chart and leave it for an hour or so for you to read, regardless of policy. Other nurses won't allow you to read the chart, despite the fact this is sanctioned by all concerned, since it is their own belief that patients should not be allowed any medical information. If you *are* curious and would like to see your whole chart, ask the nurse.

You'll probably be surprised at what you see. In the first place, very few physicians write legibly. Nurses become accustomed to each doctor's handwriting eventually and can read what would be merely scribble to anyone else.

Another surprise is the amount of information omitted that you might have thought significant. Since it is basically a legal document, only that which would be salient in a courtroom is required. A nurse or physician who is pressed for time might even omit some of the required information unwittingly. A patient has little, if any, control over what goes in his chart. Thus he can't depend on it to support a claim against the hospital.

Charts and Keeping Records

You might at some point get involved with transferring your charts from one physician to another. *Don't bother!* Whether your doctor reads your past charts or not, he will still want to take a history directly from you. He is rarely interested in what another doctor had to say on your records. Actually, you'd be surprised how little information is available from physicians' charts. If you've done your homework, you know what medications work for you, which ones you're currently taking, when your hospitalizations have been and what they were for, the dates of your last immunizations, and the locations of any X rays done in the recent past. You must keep your own records current.

When you take Johnny to get a tetanus shot, write the date

down. When you have a Pap smear, write the date down. Keep your own records. You might come across a physician who refuses to transfer your records to another physician.

In any event, if you want your records transferred, you must *write* to Dr. A. and tell him you authorize him to send your records to Dr. B. He must have *written authorization* before he can send them.

If you don't want Dr. A. to know you're going to Dr. B., all the more reason not to ask for a chart transfer, but don't feel that you're at risk if you don't give old records to the new doctor— Dr. B. might be better off without the influence of Dr. A.

The larger hospitals retain medical records on microfilm for many years, while smaller hospitals keep all charts carefully arranged in a records library. If you feel compelled to read yours after you've left the hospital, your physician can write a permission, usually on his prescription pad, that you present to the medical-records department of the hospital. Curious to see the difference between what I thought should be recorded and what the medical profession thought should be, I requested a review of my own hospital chart and was greeted by a not very friendly clerk in medical records. Her manner was rather accusing, in fact, and I realized that a request to read a chart is usually translated as an impending malpractice suit. Suspicion shrouds your request to read your chart, but it's an interesting experience that I highly recommend. And suspicion never harmed anyone.

The average patient worries only about judgmental statements on a chart. More than one has said to me, "Well, you've probably heard everyone else's side so I'll tell you mine. I really tore this place apart last night, even called the nurse a few unsavory four-letter words, but I was ..." and they go on to excuse their "bad" patient behavior.

If you're lying in a hospital bed right now worrying about the bad time you gave everyone on the last shift, stop worrying because the staff on shift now probably has no idea of your previous behavior. Patients react to stress in very different ways and we understand that. We may, as humans, consider you "demanding," or "cranky," or "nasty," or "manipulative," or "faking it," but we wouldn't write that on your chart because we wouldn't want the legal world to know we aren't understanding enough to allow you to express stress in your own way.

SHIFT REPORT

Once every eight hours, around 7:00 a.m., 3:00 p.m. and 11:00 p.m., one shift of nurses "reports off" to the next shift, often just outside your door. This is called "walking rounds." The original intent was to stand at the foot of your bed and force you into becoming a participant in your own care by "reporting" to you as well as the other nurses, which is comical since the jargon used to exchange information wouldn't give the average patient the slightest clue how he could participate in his own care. However, it does manage to frighten many patients into total submission. "His CA is up," says the nurse, meaning his calcium level is elevated, but he might have heard "Ca" used as a contraction for cancer. How would you like to be lying there hearing that your cancer is up? If you're curious, wait until report is finished and then ask what you want to know.

The most important thing to learn about report is that if you happen to want something this is the worst possible time to ask for it. One nurse will leave the reporting group to fill your request, while all the others must stand in the hall waiting for her until they can continue.

If you've bucked the system anywhere along the line, you might expect that information to be passed along during report. However, patients are rarely classified then as "good" or "bad" since the shift that is ending has only one thought in mind—get report over with as quickly as possible.

PRESCRIPTIONS

Medical abbreviations and symbols are the same, whether they're on your bedside signs, various chart forms, the physician's orders, the prescriptions he sends home with you, or the prescriptions he writes in his office. If you can read one, you can read them all, which really opens new vistas to you. The most common abbreviations and symbols are given in the Appendix and should be scanned now so that you know a little about them, when we later discuss how to read a prescription.

Suppose that two months ago you were in California where you were examined for an upper-respiratory infection. The doctor gave you prescriptions for an antibiotic, a decongestant, a cough syrup, nose drops, and an ointment to soothe your raw nostrils. You took *all* of the antibiotic as you *always* must for it to be effective. Your other symptoms disappeared within a couple of days, so you still have better than half of each of the other medications sitting in your medicine chest.

Now you're in New York with an upper-respiratory infection once again, seeing a different physician who gives you a handful of new prescriptions. The average person makes a pharmacy stop on the way home and pays heavily for whatever has been prescribed. Now your cupboard holds two sets of decongestant, cough syrup, nose drops, and ointment. The names of the medications may be different, simply because there are so many different brands just as there are so many different brands of detergent. However, there's a very good chance that you have spent your money for new medications that work no differently than the ones you bought in California.

Many medications have a short life, in which case they will be labeled with an expiration date. Others are extremely dangerous to keep around the house if you have small children or others who might not realize the harmful potential of drugs. In that case, the best choice might be to discard medications as soon as the illness has passed. But to discard *all* medications, as is advised by pharmacists and physicians, is economic foolishness. You must learn to be selective.

Labeling Prescription Drugs

It's difficult to be selective if you don't know what's in the prescription and there are some states that still don't have labeling laws. Those who are against labeling argue that disclosure of the name of the drug would be detrimental to the welfare of some patients who might worry unduly. However, the reasons for labeling prescription drugs with their names and strengths have been set forth repeatedly: (1) the patient has a right to be informed about the drugs he is taking, the desired effects, and the anticipated side effects; (2) patients with drug allergies have to know what they are taking; (3) in an emergency situation such as poisoning, overdose, or attempted suicide, identification of the drug could be lifesaving; (4) the information is valuable if the patient changes physicians or contacts the prescribing physician at a time when his records are not immediately available. There are other equally persuasive arguments in favor of labeling all drugs, but until such time as it becomes mandatory practice, you should be sure to advise your physician that you want all your medications labeled. If he intends to do so, he will write on your prescription "LAS" which means "label as such," or merely "label."

In addition, it's a good idea to label your medicine bottles with your diagnosis or symptoms at the time. For instance, Benadryl might be prescribed when you have a rash. Write "itching" on the label and then ask the physician if you can use the same medication a few months later when he is writing still another prescription to relieve itching. If you write "headache" on a bottle of Fiorinal now, perhaps a headache two or three months from now can be relieved with the same medication rather than a brand new bottle of twenty pills of some similar or identical medication. By the way, Benadryl won't *cure* what's causing your itching. Prescriptions are not always intended to cure anything—they simply relieve the symptoms. Keeping your prescriptions labeled may not save you a trip to the doctor but it can save you the expense of duplicated drugs.

If you're going to keep medications for later use you must do it in an organized, safe manner. Get yourself a small metal box from the hardware store, perhaps a fishing-tackle box, with a *lock and key*. Write "Pharmacy" on the top, put all your drugs in it, and *keep it locked*.

My neighbor walked into the kitchen one morning to find her diet pills scattered on the counter and her three-year-old perched there separating them into little piles—the partially chewed ones in one stack and the whole ones in another stack. "Yucky," she said, with the tiny beads from the capsule dribbling down her chin. Her mother reconstructed the chewed ones, counted them, and calculated that one dose was the most the child could have taken. Even that was doubtful since the child obviously didn't like the taste.

As the day wore on, however, the child became more and more "hyper" until by bedtime she was literally running in circles nonstop, babbling away. There was no way to retrieve or reverse the effects—they simply had to "wear off"—and for twenty-four hours that child never stopped moving. You simply can't count on the early-morning pilgrimages of little folk not extending into areas you didn't think they could even reach. Most medications look like candy too. *Keep that box locked!*

If you have a medicine cabinet bulging with drugs that are unlabeled now, you don't have to discard them. Any pharmacist or physician has an illustrated chart of drugs for easy identification. In fact, if you have access to *Physician's Desk Reference (PDR)*, you can identify them yourself by consulting the illustrations in the front of the book.

Let's assume though that you have tossed all the unlabeled drugs and have a boxful of labeled ones. Make a list of them and keep it in your wallet. Next time the doctor hands you a prescription, ask him if any of the drugs you already have could be substituted or show the pharmacist your list when you take the new prescription to him.

About the PDR

The *Physician's Desk Reference* is just one of many books the medical community uses for resource. It lists product information on approximately 2500 pharmaceuticals and is published yearly "with the cooperation of the manufacturers whose products are described." The book also lists indications, effects, routes, methods, dosages, frequency of administration, warnings, hazards, contraindications, side effects, and precautions. It is indexed by manufacturer, by brand name, by generic and chemical name, and by drug classification. The cost is $13 to $16 and it's available at large bookstores, usually those near universities.

However, there's a big problem when you decide to explore the drugs you are taking. If you look up some fairly common drug such as Valium, you could be frightened into never taking any medication since the *PDR* lists every possible ill effect. People do die from such seemingly benign drugs as aspirin and the *PDR* listing of most drugs is thorough enough to convince you that every drug is a potential poison.

Your best bet for reliable drug information is really a pharmacist. When you have a prescription filled, he should tell you what drugs are incompatible with it (in case you're taking any of them), whether it should be taken on a full or empty stomach, how long it can be kept in your medication box, and what effects you should anticipate. Write down what he says! Actually, this is an important part of his job and he'll enjoy teaching you about your medications. If he doesn't offer this information, find another pharmacist.

You must always remember that *every* drug has unwanted side effects of some sort and you and the physician are faced with a choice of the lesser of two evils. For instance, prednisone has a very long list of undesirable effects, but if you're really suffering from arthritis to the extent that you're immobilized, you'll probably decide that the benefit of taking prednisone outweighs the risk. As in many medical decisions, sometimes the bottom line is a dilemma focusing on quality of life versus quantity of life. You hold the responsibility for that decision.

How to Read a Prescription

The forms used for prescriptions are often a means of advertising; thus a certain pharmacy or drug company may have its name at the top of your physician's prescription pad. This is nothing more than advertising and it's safe to ignore it! The important part of your prescription begins with your name and address. Below that the form usually says "Rx," an abbreviation from Latin for "prescription." Then the doctor writes his orders. For example, "Valium 5 mg tabs #30." This means the strength of the Valium is 5 milligrams, it is to be supplied in tablet form (tabs) and you are to get 30 tablets. To price-shop, call the pharmacy and ask the price of 30 tablets of 5 milligram Valium.

Generally the larger the quantity you buy, the lower the price, so look down in the lower-right or lower-left corner of the prescription form for the printed word "Refill." The doctor has authorized as many refills as he has written, but sometimes it might be to your advantage to buy the entire amount all at once. For instance, the prescription for birth-control pills is usually written with authorization for at least five refills; the pharmacist might give you a discount for purchasing a six-month supply all at one time.

If the doctor has not preauthorized the prescription as indicated in the "Refill" square, he will have to be contacted before it can be refilled—that might be difficult after office hours! In addition, there are strict controls on certain drugs with high potential for abuse; the number of times they can be refilled within a certain number of months is limited, with or without the approval of your physician.

After the "Rx" portion of the prescription you'll usually see the "SiG" portion, the instructions the doctor wants written on the label for you by the pharmacist. For example, "SiG tabs Tq 3–4 h PRN for nervousness"—the pharmacist will label your medication "Take one tablet every 3–4 hours as necessary for nervousness."

If your physician is really progressive, he'll write "LAS and PPI," which means label the drug and give the patient the information packet containing side effects, dosages, contraindications, etc. You may have noticed these PPIs enclosed with birth-control pills; there's a strong push for legislation to supply this information with every type of prescription.

Generic Equivalents

It is estimated that more than one billion drug prescriptions are written in this country each year, 90 percent of them for brand name drugs, the other 10 percent for drugs prescribed by generic name. A drug prescribed by brand name is manufactured by only one pharmaceutical company, under patent, giving that company a monopoly. In 1980 patents on at least eighty-three of the best-selling prescription drugs in this country expired and the monopolies their manufacturers enjoyed began to disappear.

A drug prescribed by its generic or chemical name, on the other hand, is generally manufactured by several competing companies; thus the lower price. For instance, your doctor might prescribe tetracycline for you under the brand name Achromycin, Panmycin, Robitet, Sumycin, or any of several other brand names. All are generically equivalent—that is, all can be considered to have been manufactured under the same standards, meet identical or comparable specifications, and can be shown to be bioequivalent. No matter which one goes into your stomach, the therapeutic effects are the same—only the prices differ.

If you live in Florida and your doctor prescribes Robitet, the druggist is permitted by law to substitute the cheaper generic drug unless the doctor insists on no substitution. In New York, on the other hand, the pharmacist *must* fill all prescriptions with generic equivalents if they are cheaper, approved, and available. Although forty states have some type of generic law, some of the laws have been stymied by professional opposition and other problems. Since some brand name drugs cost up to seven times more than their generic equivalent, you could save yourself 45 percent of your drug bill by requesting that your doctor prescribe by generic rather than brand name, until the laws in your state become as sophisticated as those in New York.

You now know how to read a prescription, how to avoid spending money on duplicate prescriptions, and how to get one filled at the least expense. Now become friends with your pharmacist. He is a great source of information waiting to be tapped!

FOR ADVOCATES

There's a good chance that you might hear more hospital jargon than the patient because you're sitting there unaffected by mind-dulling illness or drugs. Most advocates find this a very educational experience, especially since there's always the temptation to envision yourself as the one lying in the bed.

Several times you'll say to yourself, "If I'm ever a patient, I sure will . . ." and rehearse what you'd do or say under varying circumstances. Like a foreign traveler, you'll realize how much easier it would be to get what you need and find out what you need to know, if you can speak or understand the language. Some hospitals have published mini-dictionaries to

help you with the translation. For fifteen cents you can purchase *Understanding Hospital Jargon* by writing to Harper-
Grace Hospitals, 3990 John Road, Detroit, Michigan 48201.
One hundred of the most common hospital terms are listed in
this pamphlet.

For an innovative "get well" gift you might consider giving
your patient a copy of *Taber's Cyclopedic Medical Dictionary*,
published by F. A. Davis Co. (1915 Arch Street, Philadelphia,
Pennsylvania 19103). In addition to fairly simple definitions of
medical terms, this book has excellent illustrations of body
parts; a huge appendix with metric-system conversion tables;
Latin and Greek nomenclature; a directory of poison-control
centers; medical prefixes and suffixes; glossaries of muscles,
bones, joints, and nerves; analyses of vitamins; and a five-
language phrase book just in case illness strikes in a foreign
country. This dictionary even tells you the most common
treatments for diseases and accidents so you can help yourself
through uncomplicated illnesses.

The price (around $12) and size of the book are relatively
small, considering the amount of information offered, and it's
one of the few commonly used medical books generally available to the public.

CHAPTER
10
Your Legal Rights and Responsibilities

OBSOLETE THEORIES

During World War II we, the taxpayers, happily supported the expenditure of several hundred thousand dollars on shark-deflecting amulets worn by our seagoing servicemen. Small price to pay for keeping our husbands and sons from being swallowed by sharks, we thought, and no one ever heard from an unhappy customer. The war was long ended when the amulets were scientifically tested and found to be totally useless from a shark-deflecting standpoint.

During those same years and for many years thereafter, tonsils were considered a curse of childhood—the promoters of sore throats, earaches, and runny noses—to be summarily excised by the surgeon's scalpel. Indeed, wholesale tonsillectomies were a family affair. As children, we heard about the advantages of tonsillectomies (all the Jello-O and ice cream you can eat) at about the same age we heard about the advantages of losing teeth (the tooth fairy slips money under your pillow) and we happily submitted to the indignities of hospitalization.

Surgeons pronounced tonsils as vestigial as the appendix and few of us over the age of twenty-five can lay claim to having the troublemakers. Precocious children asked the surgeon to preserve them in a jar, as trophies of a sort, but the rest of us have probably never given our missing tonsils another thought, except to exclaim that we continue to have sore throats, earaches, and runny noses—despite the fact that our tonsils have been removed.

Today the medical community thinks that the tonsils serve an important autoimmune function in the body, actually fending off certain illnesses, and the wholesale tonsillectomy business has shown a dramatic decline.

In 1976 in southern California physicians made national headlines by withholding their services to protest wildly increasing malpractice-insurance premiums. The statistical results were dramatic: there was a 58.7 percent reduction in the amount of surgery compared to the year before and also a significant drop in the death rate of Los Angeles County. In the five weeks following the resumption of surgery, the death rate per 100,000 population rose from 19.2 to 26. Surgical intervention *may* influence the death rate.

Obviously, there are inconsistencies in our health-care–delivery system which is, in fact, illness-oriented and what was thought to be life-preserving yesterday may well be considered life-threatening today. The easiest route is to throw your hands up in horror and say, "What do I know? I'm no doctor. I'll just have to do whatever Dr. Smith tells me."

But Dr. Smith holds the winning card in the medical game. On the one hand, he asks you to "Trust your doctor," but on the other hand he places pen and paper before you and requires your signature on a document that releases him, his technicians, and institutions from all responsibility should your trust be misplaced. He is legally obligated now to inform you of your alternatives while he is caring for you but the responsibility for the outcome is dumped squarely in your lap.

THE PATIENT'S OBLIGATION

You have no choice but to accept the responsibility—that much is clear. Though you may stand before the medical community and shed your dignity, your individuality, your money, and your clothes, you may not shed the responsibility for your own place on the well-ill continuum of life. That is what this chapter is all about—your obligations and how to fulfill them.

While your library may be replete with advice on how to find a job, how to raise worms for profit, how to improve your sexual prowess, how to select a building contractor, how to buy life insurance, and how to tour Europe on a shoestring, it's doubtful that it holds one book telling you how to deal with the health-care delivery system. Yet you, even though you may be grossly ill-equipped to do so, are increasingly being called upon to make the decisions regarding your own health care. This shift of responsibility appears to dethrone the physician, but actually works in his best interest. He can now say, "It was the patient's choice"—even though the patient blindly signed his rights away without knowing what choices were involved and what the alternatives were.

Hundreds of patients every week submit to one of the latest sophisticated diagnostic techniques—cardiac catheterization. This procedure costs about $550, takes place in the hospital, and harms one patient in fifty; yet there is no evidence that a differential diagnosis based on its results extends either the life expectancy or the comfort of any patient. The average patient is unaware that he has a choice, that the procedure is routinely ordered by many cardiologists, that he will most likely experience pain, that he may not survive the test, or that quite possibly the results of the test will make no difference in his treatment.

FOR ADVOCATES

The patient sitting before the admitting clerk has just had a big confrontation with reality when the legal forms were presented. Hospitalization was a vague threat before he walked in the door; the legal forms have made the whole idea seem rather ominous. Don't be surprised if his hand is shaking when he tries to sign his name—he's frightened and too shaken to concentrate on legalese. The clerk will be as grateful as the patient if you intercede and advise the patient what and where to sign, *after* you have read and approved the forms.

We wouldn't sign a credit contract without reading it or sign a real-estate deposit receipt or a political petition without reading them. But medical documents we sign willingly without even reading them as if to do so would indicate distrust.

After we have managed to back ourselves into a corner we come out shouting, "Malpractice, malpractice, I've been injured," only to have waved before us the very forms that gave the medical profession the right to do anything and everything it might deem "appropriate."

He signs the Consent for Treatment form without question, for not doing so would imply that he does not trust his doctor, and is impressed when, following the test, he is told the procedure detected a certain percentage of occlusion of his coronary arteries. It is highly unlikely that he has also been told that the vast majority of people over the age of forty have *some* degree of artery occlusion and manage to chug on well into old age. This patient did not know his alternatives.

"Sign this, please," and the admitting clerk thrusts a long form across the desk laden with legal language. It's too late to read, the operating room is scheduled, the anesthesiologist has been engaged, the waiting has become intolerable, the decision has been made; there's no point in reading it. We sign and, thereby, relinquish our right to hold the physician, the hospital, the nurse, the anesthesiologist, the technician, or the housekeeper responsible for anything that might occur while we are in the hospital.

SHIFTING RESPONSIBILITIES

In days gone by, the basic therapeutic relationship was with a kindly physician who was a friend of the family, adviser, holder of hands, and provider of medical care. The relationship was personal, individualized, and bound by trust. Respected and protected by the medical community, by our social and political institutions, and by the courts, the relationship placed the control and authority in the hands of the physician, with a consequent loss of personal autonomy, but few found this objectionable. However, when the friendly physician is replaced by the institution—the hospital, the clinic, the group practice, or the health-maintenance organization—what remains of the traditional relationship is not the individual care or the trust, but the control and authority.

Today we live in a society that places a high value on individual autonomy and freedom. We want good health care, but we also want to control our own lives. We want to be properly advised and informed, then allowed to make our own treatment decisions according to our own values.

Vivian came to us about two weeks before Christmas last year. She was a "young" patient, only forty-six, who had finished a few days of diagnostic testing with very bad news—she had lung cancer. A thoracotomy was planned for three days before Christmas for identification of the type of cell and primary site.

On the morning of surgery her husband arrived very early and she said, "You know, Earl, my chances of coming out of this feeling good aren't very great."

"You'll do just fine, Viv," he urged her.

She stared far away, obviously not wanting the conflict that she knew she would arouse. "I'm going home, Earl. I'll come back after Christmas, but this may be the last one for all of us. I can't take that risk." The surgeon sat with the family at her bedside. Such paradoxical feelings are not uncommon. Who could say whether it would or would not be her last Christmas? And if it were her last, did it make any sense to spend it in an intensive care unit with all the warmth and coziness of a quarry?

She went home within the hour, had a beautiful though poignant Christmas, returned to us two days after Christmas, and died four days later. She had made the best choice.

THE PATIENT'S BILL OF RIGHTS

The choice of alternatives, the willingness to accept a given level of risk, or the preference of one treatment over another is a matter of personal choice. Our political and legal institutions have recently begun to recognize the importance of this principle, which is defined by the patient's right to consent.

Patients' rights is not a new concept in health care; however, the insurgence in the 1970s of legal liability among health-care providers gave added impetus to the significance of informed consent. The individual has the right and the power to accept or reject certain treatments and to know the corresponding risks and benefits of his choice.

In most hospitals you'll find the Patient's Bill of Rights posted, with any luck, in a conspicuous place. The only problem is that it is usually in very tiny print and is painfully long and redundant. In its original form, it was adopted by the American Hospital Association in 1973. However, various states have expounded upon or altered in other ways the original text to suit their own values.

Basically you have the right to considerate and respectful care, the right to refuse treatment, the right to privacy, the right to reasonable response to your request for service, the right to obtain information, the right to be advised if you are to participate in experimentation, the right to continuity of care, the right to examine and receive an explanation of your bill, and the right to know what hospital rules and policies apply to your conduct. In some states, you also have the right to have your advocate make decisions on your behalf regarding your care, in which case the Bill of Rights applies to him, too.

How then, given all these rights, is there controversy? Define the words "considerate," "reasonable," "privacy," "continuity," and "experimentation." In my present healthy state, I consider cancer chemotherapy "experimentation," but if I were a terminal-cancer case, I'm not positive that I would make the same distinction. What is "privacy?" I can think of many instances when we invade a patient's privacy, but under other conditions invasion of privacy might be crucial to treatment. Such are the dilemmas of the medical community.

In summary, the Patient's Bill of Rights is a step in the right direction, but it promises nothing until one tries it—even then, it promises very little except a few "intentions" on your side. The hospital *intends* to preserve your dignity, individuality, and right to freedom of choice, but wide interpretation of the terms leaves the whole matter in limbo.

INFORMED CONSENT

Courtesy, privacy, and information are the three basic rights of all patients and the greatest of these is information! Eight of the twelve rights listed in the Patient's Bill of Rights relate to knowing or being informed, since it is an established principle of law that every human being has the right to determine what should be done with his own body. Obviously, you can't determine what should be done if you don't have all the necessary information.

What is "necessary information"? It is determined by applying the standards of a "reasonable man," that fictitious character who appears in the courtroom to decide if you have been given:

1. an explanation of your condition,
2. an explanation of the procedures to be performed,
3. an explanation of alternatives to the suggested procedures,
4. a description of the benefits to be expected,
5. an opportunity to ask questions, and
6. an understanding that you are not being coerced into compliance and that you may reject treatment if you change your mind. The disclosure is to be "reasonable" and in understandable lay language.

Dr. Silver is an expert at augmentation mammaplasty, enlargement of the breasts with silicone gel implants, commonly referred to as "a boob job." At least 50 percent of his patients come to him as recipients of a gift—$1500–$2000—and a husband's sanction to have breast implants. In fact, if such a gift is under your Christmas tree and you make an appointment with Dr. Silver the very next day, he still won't be able to take your case until the following September. This insures that you are not being "coerced." Actually, coercion has nothing to do with the wait, but is a nice secondary gain for him. You must indeed really want the surgery if you have contemplated it for at least nine months before the doctor ever sees you.

Santa Claus gave Sally just such a gift and for the whole nine months she bubbled. The first appointment finally arrived and Dr. Silver applied the standards of a "reasonable man." (1) He gave an explanation of the condition—Sally's mirror had already provided that—and his charted measurements, based on body proportions, confirmed she was a good candidate for mammaplasty. (2) He explained the procedures to be performed and gave her a brochure in very simple language, detailing the operation, including the risks.

He told her that "injection of a local anesthetic is best, since a general anesthetic is added risk and expense. The surgery takes an hour. A snug, padded dressing is applied to the breasts; there is normal swelling following surgery; the dressing is removed in three days; and the sutures are removed in ten days." He went on to tell her that she might develop a hematoma, an abnormal accumulation of blood, that would require further surgery or that she might develop an infection requiring removal of the implant and then reinsertion after the infection was brought under control.

He termed the hematoma "quite rare" and the infection "extremely rare." Another "rare" complication could be disturbance in nipple sensation, while "a more common complication" is development of firmness of one or both breasts due to constriction of the implant by increased scar tissue.

"How rare is 'rare'?" Sally wondered. Herein lies the whole crux of "Informed Consent." Dr. Silver gave her a percentage of possibility for each complication to occur, an "odds are . . ." type of statement. Mammaplasty doesn't carry ominous odds, but Sally's vision of herself as a buxom beauty had not included any risk.

Still applying the "reasonable" standards of necessary information—(3), an explanation of alternatives to the suggested procedures—he told her about silicone injections and different types of implants and also suggested the obvious alternative such as bra padding instead of having implants. And (4), a description of the benefits to be expected, which were obvious to Sally as she'd thought of little else as she waited those nine months. He gave her an opportunity to ask questions, standard (5), and then he did the most important of all—(6), he gave her the written information and time to think it over. In fact, he gave her three weeks to think it over, which was about two weeks, six days, and twenty-three hours more than she really wanted—beach season was ending!

At the bottom of the sheet that contained the information he had given her was the legal "informed consent" that she was required to sign and submit to him before surgery:

I have read the above and fully understand its contents. Any questions I have had on the above material I have asked Dr. Silver and have had answered to my satisfaction.
Signed _____
Date _____

While it is not legally necessary to have a written consent, proof of consent is necessary in a court action, and the court is not one of Dr. Silver's favorite places. He insures "proof" just in case he should ever end up on the witness stand.

REJECTION OF INFORMATION

Several studies have been conducted to assess the effects of informed consent on patients, since it is a relatively new concept which has paradoxical implications; it protects the medical practitioners from unwarranted litigation, but it also frightens patients, takes a great deal of the physician's time, and sometimes results in refusal of treatment.

About one-fourth of fully informed patients say they are more uncomfortable about a procedure after having had it explained and approximately 2 percent reject treatment. Then there are those patients who indicate no interest in detailed information, which is also their right. We don't have statistics on this because very often the lack of interest is implied rather than stated. It is a well-known phenomenon that the brain can only assimilate information with which the patient is able to cope. Many times information the doctor is giving to the patient sails right in the left ear and exits the right completely intact—not one word is deposited in the brain.

I once watched a surgeon provide the parents of a fourteen-year-old stab-wound victim with the six standards for informed consent. "We'd like to take your son to surgery ..." he began, and you could see them mentally shut the door on a roomful of too much information. Their circuits were already overloaded and they simply couldn't grasp any more than the physician's first few words. This is why one should always have an advocate present during explanations destined to end in the signing of a Consent for Treatment form. Your advocate can absorb the information that comes to you as an overload and between the two of you you're more likely to make a rational decision.

FOR ADVOCATES

If the patient cannot be counted upon to make the best decisions at all times, protect him by making sure he does not sign consents in the doctor's office before you have read them. Often surgeons present the legal forms before the patient even goes to the hospital for surgery.

Don't reject your right to informed consent. Fear of the unknown is usually the reason people don't want to hear what the doctor has to say. He won't give you any gory details that you can't handle. He will tell you the risks, which are gory only to the extent that you assume you have no alternatives. So the first question is: What are the alternatives? If you have none, then you might just as well reject any further information. Obviously, if your appendix has ruptured you have no alternative but to submit to surgery; in such a case it is safe to reject the details. But, you still might have various options as to the type of anesthesia—and some say anesthesia is the greatest risk of all.

THE FORM EVERYONE SIGNS

The California Hospital Association's Consent Manual lists some forty-five different forms covering everything from abortions to temporary absence releases, while other states have even more. Most hospitals, however, use a manual as a guideline and print their own consents to suit their particular situation.

Regardless of the state or the hospital, you can be sure that your role as a patient won't begin until you sign "Conditions of Admission," which is the valid consent necessary to preclude liability for assault and battery. If you refuse to sign it, you won't be admitted as a patient. You have no alternative; there's almost no point in reading the form.

Seven points are covered:

1. the hospital provides "general duty nursing" and is not to be held responsible if the patient needs "continuous or special duty" nursing care;
2. all doctors, pathologists, radiologists "and the like" are independent contractors controlling your care; the hospital is not liable when following their instructions;
3. the hospital is authorized to release information about you to all who may be liable for your hospital bill;
4. unless your "valuables" are kept in the safe, the hospital is not liable for loss or damage to your personal property;
5. you are responsible for the hospital bill and collection fees; your delinquent account bears interest at the legal rate;
6. you authorize your insurance carrier to pay benefits directly to the hospital; and
7. the hospital agrees to accept certain health-care-service plans. If you do not belong to one of these plans you pay the hospital bill yourself.

The hospital has very nicely slipped itself to the bottom of the liability list with this form, but that's to be expected—a similar form is printed on the ticket that lets you into the parking lot downtown. *Enter at your own risk* is the basic message and the hospital does deserve the right to try to keep its legal obligations to a minimum.

Earlier I said that there is *almost* no point in reading this form. The *almost* is crucial if you see anything on the form that is not printed. Typing and handwriting deserve close scrutiny, just in case the Conditions of Admission have been combined with any other consent. A "typical" example of this form from the California Hospital Association Consent Manual appears in the Appendix.

SURGICAL CONSENTS

These are the dangerous ones, the ones that may result in the wrong operation for you. You must read this form very carefully; don't trust the nurse, the doctor, the admitting clerk, or anyone except perhaps your advocate. Be sure the procedure written is the one you want and be very sure left and right body parts are specified appropriately. The correct body part is the *most* important portion of this form.

The surgeon and his assistant will be listed on the form in nonteaching hospitals; however, the surgeon may elect to list all physicians in his medical group. Perhaps you don't feel comfortable with some of the associates in his group practice, in which case you may cross out their names. Don't be timid! Often all the names are written in only because the clerk who types the form doesn't know which members of the group may be intending to perform the surgery. If it makes a difference to you, don't hesitate to alter the form.

In a teaching hospital you won't usually find any specific surgeon mentioned. However, the physician who explained your surgery to you should be mentioned by name. If you've requested a certain anesthesiologist (and you should have), be sure his name also appears on the consent.

"Mastectomy? What do you mean mastectomy? Who ever said anything about a mastectomy? What's that mean anyway? No . . . I won't," and Kay dissolved in tears that were release for all the stifled emotion she'd held for the week before surgery.

"I'm sure it's just a cyst," the doctor had told her as he lightly pressed the margins of the lump. "We'll cut it out in a jiffy and you can go back to work in a couple of days." He'd never mentioned malignancy and she'd never mentioned cancer—each knew the other was aware of the possibility. But it seemed tremendously remote until the word "mastectomy" appeared on the Consent for Surgery that the nurse presented to her the night before the operation. The full description of the procedure named on the form was: Right breast biopsy, possible right radical mastectomy.

It's not uncommon to see much more than you expected on a surgical consent and, although it may shock you, it will prepare you for the worst before you enter the operating room. A portion of the tissue removed is biopsied, in case there are any cancer cells lurking around; if the surgeon suspects more extensive surgery might be indicated, he'd like your consent to go ahead with it right from the start. Even if he doesn't suspect cancer, he may just like to play it safe and cover all options before he begins. You should have all options fully explained to you before you submit to surgery.

It's probably safe to have a breast biopsy in your small community hospital and also probably safe to have it done by almost any surgeon, but the same is not true for more sophisticated, extensive surgeries. If you're having something as major as a mastectomy, you should be in a large hospital where many of these operations are performed and your surgeon should be the one who is familiar with the very latest techniques and theories. There's a vast difference between biopsy and mastectomy, or D&C and hysterectomy—qualification for one does not assume qualification for the other, so make sure your consent is confined to the surgery that is appropriate to the circumstances.

If you're comfortable enough with your surgeon's judgment so that you want to give him consent to do whatever he thinks best, that's fine—so long as you understand that you have no right to disagree *after* the surgery has been completed. There is less risk and expense in undergoing anesthesia only once; this is the major rationale for signing consents to cover anything the surgeon may deem necessary. You simply have to weigh the pros and cons.

CONSENTS FOR SPECIAL DIAGNOSTICS

These consents are the ones that should make it very clear that risk is involved and that the test is "invasive" (see Chapter 8— Diagnostic Exams). They look very much like the surgical consent form. You should receive the same type of information before you sign that you would receive before surgery: an explanation of your condition, the procedure to be performed, the alternatives, the expected benefits, the opportunity to ask questions, and the right to refuse. Ask what sorts of risk you face, if all possible noninvasive methods of diagnosis have already been exhausted, and how knowledge of the results might alter your subsequent treatment plan.

Disposal of Severed Member

In the case of an amputated leg, arm, or other member of the body, some hospitals may want you to sign a release authorizing them to dispose of the part at their discretion. Be sure that "right" or "left" part is properly indicated, if you must sign one of these.

Infant Release Report

If a child is to be released to anyone other than a parent or relative by blood or marriage, it must be clear that such a release has been authorized. If some day you want your best friend to pick your child up from the hospital, you'd best be sure you have signed a statement to that effect.

Death and Autopsy

In situations involving patient death the paperwork for all is monumental and comes at the worst possible time. More often than not, the staff and family are aware that the patient's condition is terminal and, more often than not, the patient and family have discussed final details—such as designation of a funeral director, whether or not there will be an autopsy, and whether any body parts will be donated to eye banks and the like. However, the family may be reluctant to face the inevitable by communicating to staff exactly what to do in the end.

At the very least, a Release to Funeral Director must be signed immediately by whoever is entitled to control the disposition of the remains. The family should never leave the hospital until this has been done.

FOR ADVOCATES

Every year laws are revised, especially as they relate to who may assume authority for relatives. All hospitals have manuals with the latest news on legal consents. In addition, they retain attorneys to rule on ambiguous laws, so don't be shy about asking for assistance and/or a look at the laws yourself.

The Authority for Autopsy may be signed by a surviving spouse, parent, brother, sister, or other kin such as surviving uncles or aunts, in that order of priority. Most of us have our own mostly negative feelings about autopsies, but I urge you to consider the fact that diagnostic, therapeutic, or other scientific purposes might be helped by a postmortem examination. According to a spokesman for the Intersociety Committee on Pathology Information, there is a 40 to 50 percent difference between predeath diagnosis and autopsy findings. "There's no question that if a person dies and is not autopsied, the death certificate is very likely to be inaccurate."

While the implications for the future might seem insignificant once a body has expired, there are several diseases known to have hereditary risk factors which predispose the unsuspecting family members who could avoid the risks to some degree if they knew about them. In addition, mortality statistics often influence decisions regarding expenditure of research monies. For instance, based on mortality statistics, heart problems are said to be the nation's number-one killer; thus the research focus has for years been on hearts. However, if 50 percent of death certificates are based on guesswork, it is not clear that heart problems truly are the number-one killer.

CAUSE OF DEATH UNKNOWN

"Cause of death unknown" might seem like an impossible statement, but you'd be surprised at how often this is the case.

On my last day in nursing school a sixty-two-year-old patient, who had come into the hospital with a stomachache that "just won't let up," was apparently sleeping as I tidied her room. I had earlier finished bathing her and had turned the television to her favorite program, the morning routine that always ended with a nap before lunch. Possibly nothing in my nursing experience has amazed me more than seeing the mask of death on Nettie's face as I turned to leave her room. Never before or after has a patient's death been so entirely unexpected. I immediately made plans to attend her autopsy, despite the fact that I never thought I could gather the whatever-it-takes to sit through one.

The pathologist spoke into a recorder as he examined each part of her body and then examined tissues under the microscope. Each time he began to record, I anticipated hearing the cause of her death, but the findings were all normal and the autopsy was finished before I realized it was over.

"What did you find?" I asked the pathologist.

"What do you mean 'what did you find'? You were here through the entire autopsy." His look told me I had asked a stupid question.

"Well, everything was normal. At least, it sounded to me like you said everything was normal."

"Yep. Everything looked okay." He was busy sorting his instruments.

"How can everything be okay? She's dead and that's not okay."

"What do you want me to say?" he asked, amazed that I should be so inquisitive. "She died and no one knows why."

"What will her death certificate say?" I asked.

"Cause of death unknown."

Simple, matter-of-fact, and, he told me, not so terribly unusual. A broken heart, perhaps, or loss of the will to live, I wondered. She had never had a visitor, though she often spoke of a son who lived nearby.

Autopsy may not reveal the exact cause of death, but it certainly is the best effort in that direction. It's simple to say heart failure is the most common cause of death—everyone's heart does indeed fail, but did the heart fail as a result of death, or did the failure cause the death? If a patient dies as a result of cancer, knowledge of the primary site, which sometimes can't be determined without an autopsy, may contribute a significant piece of information to cancer research. "Cancer" is a vast umbrella over more than a hundred different types of the disease and autopsies may be a source of some of the most important information for "the keys to cancer."

Autopsy need not alter the appearance of the deceased and can be completed in about three hours. The written results might be delayed for several days if biopsies are sent to outside labs for pathology reports.

In some hospitals autopsies *must* be performed under certain conditions: if death occurs while the patient is in surgery; if death is sudden or unexpected; if the patient dies within the first twenty-four hours of hospitalization; or in an effort to determine the absence of criminal intent in which case the body is then termed "a coroner's case" and is delivered to the coroner for autopsy or disposition. The conditions for this vary from county to county as each sets up its own criteria for coroner's cases.

Most hospitals strive for immediate delivery of the body to a mortuary because some religions demand burial within twenty-four hours after death. The family will be required to take the decedent's belongings and sign a receipt for them. Everything, including even half-used boxes of Kleenex, will be sent home because nurses have been taught that one never knows what articles might be important or have sentimental value to the survivors.

ANATOMICAL GIFTS

Certain body parts have the potential of providing life for others, as you're no doubt well aware; however, the conditions under which they may be donated are stringent. Some states have an Anatomical Gift Act, which authorizes any individual, who is of sound mind and eighteen years of age or older, to give all or any part of his body for specified purposes.

This matter becomes particularly crucial in cases of clearly terminal traumatic injury where young people are involved. Recently, a twenty-six-year-old male came into our emergency room as a result of a freeway accident involving three fatalities. Almost immediately it was ascertained that our victim would not survive, despite all our efforts. We ran a race against the clock to save his young healthy kidneys and his heart for those awaiting transplants. However, there was no form of identification among his belongings and thus no way of contacting his family who would have to give the consent for donation of anatomical parts. We are obligated to make every attempt to give someone else a chance for life, whenever possible, but we can do nothing without a consent for donation, which is as it should be.

If one wishes to donate organs, a driver's license is a very good place to designate this since those young enough to donate useful parts are often of driving age and usually carry their driver's license with them.

LEAVING THE HOSPITAL AGAINST MEDICAL ADVICE

Leaving against medical advice (AMA) provides the hospital with a flurry of excitement. Obviously, it's a silent statement that you are an unhappy patient, unhappy with your physician, the staff, and/or the hospital. We had it happen once at four in the morning. It was the talk of the hospital for days, mainly because we all agreed we would have done the same thing had we been in the patient's position.

When you have become so dissatisfied that you are left with no alternative but to discharge yourself, the matter, ideally, should be thoroughly discussed with your physician—although his absence might be exactly why you intend to leave. Regardless of the reason, call your insurance company first to be sure they haven't made you financially captive by refusing to pay your bill if you leave AMA. This practice is dwindling, but it's wise to check it out.

The staff will attempt to persuade you to sign a form that absolves the hospital and the physician from all responsibility and ill effects that might result from your hasty departure, but you are not obligated to sign the form if indeed you do not intend to release them from liability.

LEGAL SIGNATURES

Don't be surprised or suspicious if you are asked to sign several consents, all reading exactly the same; consents have a way of straying and/or being improperly completed. Perhaps you signed a surgical consent in the doctor's office and it never got to the hospital, perhaps you signed it and your physician neglected to have a witness attest to your signature, or the clerk may have dated it today although the surgery is scheduled for tomorrow.

In many hospitals a patient may not sign any consents if he is under the influence of narcotics, which can be a big problem for those with intractable pain, who are either under the influence or suffering needlessly. If you tell the nurses you'd reject whatever procedure you have to sign for, rather than do without your pain medication long enough to sign the consent, chances are they will find a way around the rule. Notice that I said "rule" not "law." Rules aren't always a 100 percent reflection of the law.

In emergency cases, consent is implied. That is, treatment of the patient may take place without signed consent on the basis that, if the patient were able or his personal representative present, such consent would be given.

WATERTIGHT CONSENTS

There are none. A consent is nothing more than documentation of intent, one piece of evidence that may or may not be relevant, depending upon which side of the fence (or courtroom) you sit on. The important thing for you to remember is that you have a legal right to be fully *informed* before you sign any consent— and you can void the consent at any time.

FOR ADVOCATES

An eighty-year-old patient with a gangrenous leg was adamant that she did not want surgery, though the doctor had made it clear that surgery was her only hope for survival.

"Do it anyway. I'll sign the consent form. She's too sick to understand the consequences," said her daughter.

Unless the surgeon and the chief of staff are willing to document that she is "incompetent" in the patient's chart, the daughter *cannot* sign on her behalf.

Some say that "incompetent" means the patient does not agree with the surgeon or the daughter. However, you can imagine the moral dilemma a surgeon faces when he knows the patient has the right to reject treatment, the daughter is pleading with him to save her mother's life, and surgery is the only hope.

You and the surgeon are both obligated to respect the patient's wishes. Perhaps this is easier to do if you put yourself in the patient's place—it would be devastating to be wheeled off to surgery against your wishes.

Where legal consents are concerned, it is usually more difficult to be the patient's advocate than it is to be the patient. Your role is to be sure the patient has been provided with an adequate explanation of any alternatives involved.

BEFORE YOU SIGN

Be sure you have received the following:

1. An explanation of the condition
2. An explanation of the procedure to be performed
3. An explanation of alternatives to the suggested procedure
4. A description of the benefits to be expected
5. An opportunity to ask questions
6. An opportunity to reject treatment
7. A statement of relative risks involved

If you're consenting to major surgery, make sure your surgeon is a "pro" in that particular operation. Have it done in a hospital where many of this type are performed.

In cases of terminal illness, tell the staff:

1. Whether or not you want an autopsy
2. What funeral home you've chosen
3. If anatomical parts are to be donated

4. Who shall take possession of personal belongings
5. Where the family can be reached at any hour preceding death

Check with your insurance carrier before leaving the hospital AMA; they may refuse to pay your bill.

Be sure you read every word of every document.

If you are unsure of the meaning of any word, be sure to ask.

If you are indecisive, ask your advocate for advice—not your doctor or nurse.

11
The Physicians

HOW THE DOCTOR GETS TO BE ONE

One hundred and twenty five of us sat in the lecture hall three times a week, all in competition for the two A's that would be awarded at the end of the semester. The formula for achieving the A was very simple—a total score of 92 percent or better on all exams and experiments. We worked together in the lab twice a week for six hours all hoping to come up with the correct results for experiments. The lab score would be entered into the lecture score.

It wasn't by design that only two A's would be awarded; it was just that the chemistry classes were the sieves into which every premedical student was poured. The A's and B's stayed in and everyone else fell out, which is why every class was a real tournament. There was no sharing of experiment results, no conversation during lab that might reveal one's technique, no study groups to help each other achieve better test grades, no feeling of "we're all in this horrible grind together." Everyone wanted the 92 percent and everyone knew if more than a few achieved that percentage, the standard would be raised.

With each semester the number inside the sieve dwindled and the competition became a life-or-death matter—survival of the fittest. Those still in were of a single purpose, fiercely competitive, with only one thought for those who fell out: "There, but for the grace of God, go I."

Each student was an island unto himself and every other student was an obstacle to be overcome. The eleven who stayed in the sieve through all four years had barely even spoken to each other during that time.

Continuing their record for delayed gratification, they went on to compete for spots in medical school. While in medical school they competed for a good internship, then went through the internship competing for a good residency—an emotion-filled physical-endurance test of eighty-hour workweeks, zero social life, and a scanty paycheck, all with tunnel vision focused on one thing only, the "Grand Payoff," that translates traditionally into dollars.

There is no other professional training that compares in terms of sheer stress; no other ladder quite so steep; and no more fertile soil in which to produce a bitter, competitive workaholic. Having invested those precious years when their peers were enjoying their youth and having fought for survival every step of the way through their training, is it any wonder that doctors come out of training expecting a payoff? Have they not earned whatever fees they can charge?

My friend Peter and I took premed chemistry together. Now in his third year of medical school he writes, "I don't know what I'd do if I had to live one split second of the first two years over again. Many people have been rewarded for too long for being a cutthroat, and it's quite a shock to suddenly be expected to *care* for ill people." The first two years were spent in the classroom; now he's finally in contact with patients. He writes that his surgery training requires him to spend 120–130 hours a week at the hospital. "I'm putting together my ideal of medical care," he says; then I read the words of two leading Chicago physicians in the paper recently, "The practice of medicine has lost its appeal and satisfaction." Dr. Irvine Page, editor emeritus of *Modern Medicine,* notes: "A combination of forces has conspired against physicians that has destroyed their ideals of human behavior and embittered them to the point of wanting out. Many want early retirement and to hell with practice."

What will happen to Peter's ideal for medical care? I wonder, as I recall the inspiration in his voice in the early days of premed when he dreamed of being an old-fashioned country doctor. Big money was never Peter's impetus; his basic nature is one of altruism and devotion to his fellow humans. Yet he will write

M.D. after his name at a time when a good portion of the country is talking about the M.D. as a license to make money.

When Peter hangs out his shingle, he will have invested twelve years of his life in fierce competition, under incomparable stress, for the right to call himself a family practitioner. And he will have to pass a certification exam every six years to retain that right. What will be the return on his investment? I suspect the search for a return on the *real* investment is futile; however, I would gladly pay any price he cares to place on his services.

Yes, medical fees are spiraling because there is no free-market economy for doctors; yes, American medicine is on the defensive; yes, medical care is often dehumanized; yes, the elements of ethical, legal, and social issues surrounding the doctor-patient relationship demand resolution, but the system begins with the first shaking of the sieve, in the first chemistry course, twelve years before the M.D. ever begins his practice. "As you sow, so shall you reap."

MALPRACTICE

Negligent conduct is that conduct which falls below the standard established by law for protection of others against unreasonably great risks of harm. Medical malpractice suits refer to negligent conduct.

A physician (or a nurse for that matter) is under no obligation to treat a patient; however, once treatment is begun the practitioner may be held liable. The standard for care is "what a reasonable man would do under the circumstances."

In a nutshell, that's the law. That fictitious "reasonable man" dominates the scene again with everything subject to interpretation. I have seen patients subjected to what I would consider "unreasonably great risks of harm"; yet some of those same patients have told me how lucky they feel to have "the best doctor in the country." They do not consider themselves victims of malpractice in any way.

Generally, the difference between filing or not filing a malpractice claim rests on the quality of the relationship between the hospital or doctor and the patient. If you like your doctor, chances are you wouldn't recognize a "negligent act" if he committed one. If the hospital staff has promoted an aura of caring, chances are you wouldn't consider filing a suit against them. It's the lack of genuine concern and the feeling that you are nothing more than a package on a conveyor belt that is most likely to turn the wheels of your mind toward litigation. This is why the physician with a charismatic personality has a far better chance of avoiding suits, regardless of the quality of his practice.

It would be difficult for me to tell you how to file a claim against a physician—I am personally biased and feel there are few, if any, circumstances that warrant such a suit. You enter into a contract with your physician of your own free choice. You may "fire" him at any time. If you have made a poor choice, then that is your responsibility. There are good mechanics and bad mechanics, good tennis instructors and bad tennis instructors, good interior designers and bad interior designers. The same is true of physicians.

This probably sounds very harsh and cold—"If you don't choose the right doctor, it's your tough luck when he commits a negligent act"—but you must look at the situation realistically. A physician is a human being—no more, no less. The only human being who never made a mistake died nearly two thousand years ago. The only physician who will never be a candidate for a malpractice suit is the one who is not practicing. He is above all else human and, if we have conferred godlike powers upon him, which we have, and he has promoted our perception of him as a godlike being, which he has, then we are all responsible.

ALTERNATIVES TO MALPRACTICE SUITS

Dr. Worth is a gastroenterologist, one who specializes in the diseases of the digestive tract. His primary instrument is a "scope," a very sophisticated piece of machinery that has the ability to "see" into twenty-six or twenty-seven feet of the tube that begins at your mouth and ends at your rectum. If he inserts the scope through the mouth, he intends to look at the esophagus, the stomach and the duodenum (the small intestine). If he inserts the scope through the rectum, he intends to look at the large intestine.

This doctor performs ten to twelve of these procedures a day. It's a joke among the technicians who work for him that one must walk quickly while in his presence lest he pull out his scope and go to work. "Watch out for Worth or you'll end up being scoped!" To me, that is negligent conduct, generally termed "overpractice," and someone should have stopped Dr. Worth years ago. The procedure carries moderate risk and is certainly less than pleasant for the patient. It is also "invasive," but Dr. Worth often performs it before he even considers less invasive diagnostic tests.

His rationale goes like this: "Look, what do you expect me to do with Molly? Her kids have all gone off to lead their own lives, her husband works all day and then comes home and plops in front of the tv with a beer until he falls asleep, and Molly has nothing to do but sit home all day worrying about the burning in her stomach." He spoke in a hopeless tone, sorry for Molly, but irritated. "She loves it here." For the first time, I see his dilemma. We've had dozens of Mollys. I review his patients in my head and realize there's a stereotype.

Mollys are men or women usually in their late forties or early fifties. They are generally considered litigious patients. That is, we classify them as "suit-prone" and treat them very carefully because they make subtle references to indicate they carry a lawyer in their back pocket. Courtroom drama on soap operas has taught them a lot about the attention and flair that surrounds a malpractice suit.

Molly calls the hospital operator and asks for the nursing supervisor at least twice during her hospitalization. The supervisor arrives at her bedside with a very solicitous look on her face. "What can I do for you, Molly?" she says as she sits on the edge of the bed and touches Molly's hand.

"Well, I'm not a complainer and I don't want to get anyone into trouble. It's just that the nurse who takes care of me isn't really doing her job. I asked her to change the water in my pitcher and she didn't do it for forty-five minutes. Last night she didn't give me a back rub and tonight she didn't take my blood pressure. I just know my blood pressure has dropped and she doesn't even care. She acts like she's doing me a favor even to come in here." She sinks heavily into the mattress, clutches her abdomen, rolls her eyes back, and winces in pain. "Oh, I'm so sick. Why doesn't somebody do something?" and she rolls her body away from the supervisor, drawing up in a fetal position.

Molly doesn't know or care about the nurse's nine other patients, all of whom are acutely ill, and to tell her would be of no benefit. She is genuinely miserable, anxious, and in pain. She feels abandoned, out of touch with the world, and hopeless. What she *doesn't* know is that she is suffering from "the empty-nest syndrome," that her life has lost purpose—she is no longer required to feed and nurture her offspring—and that Dr. Worth cannot help any of this.

"Molly wants me to 'do something' so I'm doing something," says Dr. Worth. "I have no choice but to play the game." So he "scopes" all the Mollys in the hope of avoiding malpractice suits. The trick for him is to figure out when a Molly really is a Mary, someone who really has a physiological problem that needs attention, which is very difficult if not impossible to do, until he has exhausted all the diagnostic tests.

CLAIMS

When is an act "gross negligent conduct," when is it a "procedure to avoid malpractice," and when is it pure human error? In each of these circumstances, what should be the penalty? Is being a little bit negligent analogous to being a little bit pregnant? Who decides? How do you know when you have a real live malpractice claim? You *don't.* You may *suspect* you have a claim and feel that it should be pursued, but before you begin you should consider the consequences: What is it you really want to accomplish? Do you anticipate a change in your physical condition as a result of a suit? Can the "negligent conduct" be undone? Will the physician's license be revoked as a result of suit? Is there some amount of money that would be considered just payment for the negligence? Are there other physicians who would have acted in the same way, if they had been presented with the same set of circumstances as the one you wish to sue? How will you prove your case? Doctors "protect their own," and it's not very often that you will find one doctor willing to indict the practice of another.

There *are* cases of successful claim against a doctor, but they're the rare, blatant examples of negligent conduct. If you have one of these, go ahead and pursue it. On the other hand, if you feel you've been wronged but you're not absolutely sure you could win a court battle, you've got a couple of options.

The first option is to talk it over with your doctor. Tell him that "Based on facts a, b, and c, I think I am a victim of negligence. If you had done d, e, and f, this wouldn't have happened to me. This is going to cost me x and I think you should assume those expenses. If I had known this would happen, I would never have consented to treatment, but you didn't inform me of such possibilities."

Now you've put him on the defensive. He has no choice but to explain why he thought he did right and why your complaint is one of misperception of the facts. He may have made an error in judgment or technique; the conscientious physician feels far worse about that than you could ever make him feel. He has hanged himself mentally before you ever get to him. He feels responsible and would like nothing more than to undo what has been done. Negotiate some acceptable settlement between the two of you and let it go at that.

The second option is simply not to pay your bill. If you choose that method of complaint, you must be sure to tell your insurance carrier the circumstances and that you do not want them to pay your bill. They might pay anyway, but at least you've made known the nature of your protest.

After a few months of nonpayment a clerk from the physician's business office will phone you and ask for an explanation. Then tell the reasons why you refuse to pay your bill—this sends up a red flag marked "malpractice" and alerts everyone. What happens next depends upon the physician. He may decide never to send you another bill and hope you'll drop the whole matter; he may decide to call you in hopes of circumventing further protest; or he may decide to turn the bill over to a collection agency.

If the collection agency is his preferred route, expect to see a series of progressively more threatening letters alluding to the fact that there will be legal action. If you change addresses, the agency will follow you, even if you move to another state. When you have ignored their letters long enough (for three years in one case I know about) you may receive a phone call asking why you won't pay. Now comes your shining hour!

"This is the story and this is the last time I am willing to tell it." Give the facts ending with "This is the last time I am telling this story outside a courtroom. I have not paid because I do not feel I owe this debt. If anything, I feel the physician is indebted to me. If you wish to pursue this, the matter of who is in debt will have to be decided by a jury." Without stating it you have said, "The physician has two alternatives: answer to a malpractice claim or forget the bill." It's a good bet you will hear no more from the collection agency or the physician.

Not everyone would agree with me that this is the way to handle what you consider negligent conduct, but I can only tell you what I have done and what I would do again under similar circumstances. As much as I consider myself a patient's advocate, there is no way I can condone a malpractice suit because I feel there is no doctor *willfully* engaged in negligent conduct. Yes, there are some who are "shoddy," there are some who "overtreat," there are some who consistently use poor judgment, there are some who damage with a "slip of the knife," there are some who are careless, there are some for whom quantity of life justifies any therapy and quality of life be damned, there are some who overlook the most important clue in a diagnosis, and there are some who are ignorant—but it is doubtful that a malpractice suit will eliminate any "negligent" physicians from our society. What will? Lack of business!

Like any other business, survival is dependent upon customers. You are after all buying a service and are always free to take your business elsewhere.

ARBITRATION

Laura, a divorced mother of three, nonworking and with no savings, is surgically sterilized. Five months later she discovers that she is pregnant. Who pays the bills?

The doctor who performed the sterilization is a member of a group of doctors who insure themselves and require the patient to sign an arbitration agreement before submitting to treatment. Under this agreement, the patient has relinquished the right to sue the physician. The group of doctors can decide to rectify any malpractice claim or provide for an enforced judgment decided by an arbitration panel.

The American Arbitration Association says several million people have agreed to arbitration since 1969. In the past three years, thirteen states have passed laws providing for arbitration for malpractice claims. Basically, the arbitration process involves a panel of three arbitrators, who preside over a hearing that includes the "injured," with or without his attorney, and the physician and/or his representatives. A judge or jury is not involved, the panel's decision is binding for all parties, and the decision is not subject to appeal.

The advantages to such a system are obvious: since the wait for a court date is eliminated, the case may be resolved about three years sooner; the costs of administering justice are reduced by about 60 percent; and the simplified procedures and relaxed rules of evidence in arbitration may aid the "injured" in presenting his case. The California Supreme Court states: "The speed and economy of arbitration, in contrast to the expense and delay of a jury trial, could prove helpful to all parties." It has been said that only twenty cents out of every dollar awarded the "injured" through a jury trial actually makes it into the injured's pocket.

The disadvantages are just as obvious: the arbitration panel may be composed of a physician, a lawyer, and a businessman, who could very well be a hospital administrator, tending to place the balance of power in favor of the physician, or it might be an arbitrator chosen by you, one chosen by the physician, and a third chosen by the other two arbitrators. For claims under $1500, you have no choice of arbitrators, but if the claim exceeds that, you will be given a list of arbitrators from which to choose.

By this time you probably realize that I would sign the arbitration agreement, since I am biased against suing medical practitioners, in the belief that the properly chosen physician is never willfully negligent. However, in circumstances in which you have no control over who is providing the service (in emergencies, for instance), I would hesitate before signing an arbitration agreement. I would not feel comfortable relinquishing my right to a jury trial if the doctor is not one of my choosing.

There is some talk that an arbitration agreement violates antitrust laws in the belief that it deprives people of the right to bargain with doctors. However, it's not clear that anyone ever has exercised that right and the laws have not yet been challenged successfully.

In Laura's case, her doctor paid the bills associated with her pregnancy; he was a member of a self-insured group and the situation was rectified without need for an arbitration panel. If one could always count on such a result, the whole topic of malpractice would, of course, be redundant. A sample Arbitration Agreement appears in the Appendix.

HOW TO CHOOSE A PHYSICIAN

First, ask everyone you can think of—not when you are in need, but when you first move into an area. You need to have a "family" doctor, preferably a certified "family practice specialist," one who sees you for anything and everything, a "general contractor" of your care who refers you to specialists when the occasion demands. He's the "director" and the one who cares for your minor ailments, the one who grows to be part of your family, and the one you can trust.

The Welcome Wagon woman, the Community Greeter, or the person who welcomes you to the community with coupons for this and that is a good source of information.

Go to the nearest hospital emergency room and ask the clerk if you can file a Consent for Treatment form for your minor children. Then tell her you're new to the area and would like her to recommend a family physician. Do the same thing at the next closest hospital.

Then go to a meeting of the local Newcomers Club and be sure the subject of family physicians is brought up there. Clerks in stores, your insurance agent, the telephone installer, the postman—all are good sources of recommendation.

I'm sure you've heard that you should call your local American Medical Association, which will give you the names of three physicians from which to choose. That's a waste of time. In alphabetical order they will give three who are close to your home—this says *nothing* about the physicians' qualifications.

All physicians who are members get equal treatment. You've really gained nothing that you couldn't have gotten out of the phone directory by choosing three with offices close to you.

GETTING ON THE BOOKS

Once you've heard the same physician's name three times, you can be fairly sure he's a good choice. Call and tell his receptionist you're new to the area and would like to make an appointment so that you can get acquainted before you really need help. This may seem a waste of time and money in some parts of the country, but in other areas many family physicians limit their practice to a certain number of patients. Once that number has been reached, a call from you in dire need will get this response: "I'm sorry, Dr. Brown is not taking any new patients now."

You may be able to get on the doctor's books just by going into his office and filling out the pertinent information, such as your name, address, and your insurance policy number.

The point is: very rarely can you call after-hours or on a weekend and find a physician who will care for you, if you are not already in his records. And accidents or major illness often strike after offices are closed. No physician is obligated to treat you, no matter how desperate you are, and many have been known to refuse treatment after-hours. In fact, there's a good chance the answering service will refuse even to get him on the phone for you unless you have already registered as his patient. In addition, you can't count on hospital emergency rooms to provide you with a doctor, since not all hospitals have emergency rooms. Of those that do, not all are open with a physician there twenty-four hours a day, so call before you head for the hospital. In the first place, you're likely to receive faster treatment if you call in advance; in the second place, you wouldn't want to waste precious time driving to a hospital where there is no doctor. Naturally, you don't have a choice of physician under emergency conditions, but if you like the one who treats you, ask if he takes private patients or if he will recommend someone who does.

As a health-maintenance organization (HMO) member, you also have a choice of physicians, despite common opinion to the contrary. You can choose from among the physicians on their staff and make your appointments only with that one. If you don't like the first one you see, make an appointment with another one the next time. Actually, it's a convenient arrangement because your chart goes with you no matter which physician you see. The only problem is: all physicians on the staff rotate off-hours duty, so your chances of seeing the doctor of your choice on an emergency basis are slim, but at least there will always be someone who will see you at any hour of the day or night.

You may select a physician from those on the staff at a teaching hospital, in which case he will be the "attending physician," or you may be designated a "staff patient." In both cases you're likely to be seen by medical students, interns, residents, and house-staff physicians. This is a good chance to get a look at several and write their names down for future reference. The attending physician (if you have selected one) will direct your care, but you'll still be fair game for all the others.

The parade of doctors in and out of your room in a teaching hospital can be very distressing, especially when you can't figure out which one you should count on, but the great advantage in such a situation is that it is unlikely that your smallest problem could escape their attention. Remember, doctors are sleuths looking for good clues. The more sleuths you have the better the chances of arriving at the correct conclusion.

Don't be afraid of medical students. They're carefully monitored by senior staff members for discrepancies in their skills and they're often more thorough than those who have been in practice several years who have developed their own shortcuts.

WHO'S THE BOSS?

Don was rushed into the emergency room with a crushed leg and his face smashed beyond recognition. The physician on duty quickly summoned the orthopedist, plastic surgeon, and otolaryngologist who were on call for that night. After surgery Don was taken to the intensive care unit, where he stayed for five days. During that time all three physicians visited him, which was fine except that they all wrote conflicting orders and none of them could answer all of Don's questions. "Who's in charge?" he wanted to know, and each doctor claimed one of the others was the "boss."

Such a problem is common in teaching hospitals and HMOs but less common in fee-for-service hospitals unless your case is a very complicated one with many consultants involved. If this happens to you, take charge. Get your nurse to play advocate for you and determine who's boss. You may not care who it is, but it's imperative that someone call the shots, so keep asking until you have an answer. Then, once you know who's running the show, save all your questions for him and make sure he knows you consider him your "primary" physician.

CONSULTATIONS

A consultation can be at your request when you ask your physician for a second opinion or it might be at his request when he feels you have a problem that requires more specialized expertise than he has in that particular field. If you have entered the hospital under the care of a family physician (a specialty in itself), he will orchestrate your care, which could involve a wide variety of specialists. Whatever the situation, there are a few things you should know about consultations.

No one offers their services for free, so you can be sure you will receive a bill from every doctor who walks into your room. Your doctor may have ordered the consultation without even advising you, but you pay nevertheless. The initial visit is bound to carry a high price tag (around $100) because the consultant will do his own workup, which means he will examine you from head to toe (or at least perfunctorily) and write a consultation report on your chart. Whether or not you ever see him again depends upon why he was there in the first place.

BEWARE THE SCHEME

The physicians on the staff in some hospitals can be like a brotherhood. They may depend upon each other for referrals, they may scratch each other's back, and play a whole political ball game. As in any group, there are the black sheep of the family who for one reason or another are blackballed, with their punishment being the withholding of referrals. The concept of cliques can apply in hospitals as it does in other work situations. Dr. Worth sends all his patients with heart problems to Dr. Stone, Dr. Stone sends all his patient with GI problems to Dr. Worth, and both send their surgery cases to Dr. Boyer. It's a beautiful, lucrative venture for them all. In fact, Dr. Worth can tell how busy his hospital rounds will be tomorrow by looking at the number of Dr. Stone's patients whom he hasn't yet done a consult on today. If you come in as a patient of Dr. Worth, you can be sure you will be seen by Dr. Stone and vice versa.

How can you avoid this scheme? It's simple. When a doctor walks into your room and announces that he has been sent by your primary physician, tell him you first would like to discuss any consultations with your physician before they occur. Don't be timid!

Actually, there's a three-ring circus here because a patient with a chest pain is ripe for the cardiologist-gastroenterologist-surgeon racket. If Dr. Stone sees the patient first, he immediately calls in Dr. Worth and they do their workups simultaneously. That is, they both do all the tests for heart problems as well as digestive tract problems, because the stomach and heart are in such close proximity and the pain of a heart attack can be confused with the pain of a stomach problem. Dr. Boyer shows up in the middle of the whole thing since surgery might be involved.

This type of setup can be downright shoddy. You can control it by demanding that only noninvasive diagnostic procedures be performed (the noninvasive ones are the "cheap" ones) and also by demanding that one physician exhaust his bag of tricks and come up with a diagnosis before calling in another physician. By all means refuse to even talk to a surgeon until you have been told all the alternatives to surgery and have definitely come to the conclusion that you do indeed want to have surgery. Unless you're bleeding profusely, no surgery needs to take place so fast that you can't take the time to select your own surgeon and the hospital in which it will take place.

SECOND OPINION

"Doctors who are unsure about something will resent the question about a second opinion. To us that is a sign that something is wrong with that doctor," so says Dr. Sidney Wolfe of Ralph Nader's health research group.

Studies by researchers at Stanford, Cornell, and Harvard medical centers have found that one out of five elective operations was not indicated by symptoms or diagnostic-testing results. Dr. Eugene McCarthy of Cornell Medical College studied the importance of a second opinion before surgery. He found that 34 percent of 3171 patients who were told they needed surgery were found *not* to need the operation by the physicians who gave them a "second opinion." Requiring an opinion from a second physician before approving certain types of elective surgery brought a savings of $1.6 million in Massachusetts and a sharp reduction in certain types of operations.

In the nineteenth-century words of surgeon Sir John E. Erichsen: "There must be a final limit to the development of manipulative surgery. The knife cannot always have fresh fields for conquest; and although methods of practice may be modified and varied, and even improved to some extent, it must be within a certain limit. That this limit has nearly, if not quite, been reached will appear evident if we reflect on the great achievements of modern operative surgery."

Two facts emerge from current literature: greater restraint in the performance of elective surgery may well improve the life expectancy in this country, and no person relishes a challenge to his opinion. While others may agree with Dr. Wolfe that there is something "wrong" with the doctor who resents a request for a second opinion, I submit that both right and wrong doctors, as well as butchers, bakers, candlestick-makers, and all of us, resent a request for a second opinion, but I urge you to seek one anyway.

There are a few tricks to getting a second opinion, however, and you should know that the difference between a second opinion and confirmation of an erroneous diagnosis is subtle.

Eric was told by Dr. Stone that he had an 80-percent occlusion of his coronary arteries and needed bypass surgery. This would cost about $30,000 from start to finish. "I would like a second opinion," said Eric. Dr. Stone replied, "Why sure, Eric. That's a wise idea. I'll send in Dr. Kahn."

Enter Dr. Kahn, another cardiologist. "I've reviewed your case with Dr. Stone, Eric, and it appears you should have bypass surgery."

Two days later Eric has the surgery, is $30,000 in the hole, and it has not yet been proven that his life expectancy has been improved.

What Eric didn't know was this. Dr. Stone is on the staff of hospital X. Dr. Kahn is also on the staff of hospital X. Dr. Stone and Dr. Kahn are buddies. Do you challenge the decisions of your buddies? Can you really expect Dr. Kahn to walk into Eric's room and say, "Well, I've reviewed your case with Dr. Stone and I think he's made a bum decision. I really don't think you need surgery at all."

What should Eric have done? Getting a second opinion is no simple task, especially if you're already in the hospital and all the doctors on that particular staff are colleagues. The first thing he should have done was tell Dr. Stone he would like to be discharged from the hospital to go home and think about it for a while.

Then he should have made an appointment with a cardiologist in another city, stated his symptoms, and looked for differences in opinion. We've been taught that our medical records are necessary for diagnosis, but that's really not the case. You can hand six doctors the same medical chart and come up with six different opinions. Six different cardiologists can read the same EKG and come up with six different diagnoses. Six different radiologists can read the same X rays and come to six different conclusions. Remember, medicine is more art than science! The second-opinion doctor doesn't have to know anything about Eric's experiences with Dr. Stone to come to a conclusion. In fact, ethically he might feel obligated to support Dr. Stone's conclusion if he knows one has been made.

This is not to say that all doctors protect their own or that it is impossible to get an unbiased opinion from a second physician on the same hospital staff as the first; but it is simple fact that the second doctor will most certainly *lean toward* the opinion of the first doctor and is really put on the spot when you request a challenge to his colleague's opinion.

Don't take chances! Yes, it is a terrific nuisance to be discharged from the hospital, submit to the examination of another physician, and weigh the pros and cons while the rest of your life hangs in limbo, but there is an element of risk in *any* surgery and surgical risk is something you should not undergo except under extreme circumstances. Dr. George Crile, a retired surgeon, has written a very enlightening book, *Surgery: Your Choices, Your Alternatives,* which can give you some important information on the subject. While most books written by physicians tend to minimize the risks imposed by their own practice, Dr. Crile is a true patient's advocate and, since he has retired, is at liberty to tell you the straight, honest facts.

Suppose the second-opinion doctor Eric consulted concurred that he needed bypass surgery. The biggest hurdle has been passed and now Eric can rest assured that he isn't embarking on some ill-fated cruise when he could have stayed right on shore. He needs to choose a surgeon, but not just any surgeon. He needs the best in the business, especially when he's having open-heart surgery or brain surgery. He should go to a university library and find out who the authorities are, who is writing about hearts, and where the operation is being done. If two a month are done at Eric's local hospital and two a day at the hospital in the next city, he should travel there. If a hospital does not frequently perform a certain type of surgery, it is not going to have the expert technologists and specialized equipment that so often influences the mortality rate.

If Dr. Stone does two open-heart surgeries a day, Eric probably can safely choose him as his surgeon. If he does two a month, he's not an expert. Members of the Kaiser Health Plan have a specialty in each medical center; you and your family have to travel, but you'll go where the special equipment is used and be treated by those who treat nothing else.

Common sense tells you when it's worthwhile to travel for medical services. Obviously, you're going to want the experts for major surgery, but a general surgeon can take care of removing your gallstones and other ordinary surgery. You still don't want a surgeon who *rarely* removes gallstones, but you're more likely to find one who does it often right in your own hometown.

If you have surgery without seeking a second opinion, you're asking for trouble. Should trouble be the result, you're obligated to accept it—you didn't do your homework.

HOW TO CHANGE DOCTORS MIDSTREAM

This is the toughest problem of all. "Have a frank discussion with him" is what the experts tell you to do when you've decided you simply can't get along with your doctor. However, these "frank discussions" are emotion-laden affairs that few of us can carry off, especially when we're weakened by illness. We can't even say to our neighbor, "You know, I just don't like the way you do things," so how can we say the same thing to our physician? I submit that we can't. Nor can we switch to another physician on the staff in the same hospital because we really are stigmatized once we change doctors.

If you are ambulatory, it's not difficult to tell your physician you want to be discharged. Before you do just that, have your advocate make an appointment with a physician who is on the staff of another hospital. If you arrange it right, you can be driven from the hospital right to the new doctor. Then if he feels you need hospitalization, he'll see that you're sent to another hospital. Your treatment method might not be changed, but at least you'll have some peace of mind, and peace of mind is the thing that should be top on your list.

You cannot be admitted to a hospital without being admitted to some doctor's "service." You can't "fire" your doctor without first having another doctor who has accepted you as his patient. Few patients can call another doctor and ask him to take over their care, as a hospitalized patient, from the care of the first doctor; the second doctor simply won't walk into the hospital and call you his patient. Remember, medicine is a business and doctors don't "steal" patients from each other, even at the patient's request.

If you're not ambulatory, you can ask to be discharged and taken out of the hospital by ambulance but you need to have your advocate make more involved arrangements. The appointment with a new doctor could be sticky—you are obviously in bad condition if you have to be transported by ambulance. On the other hand, many bedridden patients can stay at home and have the Visiting Nurses Association care for them until they can get to another doctor. The nurses will only act under doctor's orders, so if you can get the first doctor to send you home with Visiting Nurses, then you can get on with the business of finding another doctor. Complicated, isn't it? All of which tells you that it is *imperative* that you find a doctor in whom you have confidence before time of need.

FOR ADVOCATES

By the time the decision has been made to switch doctors, you're at least as distressed as the patient since you've probably been the sounding board for all the unhappiness that has led to the decision to switch. And now you have the bulk of the task on your shoulders—you have to engage a new doctor:

1. You *might* be able to get one of the nurses to recommend another doctor. If not, look in the Yellow Pages of the phone directory, under the appropriate specialty in the "Physicians" section.
2. Call and tell the doctor's receptionist the symptoms of your patient. She doesn't need to know that the patient is hospitalized or what the official diagnosis is, just tell the symptoms and/or complaints, and ask for an immediate appointment.
3. When you've found someone who will give you an appointment, plan your patient's hospital discharge for the appropriate time so that you can drive directly to the new physician. Just tell the patient's nurse that you will be picking up the patient at such and such a time. She may want you to arrive at some other time, for the convenience of the hospital, but you must be firm if you are to accomplish your goal.
4. A transfer to another hospital, under another physician's care, needs professional assistance. Ask anyone at the

nurses' station if you can make an appointment with the social services discharge planner. You might be quizzed as to the nature of your business, in which case simply say you would prefer to discuss the problem with the planner only. The fewer people involved with this "sticky" problem, the better.

Enlist the planner as a confidante. Tell her the problems you've had, why your patient must be transferred, and make it clear that you don't want other options; you simply want the patient transferred by ambulance to another hospital under another doctor's care.

Part of her job is to try to convince you to change your mind about a transfer—you must be firm! In the end, she will make the arrangements for you, but it will take some time, perhaps several days.

THE PHYSICIAN'S PYRAMID

Organizational charts in hospitals are often complex, but there is always a "head honcho," a physician at the apex. In some hospitals, this position is rotated among the staff on an annual basis, in others it is an elected position, while in still others it is a position filled by a physician hired by the governing body of the hospital (the board of directors, usually). This "head honcho" is known by various titles: chief of staff, medical director, or physician-in-chief.

In very large hospitals the chief of staff has chiefs of services under him: chief of surgery, chief of pediatrics, chief of internal medicine, and so on. Each specialty is a "service." The chief of a service may be elected or appointed and is considered the boss of the attending physicians, those who attend to your care directly. In a teaching hospital a bevy of would-be physicians is at the base of the pyramid. These include medical students, interns, residents, and chief residents, in order of ascending training.

Don't confuse "chief" with "best," since this is not always the case. In any complex organization, the people who make it to the top do so for various reasons, not all of them associated with competence in their own area of practice. There may very well be someone at the base of the pyramid far more competent than the person at the apex.

If you want to speak with the chief, your chances are slim to none. If he isn't a physician busy with his own practice, he's busy with the business of running a medical staff, and his calendar is usually jam-packed; but he does appreciate hearing from you whether your thoughts are negative or positive.

If you arrive at his doorstep or call on the telephone, his secretary will intercept you. "Good morning, Mr. Adams, what can we do for you?" You have never seen a more gracious, diplomatic lady in any hospital. "I want to see the chief and I'm in no mood for waiting. And no, it isn't a good morning!" Mr. Adams looks as if he's going to drop dead from apoplexy any instant—smoke's about to roar from his nostrils.

"What seems to be the problem, Mr. Adams?" One cannot help but be calmed by her undivided, compassionate attention. Mr. Adams may rant on for two minutes or two hours, it doesn't matter. She listens and makes all the appropriate sympathetic sounds. But Mr. Adams will *not* get in to see the chief. By the time Mr. Adams runs out of anger, he usually doesn't care that he can't see the chief. He leaves with a promise from the secretary that she will inform the chief of the problem and get back to him. Then she takes the problem to the appropriate department for resolution. Yes, she'll mention it to the chief and he may even take some action. In fact, he might pay a visit to Mr. Adams if the complaint seems to warrant it.

Had Mr. Adams registered his complaint on paper, it would have been a whole different ball game. His letter would have been photocopied and circulated far and wide. *Put it on paper!* No matter what you have to say, if you've put it on paper it carries about five tons more weight and you're sure to get a written reply.

If you complain or compliment in person or on the phone, you do get a listener but if you put it on paper, it goes to a file, and what's in that file could determine some other person's future. Say you're particularly impressed with the services of a medical student: you write the chief, the chief puts a copy in his file and sends a copy to the instructor, the instructor puts a copy in his file and sends a copy to the student, the student puts a copy in his file and smiles for weeks, maybe even months, maybe even twenty years later when he remembers what a kind thing you did while he was struggling through medical school.

At the end of the semester, the instructor pulls out the student's file, sees your kind letter, decides the student must be great and gives him an A. Two years later the student applies for staff privileges at the same hospital; the chief pulls your letter out of the file, decides the student must be good, and hires him. Had you paid the same compliment over the phone, only the secretary would have known how fine the student was.

Now when you apply that to a complaint, you can see how important the impact of a written statement can be. It matters if it's on paper!

PATIENT ASSISTANCE

A patient ombudsman (or advocate) is the latest addition to hospital staffs because it has been recognized that the public demands the right to participate in the decisions affecting health care. Eventually such a person will probably be required to submit to some sort of specialized education and certification. However, currently he is more often someone chosen for his ability to "keep a cool head when all others about him are losing theirs." That person's office is where you'll be asked to take your complaints more often than not, but if you want to register a complaint with great impact, write to the physician-in-chief. And remember, the patient advocate hired by the hospital is a hospital employee first, an advocate second, and cannot be expected to care for the patient as the patient's personal advocate would.

FOR ADVOCATES

You, being vitally interested in the patient's care, are likely to look upon the whole situation more subjectively than anyone. As the prime critic of the quality and quantity of care, expect to begin feeling a bit paranoid about the physician's relationship with you. Traditionally physicians have had a monopoly on health care and have been accused of imposing a "conspiracy of silence." Your questions might be interpreted as lack of trust.

First, you need to be sure that your subjectivity hasn't blinded you to reality. Did it *really* take the doctor too long to find the patient's diagnosis or did it simply *seem* like forever? Is he *really* being abrupt or are you simply supersensitive because you're upset?

Once you're clear on what reality is, then you have to put on your mental armor and keep telling yourself that your first responsibility is to the patient and if the doctor seems to dislike your concern, that's *his* problem. Understanding that the role of the physician has changed in recent years, you can allow for his feeling that maybe you are intruding on his territory and suggesting that he is not as competent as he believes he is.

To insure the best relationship with the doctor, introduce yourself as the patient's advocate (he knows what the term means) and assure him that he will be subjected to only one advocate for the patient. There is nothing more annoying to him than having to communicate with a whole flock of people inquiring about the same patient.

GLOSSARY OF PHYSICIANS

Allergist: for asthma, hay fever, eczema, certain skin disorders; many specialize in only one allergy.

Cardiologist: specializes in hearts; some internists are also cardiologists and vice versa.

Dermatologist: specializes in diseases of the skin; some do hair transplants, some specialize in skin cancer.

Endocrinologists: very scarce, specializes in metabolic disturbances, especially diabetes and obesity.

Family Practice: a doctor in general practice whose extended education and practice qualifies him for certification as a family practitioner, the "general contractor" of your care.

Gastroenterologist: specializes in the GI tract (stomach and intestines).

Gynecologist: treats the female reproductive system; some follow women through pregnancy, in which case they are called obstetrician/gynecologists.

Hematologist: specializes in blood disorders—this is the fastest-growing group of specialists; many also treat cancer and are called oncologist/hematologists, or vice versa.

Internist: embraces cardiology, endocrinology, gastroenterology, nephrology, and hypertension; most specialize in one of these areas.

Nephrologist: specializes in diseases of the kidney.

Neurologist: treats diseases of the nervous system; some are neurosurgeons, some are not; this is the one you want for any brain surgery.

Obstetrician: delivers babies, see Gynecologist.

Oncologist: specializes in cancer; most specialize further in particular types of the one-hundred-odd known today.

Opthalmologist: treats eyes.

Orthopedist: sometimes called orthopods; specializes in bone problems; most are also surgeons, each with a specialty such as knees, backs, hands, etc.

Otorhinolaryngologist: specializes in ears, nose, and throat; he's the one they call "the E-N-T man."

Pediatrician: treats infants and children, usually until the age of sixteen.

Plastic Surgeon: does reconstructive surgery: skin grafts, "nose jobs," mammaplasty, etc.

Proctologist: specializes in colon and rectal disorders.

Psychiatrist: specializes in mental illness; some specialize further in adults, children, hypnosis, biofeedback.

Pulmonary specialists: the "chest man" for diseases of the lungs.

Radiologist: specializes in making diagnoses and devising treatment plans involving the use of radiation.

Rheumatologist: specializes in arthritis.

Urologist: specializes in problems in the urinary tract; some specialize in diseases of the prostate.

Surgeons: not so long ago you went to a general surgeon if you needed an operation, but nowadays that's not always the case.

There are still some general surgeons who do minor operations like hernias and gallbladders, but most specialize. Three that haven't been mentioned previously are:

Thoracic Surgeon: chest.

Vascular Surgeon: veins and arteries.

Head and Neck Surgeon: sometimes plastic surgeons who have further specialized.

CHAPTER
12
All the Other Staff People

WHO IS THE NURSE?

Or rather, which one is the nurse? You've heard the old grousing, "I never saw a *real* nurse the whole time I was in that hospital." Maybe you didn't, it's a real possibility, then again maybe you did and just didn't recognize her.

A friend who works in a southern California hospital told me of its interesting uniform policy: the respiratory therapists wear green, the volunteers wear coral, the students wear blue, the pediatric nurses wear prints, the operating room nurses wear gray-green, the ward nurses wear pastels, and the housekeepers wear white. With that assortment walking into your room, how on earth would you know who is the nurse? Ah, you think the nurse is the one with the little pointed cap? That could be, but not many nurses wear caps and in hospitals where it's optional, you might find the nurses' aides wearing caps and the registered nurses going bareheaded.

It's even difficult to discern the "real" nurse by what tasks you find her performing—in days gone by you wouldn't have found the registered nurse emptying bedpans but today it's a common sight. You can't tell R.N.s by what they do or what they wear, so you're left guessing unless you read name tags well— if, in fact, they are wearing name tags.

It might help you to know where nursing is today—in transition. For several years team nursing was the preferred mode.

The registered nurse (R.N.) was the team leader and the licensed vocational nurse (LVN), licensed practical nurse (LPN), and the nurse's aides (NA) were the team members. The R.N. passed medications, took physicians' written orders, maintained IVs, did the paperwork, and directed the activities of the ward.

The team members did the "hands on" care, under the supervision of the registered nurses. While the system worked well in theory, there was one major flaw—the personnel with the least training were the ones providing the care to the patients, while the highest-trained personnel were "nursing the system" (doing the paperwork). Not only was the risk to the patient substantial, the lack of job satisfaction caused the dropout rate from nursing to exceed that of any other profession, with over half the registered nurses in the United States not practicing today. In addition, the public became increasingly aware of the quality of health care available to them, and now consumer consciousness speaks louder each day.

The patient demands higher-quality care, the government demands a lid on the cost of that care, and registered nurses demand an opportunity to return to the bedside to nurse the patient rather than the system, which leads us to where we are today—the team approach to nursing is on its way out. While there are many institutions in which there might be one R.N. leading two aides or LVNs in the nursing tasks of thirty-five patients, more commonly you will find R.N.s, aides, and LVNs all doing patient care at the bedside.

Statistics have proven that R.N.s produce the most work for the dollar. Since they are also the only nursing classification educated to care for the patient as a total person, rather than simply as a body, eventually it can be expected that aides and LVNs will be phased out of acute-care hospitals and all care will be delivered by registered nurses. Fortunately, this does not mean that all aides and LVNs will be out of jobs—the education system provides for their eventual advancement to licensure as registered nurses.

PRIMARY NURSING

If you're lucky enough to be in a hospital where primary nursing is practiced, you'll know it as soon as you're admitted. One of the registered nurses will introduce herself as "your primary nurse." She'll be the nursing "boss" throughout your stay. Not only will she direct your care and write nursing orders, much as the physician writes orders, she'll be the nurse who will perform the bulk of your care. She works with an associate nurse, who is responsible for your care in her absence, and will be involved in everything that happens to speed you toward recovery.

FOR ADVOCATES

Since a registered nurse practicing primary nursing holds complete accountability for your patient, she'll be grateful to have you as an ally. Introduce yourself to her as "the patient's advocate." She knows *exactly* what that term means and is trained to make advocacy as easy for you as possible. The primary nurse is the "nurse of tomorrow," the best thing that could happen to you and your patient.

Unlike the fragmented nursing that is currently so common, primary nursing care focuses on *you*, with only one person responsible and accountable for making sure all of your health needs are addressed. If you think you might have a complaint, your primary nurse is the one who can fix things for you. She's even trained to begin anticipating your future needs from the day you enter the hospital, so if you need help after you go home or need some hospital appliance, such as traction, at home, she'll be working toward insuring that you have it when necessary.

There are 128 hospitals across the United States that have all-R.N. staffs doing primary nursing and, as the public demands it, the number is bound to grow. Those patients who have been cared for in a primary-nursing setting find it difficult to accept anything else.

THE PYRAMID

The growth of the health-care industry is one of today's startling economic realities. In fact, health care is the second largest American industry. Picture 5 million people, which is the work force supporting the industry, all standing in a pyramid. At the pinnacle are the 360,000 physicians who are the most highly rewarded, large group of individuals in history. Just below them is a smaller group of scientists and an expanding army of administrators. The next level includes the nursing profession, composed of nearly 1.3 million persons; below them is a growing group of technologists supported by an even larger mass of technicians. At the base of the pyramid is the largest group of all, the nurse's aides, dietary helpers, transporters, housekeepers, and many others with the least attractive, lowest-paid jobs in the medical industry. This pyramid epitomizes the rigid framework of power, privilege, and economic reward that characterizes the jobs health workers do. It is a stratified hierarchy of decreasing power and privilege from apex to base.

As in all industries, there are varying degrees of competence, education, and economic reward within each stratum. Your own criterion for excellence might be totally different from the next person's. However, since the future of patient care is hanging in the balance right now, it would behoove you, the consumer, to learn a few facts on which to base an opinion about your health-care providers.

You're most likely to have contact with the large group of housekeepers at the base of the pyramid. Interesting stories circulate about housekeepers in a hospital and most are far more knowledgeable than one would think. They are required to attend many educational programs on safety and infection control and must be aware of volumes of regulations concerning their work. They are a "certain breed of cat"; perhaps the average person would find their type of work intolerable. Usually they are very kind, compassionate, people-oriented individuals, and the heart of the hospital "grapevine."

One thing you need to understand is that they always will want to help you, but they can't. They are not allowed to engage in patient care (for numerous reasons), and a request for service from you will only frustrate you both.

You'll come in contact with people who move you from place to place within the hospital. They may be called "orderlies" or "aides"; they too are under constraints that prevent them from doing anything for you other than transporting you.

You're also likely to come in contact with dietitians, occupational therapists, physical therapists, social workers, discharge planners, respiratory therapists, lab technicians, radiologists, X-ray technicians, ward clerks, unit secretaries, emergency medical technicians, tv repairmen, researchers, candy-stripers, engineers, coordinating clinicians, maintenance technicians, nurse's aides, security guards, central-service technicians, pharmacy technicians, nuclear-medicine technicians, phlebotomists, volunteers, and chaplains.

To help you figure out who's who, scan the chart at the end of this chapter. It won't tell you all you need to know because there is no consistent title nationwide for people doing the same task. For instance, the person who answers your call bell may be called a ward clerk, unit secretary, unit manager, or any number of similar titles. The nurse in charge of the floor may be called head nurse, charge nurse, area supervisor, nursing supervisor, clinical specialist, coordinating clinician or again, any such similar titles.

Many hospital workers belong to unions—there is quite an array of them represented in every hospital—so the task of one person cannot be performed by another person. For instance, if a nurse mops up some orange juice in your room, she is "taking work away" from the housekeeper and if the volunteer brings milk to you from the kitchen, she is "taking work away" from the dietary aide. This can be a pain in the neck for you, but you're involved in a complex bureaucratic organization.

Among the nursing staff you might encounter similar situations. It could be that only one nurse administers medications, another gives your bath, and yet another makes rounds with the physicians.

How on earth are you to know who is responsible for what? You can be sure that one registered nurse is the "boss." She has been assigned responsibility for a certain group of patients, regardless of who actually delivers the care—she is the one you should ask for right away. At the beginning of each shift, find out and then ask for her by name; she will see that the right person is sent to you if you need help. You may never see her, but your care will be markedly improved if she knows that you know who she is. It is a sad state of affairs, but you can help the problem by making lots of noise about it. Primary nursing is what you want, with one nurse doing everything you need, totally responsible for you and perhaps three other patients.

HOW A NURSE GETS TO BE ONE

A registered nurse must pass state board exams once and complete thirty hours of continuing education every two years (in most states for the rest of her professional life) in order to renew her license. That's basic, but the education she has obtained before she takes her state board exams varies tremendously.

If you ask a nurse how she got to be one, she may reply, "Through a two-year college program," or "Through a three-year hospital program," or "Through a four-year college program"—all are partially true. How a nurse gets to be one varies considerably across the nation.

Actually, hospital-based nursing programs are being phased out and in some states one must have a baccalaureate degree to be a registered nurse. The two-year programs in community colleges actually take three years because one must have about a year of prerequisites before application is considered. And the four-year programs actually take five years for most people.

Further education qualifies a registered nurse to be a public-health nurse, a school nurse, a clinical specialist, or a nurse practitioner. Other nurses specialize in research, in administration, in infection control, or various other areas. Whatever the specialty, the criterion for licensure is the state board registration.

Licensed vocational nurses on the West Coast are the same as licensed practical nurses on the East Coast. Their education consists of one year, usually at the community-college level, focusing on the technical skills of nursing.

Nurse's aides are trained in hospital programs, high-school courses, or "on the job." Their duties are limited to functional tasks such as bed-making, bathing patients, and filling water pitchers.

This year, the published dropout rate for nurses is 70 percent, which says something about the disenchantment associated with nursing right now. Working holidays, weekends, nights, and rotating shifts appeals to fewer and fewer nurses. The Florence Nightingale image that once sparked their interest fades in proportion to the cost-containment programs in hospitals that demand more patients per nurse, resulting in less care per patient.

FOR ADVOCATES

You already know where to go if you have a complaint about the medical staff. For other complaints such as those related to nursing care, your best bet is to ask for the nursing supervisor. She'll route it to the right place and get results for you. Don't be timid! Her primary objective is high-quality care, but often she is so buried in paperwork she doesn't know if something is amiss unless you tell her.

Some staff members are inclined to get suspicious if you are with the patient for hours at a time and you'll sense their hostility. In fact, you'll feel like an intruder with some dishonest ulterior motive.

Be sure to treat this as *their* problem rather than yours. Perhaps they lack self-confidence and fear that you might catch them in some error. Perhaps your conversation suggests you work in the medical profession—you might even be a nurse in disguise—and they wouldn't want you to be more aware of the patient's needs than they are. If you come across a staff person who seems to want you to leave, you should probably plan to spend the bulk of your visiting hours with the patient when that staff person is there. This may be personal bias, but it's been my experience that the less competent people are the ones who want visitors to stay away.

The majority of staff members will enjoy talking with you

and answering your questions, as long as you make casual conversation brief. Generally, they have far more tasks to complete than their shift allows.

WHO'S WHO

This is a list of those with whom you might come in contact during hospitalization:

Audiologist: B.S. degree (M.S. degree for certification); licensed by the Board of Medical Examiners; specialist in speech and hearing problems.

Audiometrist: completion of certain courses in college or university; certified by the state; a technologist who operates speech and hearing machinery and functions as an assistant to audiologists.

Clinical Laboratory Technologist: minimum of B.S. degree; licensed by the state; directs laboratory technicians in the performance of various lab tests.

Dietician/Nutritionist: B.S. degree plus six-month internship; works with dietary aides to produce the meals and teach nutrition to patients and staff.

Emergency Medical Technician (EMT): one to two years post–high-school training; ambulance and emergency room attendant with basic life-support training.

Hospital Administrator: M.S. degree; runs the business end of the hospital; ranks alongside the physician-in-chief on the organizational chart.

Medical Record Technician: one to two years of college; certified by the state; transcribes physician's notes and insures the maintenance of patients' charts and hospital statistics.

Microbiologist: minimum B.S. degree, graduate work usually required; conducts certain laboratory tests.

Nuclear-Medicine Technologist: B.S. degree; directs nuclear-medicine technicians (associate degree) in the performance of certain diagnostic tests.

Occupational Therapist: B.S. degree or two-year M.S. program; conducts occupational-therapy programs in rehabilitation centers.

Paramedic: two years of training or more, sometimes a specially trained fireman or nurse; akin to an EMT, with more extensive training in life support under emergency conditions.

Pharmacist: five to six years beyond high school, including graduation from a school of pharmacy; leads pharmacy technicians in the preparation and dispensing of drugs; administers medications to patients in some hospitals in the eastern parts of the nation.

Phlebotomist: may be either a lab technician or a nurse; specializes in drawing blood samples.

Physical Therapist: B.S. degree, a postbaccalaureate certificate, or M.S. degree; licensed by the Board of Medical Examiners; directs physical-therapy aides in performing certain treatments.

Psychiatric Technician: up to two years in associate degree program; licensed by the Board of Vocational Nurses and Psychiatric Technician Examiners; works under a registered nurse specializing in care of psychiatric patients.

Radiological Technologist: two-year course in an approved school; certified by the state; performs X-ray department functions.

Respiratory Therapist: two to four years post–high-school training, dependent upon goals; may be registered or certified; performs respiratory tests and treatments that are performed by registered nurses in other hospitals.

Speech Pathologist: M.S. degree plus one year experience in the field; licensed by the Board of Medical Examiners; specializes in treatment of speech problems.

Social Worker (clinical): M.S. degree; licensed by the Board of Medical Examiners; functions in counseling and linking patients with community social-service organizations for care after hospitalization.

If you're wondering about the basic qualifications of those caring for you, a rule-of-thumb glossary gives you some idea:

-ologist indicates at least a Bachelor's degree
-ist can mean training anywhere from a year to a Ph.D. or M.D.

technician means two years training or less
aide indicates on-the-job training or a short vocational-school
course.

If you come upon a physician's assistant in your wanderings, he is the result of an idea conceived by a prominent cardiologist in the late 1960s when there was a severe shortage of physicians in rural areas. Today, only 16 percent of the 7500 P.A.'s practicing in the nation are in rural areas; there is a contention that they will help keep the high cost of getting sick from skyrocketing faster than it already has. His education is less than that of a registered nurse, but more than that of an LVN; he can usually be found in a physician's office handling physical examinations or minor ailments.

To confuse you further, a scrub nurse is the person who stands beside the surgeon passing instruments. Though she may be a registered nurse, more often she has far less training than an R.N. The R.N. is called a Circulating Nurse. She assesses the patient's condition before the operation, makes sure the legal paperwork is in order, insures that all the correct instruments are ready, and directs all the activity during the operation.

Then there's the anesthesiologist, who is actually a physician, and the anesthetist, who is a registered nurse with advanced training. The psychiatrist is a physician and can write prescriptions, but a psychologist cannot. A radiologist is a physician who specializes in "reading" X rays, but a radiological technologist actually takes the X rays. The ophthalmologist is a physician who can treat eye diseases and do eye tests, but the optician prepares lenses. Confused?

I bet you thought an orderly was a "junior doctor," the real thing in the making. Not so. He's an aide. And have you heard of a cast technician? He's the one who works in the emergency room or orthopedic office and has been trained to apply casts to sick limbs.

Do you know the difference between administrative assistant and assistant administrator? In most bureaucracies, the second has no clout while the first does; it's very difficult to judge anyone by a title.

13
The Patient's Paperwork

HOSPITAL AND HOTEL ARE NOT SYNONYMOUS

"Whaddaya mean how was my night?" he snarled, spitting the thermometer onto his navy-piped, red satin pajamas. "How the hell do you think it was?"

His stunning blonde friend retreated to the corner, embarrassed by the outburst, wishing her corporate tycoon lover would act less like a spoiled adolescent. Each day of his hospitalization she felt more and more intimidated by a Leon she had never known before.

"Tell her about it, Jean, just tell her how I slept last night. I'm getting out of here. Just get me the doctor. This is no hospital, this place is a damn looney bin. Why, if I ran my corporation like this we'd all be down the drain tomorrow. Tell her, Jean," he commanded.

"You didn't sleep well?" I asked redundantly, wishing he'd keep quiet long enough for me to hear his heartbeat. His blood pressure was elevated, a sure sign of anger. The thermometer slipped to the floor, shattering, scattering tiny beads of mercury under my feet.

"Now, Leon, darling, calm down, I'll get the doctor," and she drifted toward the door, sleek Halston dress just slightly brushing her perfect model's body, the waft of Nuit de Noël lingering behind.

"What was the problem last night, Mr. Mitchell?" I asked for it and I got it! A floodgate opened, releasing a drenching tide of venom and hostility he had been storing for three days while he submitted to an exhausting routine of diagnostic tests.

"I'll tell you the problem. I don't belong here. This is a damn prison. Now look, all I wanted was a lousy ham sandwich, you'd have thought I was asking for that nurse's virginity. I can't sleep when I'm hungry. Is that so hard to understand? Who the hell does that nurse think she is anyway?" His chest puffed out, his jowls hung lower, and he heaved his massive body to the side of the bed, tumbling the pitcher of water to the floor as he reached for the morning *Times*. Almost to himself he grumbled, "She wouldn't do a thing I asked. Damned odd—Orientals are usually such good servants."

Servants? Six years of education to be classified as a servant, a toter of ham sandwiches to male chauvinist pigs? Wait till Yoshi heard what a poor servant she was.

It would do no good to tell Leon he couldn't have a ham sandwich because his life was hanging on the brink of extinction waiting for just such small things to push him over the edge. The doctor's order called for a salt-free, clear-liquid diet, which Leon knew full well, but he had not learned that a hospital is *not a hotel!* Hotels were a way of life for him and room service had better be prompt.

Leon is not alone in his misconception of the primary function of a hospital. Nurses do have difficulty resigning themselves to the fact that the hospitalized patient's expectations are often those of the hotel guest. "I was there for an hour before anyone even bothered to unpack my suitcase," said one angry patient who, by the way, was fully ambulatory and no worse off than when she packed the suitcase herself two hours earlier.

Perhaps the proclivity to relate the hospital experience to a hotel sojourn is the terrified mind's way of saying "I'm not sick, I'm just having a well-deserved rest in this hotel they call a hospital."

WHAT CAN GO HOME WITH YOU

We once had a patient who had occupied the same room for about three weeks, but it looked as if she had been there three years. Dead flowers, old newspapers, and cards polka-dotted the room. She loved clutter and we liked our patients to feel at home. However, finding her among the clutter was becoming a problem, so one day when she was sent to the X-ray department we decided to dispose of at least half of it, which was an interesting project. Every nook and cranny of the room was stuffed with goods: silverware, napkins, packets of sugar, pepper, salt, mustard, mayonnaise, thermometers, plastic cups, water pitchers, paper medication cups, Band-Aids, plates, safety pins. Every item brought into her room for three weeks had been stashed, probably for removal when she was discharged. In fact, she had sixty-three sets of silverware in her suitcase, one for every meal that had been served to her.

This doesn't mean that a hospital gives nothing away, but you both should agree on what you may take with you when you are discharged. As a rule of thumb: anything plastic may go home with you because most plastic cannot be reprocessed to suit infection-control standards. This includes the admitting kit, which usually contains a plastic washbasin, water pitcher, cup, soap dish, and emesis basin. Some admitting kits also include a thermometer which is disposed of when you leave and that you might as well take home with you.

In fee-for-service hospitals, any item charged to you may go home with you: elastic stockings; sheepskin mats; heel and elbow protectors; Ace bandages; colostomy supplies; elastic braces; disposable instruments such as scissors, tweezers, and clamps; special dressings brought into your room in bulk; urine-testing kits such as Clinitest or Ketodiastix; lotions, powders, and mouthwashes; and even your plastic bedpan and urinal. Once any item has been brought into your room, it's considered contaminated and can only be used again in the hospital if it can be sterilized. Labor costs often prohibit sterilization, so if you don't take it home, the trash compactor gets it.

Before you leave the hospital, your advocate should stop by the business office and ask if they need you to sign or pay anything. That's when you find out how comprehensive your insurance is.

FOR ADVOCATES

On the day of discharge:

1. Phone the nurse and ask what time you should be there and at which entrance you should park your car.
2. See the secretary at the nurses' station and ask her for your patient's discharge slip.
3. Gather up some of your patient's belongings so you don't have to make too many trips, drop them off in the car, then go to the cashier on the main floor near the lobby, and present them with the discharge slip. They'll probably have you sign a form or two, then go back up to the secretary and tell her you are ready to take the patient. She'll see that a nurse and wheelchair are sent to the patient's room.
4. You carry the belongings, the nurse wheels the patient, and you're on your way.

THE BILL

More often than not you're sent on your way with the bill following you home a few weeks later. "I came home from his funeral to find a seven-thousand-dollar hospital bill in my mailbox," lamented one woman. It does seem harsh and cruel that one pays whether the patient survives or not; however, the harshest part is receiving the bill when all your defenses are at a low ebb.

A hospital bill is *always* a shock to everyone, without exception, even if the insurance pays. Unfortunately, the business office is just like your department store's business office; they know nothing about you or your personal circumstances. They simply do the accounting and mail the bill.

There are some similarities between a hospital and a hotel, I must admit, and one of these is the bill. Look at your hospital bill just as you would your hotel bill. It does not matter that insurance is forking over the cash, there are still errors that push the cost of hospitalization up for everyone.

How do you check your bill? Stop looking at it as a calamity and pick it apart piece by piece. The billing procedure is so complex you need to be a scientist to figure it out, especially since most hospitals bill by the Relative Value System (RVS) code. That is, a unit number is assigned to each procedure and item, there is a dollar amount commonly assigned to each type of unit, and then the translation takes place ending up in dollars and cents on the far-right-hand column of your bill. Expect to see the itemized accounting categorized into hospital departments. First is the room rate, which includes meals, general nursing care, and the most basic of services. Check to see that you are charged for the correct number of days.

Pharmacy Costs

The pharmacy section of the bill is very interesting. If you bring your own Tylenol into the hospital with you, you probably paid around $2.20 for a bottle of 100; we send these medications home, since we can't be sure what is in the bottle, and charge you thirty cents for each Tylenol from our pharmacy. We charge you thirty cents for each Dalmane, although you probably paid about $3.00 for a bottle of 30 from your corner drugstore. Every injection of Demerol costs you around $2.50 in the hospital; the estrogen injection we charge you $9.00 for can be purchased outside the hospital for $2.20. Someone has to write the requisition for your meds, someone else puts the order together, someone else delivers it to the floor, someone else puts it in your medication drawer, the nurse gives it to you, then there is all the paperwork behind it, all of which adds to the price.

Also, on the day you leave the hospital a nurse may hand you some prescriptions the doctor has left on your chart. "Get these filled on your way home. You've got to keep taking your medications so you don't have a relapse." The path of least resistance is the one we all choose; you're likely to decide to get the prescriptions filled at the hospital pharmacy so you don't have to make a stop on the way home. *Don't do it!* Even with my employee discount, there's no more expensive place for me to buy drugs than my hospital pharmacy. The pharmacies in large medical-office buildings are also notoriously costly. They pay a premium for the building space they occupy, they usually will deliver to the home if requested, and such costs are naturally passed along to you.

If you're a member of a health-maintenance organization with a prepaid health plan, then there's a flat fee for your drugs, usually about a dollar, and of course that's where you should get your prescriptions filled.

There is really no one inexpensive place to purchase your prescriptions—marketing techniques for drugs are quite similar to those used in the grocery store. Both have "loss leaders"; the company may lose profit on a very popular item when they sell it at a much lower price than their competitors, but chances are they are yanking up the profit on other less popular items. For instance, the pharmacy in a very large discount-store chain sells birth-control pills for $1.56 less than the pharmacy around the corner from my house, but the cost of antibiotics from the same chain is $3.10 higher than at my corner store. As with any other commodity you purchase, the savings can be substantial if you "shop." Use the phone book and call around for the best price on the prescriptions you have in hand. See Chapter 9 for more about your prescription.

Your pharmacy items will be lumped together on the hospital bill, usually by the day. You will have no way to check to see that you got what you're paying for. The only time you have any recourse is if you did not receive any meds and find pharmacy listed on your bill.

Central-Service Charges

Now look at the central-service items listed. When your nurse brought supplies into your room, she first removed a little sticker that identified the item and then stuck it on a card with your name. The card was sent to the accounting department once a day and the clerks there had no idea whether or not you actually used the item—if it came into your room, you're paying for it. For a Band-Aid, the cost is so small it doesn't matter too much whether or not it was used, but for items like heating pads, respiratory-therapy equipment, crutches, a walker, and complex surgical dressings, the cost is considerable.

One of my pet gripes is the cost of using a hospital's heating pad. Outside the hospital you can buy a good-quality pad for about $7. Inside the hospital you are charged for using theirs at the rate of about $28 per day every day; if you no longer need it but no one bothers to return it to the central service department until you're discharged (this *often* happens), you pay $28 a day for it to sit in the corner of the room.

The hospital's pad costs about $200 because its of special construction, which is why you pay plenty, but you can police your bill in advance of payment day by making sure a nurse removes all unused equipment from your room promptly.

Respiratory-therapy equipment is interesting, too. One setup costs as little as $5, a one-time charge to you, while another costs $800 at a $24-a-day charge to you for however long you use it. Both do exactly the same thing for your body; if you brought a cola bottle from home and blew in it several times a day, you could accomplish about the same therapy as with the expensive equipment.

If you're to be hospitalized for longer than five days, the nurse will put a fluffy white pad on top of your sheets so that your body will have cushioning on which to lie. It costs about $30. These are called "sheepskins," which they are not, or perhaps "Tomacs," a trade name. In any case, it's yours when you leave (if you aren't in an HMO), so take it home and make a bathmat out of it. Or save it for the next time you're hospitalized. They launder easily in a washing machine and, if you don't take them home, they're discarded.

Miscellaneous Charges

Don't be misled by the dates attached to the charges. You might have had surgery on the seventh of the month, but the bill may say the eighth, because that was the day the charge was posted to your bill. Perhaps you went home on the twelfth, but a pharmacy charge may appear on the thirteenth, which is the day the charge was posted.

Some things are checkable. You're charged for the operating room, anesthesiology, and the recovery room in terms of how long the services were required. If the doctor tells you your operation took ten minutes, but your bill says your operating room time was one hour, scream. Every fifteen minutes in the operating room racks up a considerable bill.

If you're charged for three units of blood but you know you only received two, say so. Someone made a mistake, and the cost of blood is very high.

If you're charged for three hospital days and you only stayed two, speak up. Your chart probably made it to the office a day late, or someone forgot to notify the business office that you left, especially if you left against medical advice (AMA). When looking at room charges, remember that the "day" starts at 11:00 a.m. and a "half-day" usually ends at 5:00 p.m.

The bills that come rolling in after hospitalization don't end with the hospital bill. You'll hear from the assisting surgeon, the anesthesiologist, any consultants, your own physician, the radiologist, the physical therapist—and that may not be all! You can have some small impact on the cost of your hospitalization. (See A Guide to Cutting Medical Bills in the Appendix.) In fact, the impact may be rather large if you do such a thing as refuse treatment in the intensive care unit where the cost of every hour is astronomical.

Generally, the fact that your insurance company pays most, or all, of your bill leaves you so relieved that you file the bill away in your memory box to laugh about some years later. But that's one of the reasons the cost of health care is so high. The patient isn't paying enough attention. "What can I do? I'm at their mercy!" This is like taking your car to the service department and giving them carte blanche to "make it well." Most people do that just once before they realize unmonitored repairs are financial idiocy.

Until the public stops considering medical bills a natural consequence of making it through life, it's unlikely that the escalating costs will be slowed. Ask questions, consider it your social obligation to monitor your medical bills and to question your charges in advance. Consider your medical bills analogous to your car-repair bills—don't just shell out and shut up.

TO QUESTION YOUR BILL

As always, anything in writing receives far more attention than a phone call. We received a letter from the widow of a long-term patient. The hospitalization had been about two months and the bill was pages long. She had written to protest what she felt was an overcharge of too many units of blood. "I can't see why they had to give him any anyway, since the only blood that was missing was the stuff you kept taking out of him for all those blood tests. He wasn't bleeding anywhere. Why did you take so much? And why should I pay for it?" She ended by saying she would pay for two units, but not the third.

The letter went first to the business office for reply, then to the physician-in-chief for his reply, and then to the director of nursing. It ended up with the physician of the late patient who called the widow and explained the details of her husband's death. She had simply thought that we might have contributed to his demise, although she only intended to let us know of her doubts about the third unit of blood.

If you hate letter writing, a phone call to the billing department can settle any dispute over your bill. Have the bill in front of you so you can refer to it as they check the original. Make your questions specific and get the name of the person helping you and exactly when they intend to get back to you with a reply. Don't bother calling during the lunch hour or after 4:00 p.m. because you'll be very low priority.

HEALTH-CARE CRISIS

The little red bicycle sat upright in the deepest end of the pool, the sparkling, clear water magnifying its lethal image. It is April; the bike has been there since November. The rider, three-year-old Mindy, has been in an intensive care unit since that November day when she and the bike slipped over the edge of the pool.

Mindy drowned. Although most of us consider "drowned" a terminal word, synonymous with dead, such was not the case for Mindy or hundreds of others, despite the fact their medical records still contain the word "drowned" as the official diagnosis.

No one knows how long Mindy was at the bottom of the pool; at least a minute, perhaps ten minutes. She was resuscitated by the rescue squad and transferred to the nearest hospital where she lies today in the same state as that first day, showing "no significant evidence of recovery."

Mindy's medical problems are such that she is not a candidate for care anywhere other than an intensive care unit and, putting aside all other implications of this case, the nursing care alone will cost $48,080 this year. Cost of occupancy in the bed is predicted at roughly $365,000, with equipment, supplies, treatments, and tests necessary to meet her needs at about $24,800. Conservative estimates place the physician's bill at approximately $3900 for the year.

"Brain death" and "pulling the plug" do not apply to Mindy's case, since she is not being kept alive with mechanical equipment. A nursing home is not appropriate because she has episodic problems which require intensive skilled nursing. Institutionalization is not appropriate, again because of the episodic problems.

Mindy is only one small drop in the ocean of what the media term our "national health-care crisis" and "crisis" is traditionally translated into dollars or, more appropriately, lack of dollars.

In 1978 we spent $161 billion on health care, $57 billion of it funded through the government, $41 billion of it paid for by corporations, and the public picked up the tab for the remainder directly. Of course, it also picked up a portion of the tab for the government as a taxpayer and helped out the corporations as an employer or employee.

One-tenth of the entire federal budget supports health programs; one-tenth of the nation's total output of goods and services is spent on health services; between 1973 and 1978, physicians' fees rose 42.6 percent. Medicaid is a $21-billion program and the nation's health-care bill has increased threefold since 1970. Two billion dollars of each year's Medicaid money is either wasted or misspent and hospitalization eats up 80 percent of the health-care dollars we spend. Look at your newspaper today or any day and you too can gather startling statistics indicating that we are indeed in a health-care crisis, in terms of dollars, as well as in the provision of *adequate* health care for everyone, including the indigent and those in rural areas.

Sophisticated analysts could write volumes on why we are in crisis. It is somewhat of an oversimplification to narrow it down to three basic causes, but these causes are those in which you, regardless of your age, sex, race, or health status, probably have a large stake: (1) poor use of resources, (2) backward incentives, and (3) resistance to cost-containment steps.

Our resources are mind-boggling and growing all the time. The most newly developed technological icon to immortality, the whole-body scanner, known as the CAT (computerized axial tomography) scan, is not only a boon to patients but a status symbol to hospitals. "Ah yes, well we just installed our CAT, at a cost of one and a half million dollars," says the hospital administrator. The new physician in town, eager to be on the staff of the most progressive hospital, joins the team and brings all his patients there. The administrator's beds get filled up and the hospital operates "in the black" that year—good business tactics, after all.

Atlanta, Georgia, has seventeen CAT scanners for 1.5 million people, while Connecticut has six scanners for 3.2 million people. Do the people in Georgia enjoy better health? No, but they do enjoy larger medical bills. The epitome of "poor use of resources" is demonstrated in a West Coast city where three hospitals occupy the crest of a very small hill—so small that you could hit all three hospitals if you stood in the middle of the street and gave your best pitch to a baseball. The proliferation of nuclear-medicine equipment on this hill has been nothing short of phenomenal—four sets of the same kind of equipment at a cost of $150,000 for each set. "A medical arms race," the newspaper calls it, as each hospital competes for the right (the government requires "proof of need" for a "permit" to install such costly equipment) to place the $1.5-million CAT scanner among its equipment.

In some parts of Maine where the number of surgeons is high, the number of operations performed is more than double the number in other parts of the state. Does that mean there's better health in those parts of Maine where the surgeons congregate? Not necessarily! Studies indicate the greater the number of surgeons and specialists in an area, the higher their fees, and there is little more that can be said for those areas where they congregate.

The average hospital stay on the West Coast is 6.4 days, in New England, 8.1 days, and in New York City, 9.8 days.

Does that mean you'll be healthier if you live in San Francisco? Well now, there are no statistics to support the notion that *more* health care improves the quality or quantity of life. More is not always synonymous with better. The goal is quality care in a cost-effective framework, but as a nation we are pitifully short of the goal.

For more examples of poor use of resources, examine your own health-care habits. Though you probably have been taught the contrary, the annual physical examination that is commonly held to ward off major illness will not protect your friend who had his annual "checkup" yesterday and today has a heart attack. Why? Because most often our diagnostic equipment is not sensitive enough to pick up diseases that have not yet manifested symptoms and for many of those diseases that can be detected before symptoms, life expectancy is not enhanced by early detection.

Advocates of preventive medicine, who are also proponents of conservation of our medical resources, advise you to do the following, in the absence of any signs of ill health: Have two check-ups when you're in your twenties, three in your thirties, four in your forties, five in your fifties, and upon doctor's advice thereafter. In controlled studies, little difference in mortality or morbidity rates were found when comparing large groups of individuals who received regular physical examinations with those who sought medical advice only for symptoms.

BACKWARD INCENTIVE

Paul M. Ellwood, Jr., medical administrator of the Kenny Rehabilitation Institute in the mid-1960s, made this observation: "We found that the more successful we were in rehabilitating people, the sooner we discharged them from the hospital and the more money we lost. It was almost as if we were rewarded for keeping people in the hospital." The incentives were backward, *are* backward.

Under present comprehensive insurance and reimbursement arrangements, neither consumer nor provider is rewarded for intelligent use of costly resources. Our individual health-care insurance costs are being paid mostly through a compulsory levy that's pre–take-home pay and pre–income tax—it comes out of our pockets before it gets into our pockets—and we pay scant attention to it unless the health-care provider says, "That'll be two hundred dollars please. Pay before you leave." To which the average person exclaims, "Two hundred dollars. Good heavens, my insurance company covers me. Bill them, please!"

If you need a gallbladder X ray, your insurance only covers you while you're hospitalized so off you go. "We might as well remove that mole from your foot while you're in here," says your doctor, and the X ray that would have cost about $50 on an outpatient basis ends up in a five-day hospital stay costing around $4000. That's what's known as "backward incentive."

When you're in a hospital bed, the hospital gains, the physician gains, and the purveyors of supplies and equipment gain. When you're in your own bed, they all lose. It's that simple— "backward incentive."

"Your heart shows some irregularities on your EKG," says your cardiologist, and you go into the hospital for a cardiac catheterization. It turns out that your need for coronary-artery–bypass surgery is marginal. If you have it done the surgeon stands to gain plenty. In fact, some such surgeons gain by around $3 million a year each. If you do not have it done, though, he gains nothing. That's backward incentive.

The third basic reason for our health-care crisis, the resistance to cost-containment steps, comes quite naturally from the health-care providers, but also from the public, since we make no rational judgment on whether the investment is worth the result. In other areas people will stop spending if there is no promise of success, but in health care people will spend thousands regardless of the hope for success. There is simply no interest in cost effectiveness. We will keep spending on research and on intensive care until the effort either fails or harm results.

Twelve years ago there was no such thing as an intensive care unit. This year the salaries of the nurses required to staff an average six-bed ICU will cost close to $250,000. The bill of a typical ICU patient is estimated at $1000 to $3000 *each* day, whether or not the patient is expected to survive. What will be the return on that investment? Many would say, "If it's my husband's life that is saved, that's enough return on the investment." If there is no chance for recovery, does it make sense to prolong life at $1000 to $3000 a day? Whom shall we save? What sort of price tag can one place on human life? What portion of the nation's resources and the government's budget should health care command?

Mrs. Benson is a good example of the dilemma. She's seventy-eight years old, supported by Social Security, and the majority of her medical bills are paid by Medicaid. Her only child is a son who has identified himself as her advocate. Mrs. Benson came to us with an enormous hernia that she had been able to ignore most of her life; however, it had recently begun to obstruct her bowel. Her request was that we do nothing but keep her comfortable.

Her physician recorded on her chart that her demise was imminent (his words) if she did not submit to surgery and, while she continued to reject that option, her son signed the Consent for Treatment form. "She doesn't understand the gravity of the situation," he told the nurses. "I insist she go to surgery." Nurses, being patient's advocates above all else in this situation, refused to witness his signature and refused to prepare her for surgery as the physician had ordered. The case became a morass of moral and ethical dilemmas.

If we remove the emotional aspect and simply focus on the cost of this case, which will be paid for by the taxpayers, the key concept is "hope for success." Mrs. Benson has a *terminal illness* which the surgery cannot eradicate. Following surgery she will almost surely be an ICU patient, possibly on a respirator. She will have a colostomy and require nursing care for the rest of her life—if she is ever able to return to her home, which is highly unlikely. There is at least a 50 percent chance that she will not survive the surgery, a 50 percent chance that she will spend weeks in ICU on a respirator, and a 99 percent chance that she will not be alive next Christmas with or without the surgery. "Hope for success" depends on how "success" is defined.

Mrs. Benson *was* taken to surgery, despite her objections, and died in ICU eleven days after the operation. Her bill amounted to $23,000, all paid by the taxpayers.

How much of the nation's resources should be devoted to treating illness and how much to preventing it? How can health care be made more humane and efficient? Who should pay for health care and how? And who should share in the decision-making process that has traditionally been a monopoly of physicians?

Such questions have caused health care to become a major political issue, especially since the nation's total outlays for health have been climbing at twice the rate of inflation.

FOR ADVOCATES

You can try bullying your patient into signing a Consent for Treatment form he doesn't want, with the anxiety the patient feels if he does not comply with your wishes probably matching your anger at being in the middle, between the patient and the physician. Ask to speak with the chaplain, even if you are not accustomed to doing this, since you need an objective listener to hear you out and perhaps assist you in arriving at some solution.

RESOLVING THE CRISIS

The nation's policymakers will soon have to make some fundamental choices about our health care, though it's not as if they've been sitting on their thumbs as escalating costs would suggest. Indeed, the 1973 Health Maintenance Organization Act was designed to decrease the costs of the Medicare and Medicaid programs, which it has not. (The act essentially says that any employer who provides medical benefits and has over twenty-five employees must offer those employees the choice between a prepaid health plan and a fee-for-service plan.) This is not to say it never will decrease costs; in fact, more than 7.3 million persons were enrolled in HMOs in 1978, up one million over 1977.

Another alternative to the crisis is national health insurance (NHI), which is the really big political football these days. We are the only major industrial nation without NHI, a form of socialized medicine; it is said that it could save us $23 billion within two years after it is initiated. The nation's policymakers have been unable to agree on the basics of a plan, which is why political campaigns rely heavily on this issue these days—you know how long major national legislation takes.

In addition, legislation is impeded by our free-enterprise system in which those who derive their income from their profession (physicians, equipment manufacturers, insurance carriers, and labor unions) resist any change that would alter their standard of living. NHI would certainly have a major impact on the incomes of those who have a vested interest in the health-care industry. Thousands of lobbying dollars are strategically placed to block NHI, which is why it is not likely that we will wake up tomorrow and find national health insurance available.

In the meantime, you do have a choice between fee-for-service and prepaid health insurance and you need to be well informed enough to make the wisest choice—your health and your pocketbook are at stake.

HEALTH-MAINTENANCE ORGANIZATIONS

Of the 185 health maintenance organizations functioning in July 1978, 34 were in California, 11 in Wisconsin, and 7 in Pennsylvania. The other 133 were sprinkled throughout the country. This means you might be one of the 70.3 percent of Americans polled who have never heard the term HMO, though such plans have existed for more than a century. You might have heard the term "prepaid," which is the same concept as HMO, or you might know it as a specific group such as Kaiser, the nation's largest HMO and the prototype for all others.

In brief, an HMO is a medical supermarket that guarantees

a broad range of services and pays its physicians salaries and/or a division of the profits, all for a flat fee to you, paid on a monthly basis. Some HMOs are run by consumers, some by corporations for profit, and others by groups of physicians. The HMO tries to prevent you from becoming ill because, if you do, you may end up in their hospital and cost the organization more than your membership fee. Remember the term "backward incentive"? This is *not* backward incentive! Office visits are free simply because they want you to seek help before a problem arises that requires hospitalization. Their income depends upon your staying well. When you're sick, you lose and they lose, which makes quite a bit more sense than others profiting from your ill health.

In the past five years the government has spent $170 million in grants and loans to help HMOs get started, largely because of these interesting statistics: HMOs cut hospital use by about 30 percent; participants in HMOs undergo about half the amount of surgery as the population as a whole and have lower mortality rates; 70 percent of the HMO's premium dollar is spent for outpatient care; total cost to the participants is lower by 25 to 30 percent; there are 457 hospital days per one thousand participants in contrast to the 882 days per thousand people covered by the private insurance companies; and the average length of hospital stay for an HMO patient is 6.1 days, as opposed to the 7.4 average for the fee-for-service population.

This is only the beginning of the statistical evidence that supports the notion that the answer to the nation's health-care crisis might well be the widespread availability of HMOs. They are most assuredly an avenue to medical-hospital cost control.

THE OTHER SIDE OF THE COIN

HMOs have been accused of skimping on their services and of skimming their participants from the healthier segments of the population, of constraining the physician's independent professional judgment, and of destroying the doctor/patient relationship—none of this is supported by statistical evidence. The consumer is a package on the conveyor belt through the American health-care system, be it fee-for-service or health-maintenance organization. Many participants in prepaid plans would find it difficult to be persuaded that the benefits of an HMO don't outweigh any disadvantages.

And by the way, Mindy, the three-year-old drowning victim, is a real patient in a health-maintenance organization. Her father's employer pays the monthly premium to the plan, her parents have no financial obligation of any kind, the health-maintenance organization is financially sound, the quality of her care is unexcelled, and you, the taxpayer, are not contributing one cent of your earnings to her care—this says quite a bit about the possibilities of resolving our health-care crisis through HMOs.

In December 1978, Sylvia Porter, nationally syndicated columnist, wrote a comprehensive series of columns on HMOs entitled "Breakthrough in the Health Care Field," which answers many questions you might have. If her columns normally appear in your local newspaper, you might ask them for reprints. Otherwise you may obtain information by writing to the Office of HMOs, Department of Health and Human Services, in one of ten regional cities: Boston, New York, Philadelphia, Atlanta, Chicago, Dallas, Kansas City, Denver, San Francisco, and Seattle. Or call the HMO information toll-free number (800) 638-6686.

YOUR HEALTH INSURANCE

"The hell with it," he growled. "It would take me three days to fill out all these papers. I'll pay the bill myself!" He fell into the trap known as "path of least resistance" and saved the insurance company a bundle.

In the past, there has been no one to help us file insurance papers and most of us really didn't know much about what medical services our insurance carriers obligated themselves to pay. In fact, this is often by design.

I call my employer. "I'd like a copy of the medical-insurance policy." The clerk tells me she has none, that I must call the carrier. I call the carrier. "What do you want that for?" he asks. I tell him I'd like to be able to plan for the cost of the surgery I'm anticipating. "You'll have to get a copy of the policy from your employer," he tells me.

I call the clerk again. She tells me she's never seen the policy but she'll see what she can find out. Two weeks later she calls and tells me, "We've never had anyone ask for one. What do you want it for? No one's ever seen one around here. Call the insurance company back and insist that they send you the policy." I call the carrier back. "We don't give out that information, ma'am," and his voice is suspicious. "You'll have to get it from your employer. They bought the insurance, they're paying for it, and whatever coverage they bought is what you'll get, so why are you even asking?"

A year has passed and I have not seen a policy. I have seen a flock of "rejects" from the carrier, bills they feel are not their obligation or those they feel they will pay only partially, because they "exceed the accepted rate for your area."

"How does insurance billing work?" I asked the business office manager of the hospital where I work. She laughed. "Have you got six months while I explain it?" she asked.

Much as one takes income-tax records to a tax preparer each year, you may now take your medical bills to a company specializing in maximizing the amount of money you receive on a medical claim. As a subscriber to such a service you are entitled to have your medical bills scrutinized for accuracy, the claims filed and monitored, and follow-up work performed. It's estimated that the increased benefits to you are most often around 35 percent, simply because experienced people file your claims and keep track of what you are actually owed versus what the insurance company usually pays. If there's a discrepancy, the filing service works with the insurance carrier to settle it for you.

Look in the Yellow Pages of your phone book for these services, usually under the heading Medical Organizations. Or you can handle the whole matter by mail: Medical Claims Filing Service, 3512 South Silver Springs Road, Lafayette, California 94549, (415) 283-1365. Fee schedules vary with these companies, but most charge around $100 a year, on a subscription basis, to handle all of your health insurance problems, and/or you can choose to have them handle only one hospitalization for about $45.

If you have a stack of old bills lying around, waiting for you to get the energy to tackle them, the filing services will handle it for you and charge about 20 percent of the amount of money your insurance pays off.

MEDICARE

You may be eligible for Medicare in which case you should know the following: Medicare and Medicaid pay what they feel like paying when they see the bill. "It usually works out to be about half the bill, regardless of what items are on the bill." Probably that is not the way the matter is seen by those who run Medicare and Medicaid, but that's what it looks like from the patient's end.

The Department of Health and Human Services has provided a raft of handy little booklets to guide you through their system. The key word is "reasonable." They pay certain "reasonable charges"; what is reasonable is determined by the Medicare carrier—the organization selected by the Social Security Administration to handle claims in the area where you receive services. Today, that's the "Blues"—Blue Cross and Blue Shield. Next month the carrier may change.

The social implications of our health-care system could fill volumes and really are not appropriate here, but I would like you to know one important thing: if you do not "sign up" for Medicare in the three months before or after your sixty-fifth birthday, you are not eligible to do so until the "general enrollment period," January 1 through March 31 of each year. If you land in the hospital four months after your birthday, but before January 1, Medicare will not cover your bills. It's that simple.

Also, you pay a penalty for not enrolling in the plan when you're sixty-five. First of all, the coverage doesn't start until July of that year and your premium will be 10 percent higher for each twelve-month period you could have been enrolled but were not. Say your birthday is January 10, you don't even think about enrolling in Medicare, someone tells you about it on April 14, and you go down to the Social Security office to enroll. Sorry, you have to wait until January. January comes, you enroll, and on March 15 you land in the hospital, but Medicare is not obligated to pay bills you incur before July of that year.

Medicare is two-part insurance: hospital insurance and medical. The first is financed by contributions from employees, employers, and self-employed people. The last is financed through monthly premiums paid by those who sign up for the insurance. Under certain conditions you are automatically eligible for hospital coverage. Eligible people get free hospital and are automatically enrolled in medical and billed for medical. Those *not* eligible for free hospital can buy it, but they must also buy the medical, and enrollment is not automatic.

In other words, whether you get it free or purchase hospital insurance through Medicare, you can't have hospital insurance without paying for medical insurance.

To find out where you stand and what your options are you should call your Social Security office sometime within the three months preceding your sixty-fifth birthday. If you're eligible for hospital coverage, enrollment for medical insurance is automatic and you will be billed for the premium unless you make other arrangements with the Social Security office. Confusing, isn't it?

There's another hitch! Suppose you want to cancel your insurance. It must be done in writing, but that does not release you from financial obligation for the premium immediately. Your coverage and premium payments don't stop until the *end* of the quarter following the quarter in which your cancellation notice is received. For instance, on March 30 you decide you no longer want the insurance, you write to Social Security but they don't receive your notice until April 3, the beginning of a new quarter. Your cancellation is then not in effect until the end of September and you will have to continue paying the premiums until then. Any expenses are also covered until then.

MEDICAID

Although Medicare is a federal project entirely, Medicaid is supported by your federal, state, and county taxes. You may know it by another name—in California it's called "Medi-Cal." It's administered by local county welfare offices and has criteria different from Medicare. Whether or not you are eligible is up to the county welfare department worker.

If you expect Medicare or Medicaid to pay your bills, you must tell the business office of the hospital your intent *immediately* upon your arrival. In many cases, the providers of your medical care must first consult with the state before proceeding, if they are to be paid. If you have "stickers" or a card or forms to be filed, bring them with you. It would be devastating to have insurance but not be reimbursed for your bill simply because you didn't tell anyone early enough that you were covered.

THE PATIENT-CARE COORDINATOR

Someone with this title or a similar one is employed by every hospital to unravel the mysteries of insurance coverage, to help you with your plans for care after hospitalization, and to help you or your advocate avoid having to foot the whole bill on your own. In large hospitals, there are several of them, sometimes called "social workers." Don't be put off by the title, which has implications of poverty, since most people now know you don't have to be poor to be covered by Social Security hospital insurance.

The amount of information used in the work of the patient-care coordinator is staggering, but even more staggering is the forty-one-page list of criteria which speaks to the issue of whether or not your medical condition warrants hospitalization. If you don't meet the criteria, you cannot stay in the hospital. It doesn't matter if you are unable to care for yourself and have no living friends or relatives; if you don't meet the criteria, you must be discharged.

BUYING PRIVATE INSURANCE

"My insurance covers everything" is what most people say, but few really do have that sort of insurance. As women join the work force and the two-income family becomes the "norm," you often have several medical-insurance alternatives. By law, the employer must provide the employee with a choice of insurance:

a prepaid health plan or a private carrier. At the same time, the spouse may be offered insurance of two different types, bringing the choice up to four.

Take out a piece of paper, make four vertical columns, head each with one of the insurance plans, then start a list down the left side: maximum benefits, deductible, maternity benefits, laboratory benefits, extended (or convalescent) coverage, major-medical percentage, coverage for dependents, outpatient services, payments to physicians, mental-health benefits, prescriptions, accidents, duration of hospital coverage, eye exams, and dental benefits. Fill in each of these major sections and then compare the four.

You might find that you both have been offered the same prepaid health plan, such as Kaiser, but the coverage could be different. Each employer buys the coverage plan he wants; one might have full hospital, physician, prescription, and dental benefits, while another might have a higher deductible, some certain fee for prescriptions, and no dental. There are all sorts of plans with all sorts of variations on the theme.

How should you decide? Consider your circumstances. If you have a chronic illness that requires periodic hospitalization, you'll want the plan that gives you the best benefits while you're hospitalized. If you have young children who have allergies, you'll probably want the one that offers you the most for doctor visits.

Usually you'll find that you can't have your cake and eat it too. If the deductible is low, the payoff in some other area will probably be the least desirable. Or, if you have poor coverage for prescriptions, the payoff for lab work may be fantastic.

It also helps to know a bit about the carrier of each policy. For instance, certain companies have a reputation for responding quickly to claims while others leave you dangling for months. Some always pay 100 percent when they say they will, and others continually reject your claims with a little note that the charge exceeds "reasonable" charges for your area.

If for any reason you think you might want world-famous Dr. So-and-So to treat some condition one day, then forget the prepaid plan because that one almost always limits you to the doctors on its own staff, be they famous or not.

For the best of all worlds, it helps if one spouse elects the prepaid coverage and the other elects the private coverage. That way, you always have the option of going to any major institution in the world for very complex problems, while still maintaining the easy prepaid plan.

One thing is sure: *you cannot afford to be without medical insurance!* If you have to borrow money to buy it, then do so. Look at it this way—not one of us is going to get out of this life alive and very few of us are going to die of a "run-down motor." We're all going to be involved in some heavy medical bills before we leave this earth and our last medical bills will be the largest— it's not so easy to die. Dying is a long, slow process, very seldom "sudden," and the medical bills are in direct proportion to our fight to avoid the one absolute in life—physical life is finite.

DOUBLE INSURANCE—DOUBLE PAYOFF

There are two schools of thought on this issue: First, you've paid for two policies so you ought to be able to collect all benefits from both, and second, the insurance carrier agrees to pay only those costs for your illness that you would have to pay out-of-pocket. If another carrier pays your bills, then you really aren't paying anything out of your pocket, thus the first company owes you nothing.

This is a moral dilemma you'll have to solve on your own, but I will give you one tip: it is not likely that insurance company X has any way of finding out if you've already been paid by company Y. Another tip: the more the insurance companies pay out, the higher our insurance rates climb, and the less we all take home out of our paychecks!

IN DEFENSE OF THE INSURANCE COMPANIES

With a family of teenagers, we have a fleet of automobiles around and you can imagine the high cost of the insurance bill. It's twice the cost of the medical-insurance bill yearly, and yet we've never filed a claim on auto insurance.

An insurance policy also goes along with home-ownership— you can't get a mortgage without getting fire insurance. For twenty-five years we've paid the insurance, now little less than our medical insurance yearly, and we've never filed a claim. We call ourselves lucky. We don't want the insurance company to have to pay. We gladly throw our dollars down the drain. We have, after all, bought "insurance," which is just the way you should look at your medical insurance. In a lifetime we could never repay our medical insurance carrier all that it has paid for our hospital sojourns; there are millions more Americans in the same position as us. Yes, medical insurance costs a fortune, but I can't think of any better place to put your money. And if you never have to file a claim, rejoice and consider it money well spent!

FOR ADVOCATES

Elderly patients are confronted with one of life's most complicated tasks when they are least able to handle it—filing insurance forms. If they could wait until they've regained some of the strength lost in hospitalization, the forms wouldn't seem so complex. However, the sense of urgency to pay the doctor and hospital seems to be common to senior citizens.

If you can convince your patient that the doctor and hospital will wait to be paid, fine. Chances are he will convince you that *all* bills must be paid on the tenth of the month, including the medical bills, and the job will fall into your lap. Don't despair, you may be able to put the monkey on someone else. First gather up all the bills, count how many different doctors or firms have to be paid, then phone the insurance carrier and ask for twice that number of forms. When the forms arrive, fill out the top portion and send two forms to each creditor. If you're lucky, the business office of each will complete the forms, send them to the insurance carrier, and checks will arrive in about a month.

If you're not lucky, the forms will be completed and returned to you. You should then send them to the insurance carrier *after* you have obtained photocopies for your records. (Most public libraries have photocopying machines, by the way.)

You should keep a list of which creditors are owed, how much each bill is, the percentage insurance is to pay, the date you sent the claim form, the date you receive payment, and how much is left for the patient to pay. Quite often something in the system goes awry and you'll need to consult your records to be sure you receive what's due. In addition, records help at tax time since a portion of the bills not covered by insurance can be deducted on your income tax.

If Medicare or Medicaid is involved, the forms are even more complex than those of private insurance carriers. Your best bet is to set aside a whole day for the project and begin by taking all of the bills to the local Social Security office. You may wait in line a long time, but someone will help you eventually with the intricacies of the forms and the time will be well spent.

Most important of all, keep a photocopy of all the original bills and all claim forms you submit. Lost and/or underpaid bills are not at all uncommon.

Of course, you can avoid the entire problem by engaging the medical claims filing service

CHAPTER
14
Alternatives to Hospitalization

Healing is a matter of time, but it is sometimes also a matter of opportunity. —HIPPOCRATES *(460?–377 B.C.)*

Time, that aged nurse, rocked me to patience. —JOHN KEATS *(1795–1821)*

Remember that time is money. —BENJAMIN FRANKLIN *(1706–1790)*

And of course, there's that age-old advice, "Time heals all wounds," which is not to suggest that you should let the body "do its own thing." However, if you treat a cold for ten days, it will probably disappear. On the other hand, if you do nothing for the cold for ten days, it will also probably disappear.

Jim had a lump on his neck. He was afraid of lumps—we all are. "Lump" sounds almost as menacing as "cancer" and we equate the two. "It's probably nothing," I told him, as thyroid cancer played dissonant chords through my brain. "You should have it looked at now. I'll get you in to see someone fast." "I hate doctors," he told me. "Haven't got time. Sorry I ever told you about it."

Eventually he saw a doctor and had a thyroid scan, but the outcome was questionable. "Have another scan," I nagged. "See another doctor. Don't just sit there. Does it hurt?"

"A little, but only when I swallow. It's nothing. Look, I'm a busy man. Get off my back."

"You'll be busy pushing up daisies someday." I arranged an appointment with another doctor. He went, but only long enough to grow tired of the wait and to leave without seeing the doctor. He was indeed a busy man.

Two weeks later the lump was gone. What was it? Who knows? Jim spent about $100 on the lump that is now gone. This is often all you can say about some medical problems: they do cost money if you explore them.

Mrs. Reece was admitted for diagnostic tests on the same day that Amy Thompson was admitted. Both were in their late sixties, both had the same symptoms, both turned up with the same diagnosis—cancer. Amy said, "I'll go home. Let time take its course," and she died six weeks later. Mrs. Reece said, "I'll try anything," and they gave her "the works." She died four months later.

"Do something," the public demands of the doctor, as though the slightest malfunction of the body is an evil spirit to be exorcised, yet many malfunctions are exacerbated by treatment when time might have cured them.

"Any woman who telephones with a complaint of a breast lump must be seen by a surgeon within two weeks. That's our standard," so spoke the physician-in-chief of a health-maintenance organization. "Time is of the essence."

How should you know when time will heal? By intuition? Obviously, if you're vomiting blood or passing out, time isn't the answer, but when you're in doubt, a good rule of thumb is to wait two weeks. If the condition remains unchanged it's probably worth investigating.

On the other hand, if a physician tells you he can treat you or "wait and see how it goes," then wait and see—time is on your side. It's ultimately up to you whether you consider time or the physician the healer.

EASTERN HEALING ARTS

Chinese parsley helps high blood pressure; cooked horn of deer helps the blood; the tail of a deer makes you feel strong; tiger balm relieves dizziness, sinus congestion, and car sickness; and if you need energy you can scrape tiger balm into your skin with a piece of jade.

Acupuncture and acupressure work on "slow pain," like arthritis or migraine headaches. Acupuncturists work on unblocking blocked mind-body pathways. "Every organ has a sound," the acupuncturist told me. "Laugh, cure yourself, the sound for the heart is laughter."

"Acupuncture in combination with minor changes in diet and physical exercise can restore health if the environment is healthy," said Dr. Marc Lappe, chief of the California Health Department's Office of Health, Law and Values.

Bookstores are replete with information on the various healing arts practiced in the Eastern world, most focusing on herbs, exercise, diet, and meditation. It works for some; it's up to you.

HOLISTIC (WHOLISTIC) HEALTH

"Basically all healing is self-healing. No other person will ever heal you. The body has its own healing processes." Thus say the proponents of holistic health, a movement dedicated to the principle that good health is not only the absence of disease but a sense of physical, spiritual, and mental well-being and that each person can and must take responsibility for his own well-being.

Like other manifestations of self-awareness and consciousness-raising, the holistic-health movement is flourishing in California. The major emphasis of the practitioners, some of them M.D.s, is on teaching ways that people can learn to keep themselves healthy without having to depend on someone else. Armand Brint of the Berkeley Holistic Health Center says: "The thrust of the whole holistic-health movement is the person taking responsibility . . . it's trying to cut through the mystification of disease and health that has been perpetrated over the past hundred years."

As a student of holistic health you might be exposed to such varied knowledge and skills as Shiatsu massage, stress management, yoga, belly dancing, rolfing, deep-tissue manipulation, Bach flower treatments, chanting, laying on of hands, and nutrition. The choice is yours.

DO-IT-YOURSELF MEDICINE

Although nobody is yet ready to make a dollar estimate, the do-it-yourself vogue in medicine is becoming big business. The home pregnancy test, at $10, is perhaps the fastest-selling item, selling a hundred thousand tests a month since January 1978. Charles Sobolewski, vice-president for operations of North American Biologicals, predicts this one test will be a $20-million to $50-million market ". . . if you consider the number of women of childbearing age and how many sexual encounters occur a day."

Health-conscious consumers can run to their local supermarket and diagnose their hypertension with fifty cents placed in the coin slot of a blood-pressure machine. The market for these is anticipated to be $30 to $40 million, with predictions it could go up threefold. A wide variety of early-warning kits and tests for detecting everything from diabetes to urinary-tract infections can be bought at the corner drugstore. The list may soon include tests for such diseases as gonorrhea and arthritis. The choice is yours.

ALTERNATIVE BIRTH CENTERS

More traditional than the hospital alternatives previously mentioned, alternative birth centers (ABCs) are generally housed in hospitals, though the atmosphere is intended to resemble anything but a hospital. Essentially, re-creation of the home atmosphere is intended to decrease the shock to parents and baby of the cold, clinical, technological environment of a hospital. Instead of the delivery table, the baby will be born in a bed just like home, with a couch nearby, plants, a rocking chair, and father standing close at hand. Rather than hastening the newborn to an isolette, as is common practice in the traditional area of the hospital, baby will be cuddled by Mom and Dad in his first few minutes on earth. The three will be together during a candlelight dinner that evening, there, in a special area of the hospital. Emergency services are right next door, which is why the ABCs are usually housed in a hospital. "The best of both worlds, home and the hospital," say the proponents. The choice is yours—if there's "room at the inn" when delivery time approaches.

OUTPATIENT CLINICS

Also hospital-attached, outpatient clinics are equipped to handle minor surgery, but you might have to insist on having it there. The advantage of surgery there is that you avoid the obnoxious hospital routines, such as nurses walking into your room with a flashlight all night, the patient down the hall screaming, the intercom paging doctors around the clock, and a few other nuisances of inpatient status. Although it is not for every surgery, outpatient surgery is "the best of all worlds" if you're having tubal ligation, a D&C, some hernia repairs, minor eye surgery, a tonsillectomy, tissue biopsies, cosmetic surgery, dental extractions, or an abortion.

You arrive early in the morning, have surgery, and sleep for about three hours before going home. Be sure to take someone with you to drive you home. Don't consider outpatient surgery unless you can have someone around the house to help you while you recuperate. Anesthesia drags you out; even if the surgery is minor, you won't be up to par for a few days.

FOR ADVOCATES

In outpatient-surgery departments, ask to stay with the patient until shortly before surgery. Then ask how long the surgery and recovery will take so you won't be sitting idly in the lobby for hours.

Outpatient surgery has doubled in the years between 1976 and 1978, which probably has something to do with the demystification of the medical arts. If you know the danger signs to watch for following surgery, there's often no reason why you won't fare better at home where the stress of an unfamiliar atmosphere and routine is absent—to say nothing of the stress of invasion of your privacy. This is particularly important in the case of young children who have often been severely traumatized by hospitalization during the early years.

VISITING NURSES

If your condition is such that you still need a nurse, perhaps for insulin injections, a catheter change, some cancer chemotherapy, a colostomy irrigation, or change of a surgical dressing, the perfect answer is to go home and have a Visiting Nurse come in on a routine basis. In fact, if your doctor orders it, the discharge planner of the hospital (usually the same nurse who takes care of your insurance problems) or your primary nurse can set you up for physical-therapy treatments at home and for a home aide to come in and clean, do laundry, errands, or even cook meals. But you must need the services of a registered nurse before you qualify for any other care, at least if Medicare or Medicaid is to pay for it.

Meals on Wheels can deliver you a sack lunch and a hot meal once a day for about $5. There are organizations that will arrange to transport you to the hospital for radiation or any kind of outpatient treatment. The American Cancer Society will loan you all sorts of equipment such as electric beds, commodes, safety-grab rails, and walkers. You can even arrange to have an organization phone you each day to make sure you're doing okay. The services available fill volumes in major metropolitan areas, but they don't come to you unless you request them. Ask the discharge planner for anything you might need at home—chances are she has the resources at her fingertips—but you must ask.

Insurance policies vary widely on what home services they cover. If you're not dependent upon insurance, the Yellow Pages of your phone directory can lead you to things you never thought existed. Hospital-supply houses sell and rent innumerable items for home care and messenger services will pick up and deliver packages, messages, or meals—the list goes on and on.

As you can see, I'm prejudiced. My personal bias is that you should avoid hospitalization until all other alternatives have been exhausted.

THE NURSING HOME

Mr. Sills was found in a coma on the floor of his mobile home one day. No one knew how long he had been there. He was an eighty-three-year-old gentleman in very sad shape from a diabetic condition when he arrived on our ward. His children were hastily summoned; it appeared he would not survive the night. He did, however, and went right on surviving, even thriving, though he was too weak to walk and certainly unable to care for himself when he no longer met the strict criteria for staying in the hospital.

The patient-care coordinator made plans with his children to admit him to a nursing home close to one of their homes, although he continued to tell them he had no intention of going.

On the day of his discharge the ambulance drivers wheeled the gurney into his room and Mr. Sills very calmly told them, "I'm plain not a-goin'. I will have you arrested for kidnapping, you know. Can't anyone hear when I say I am flat out not goin' to any nursing home? Get out of here and stay out of here." The drivers shrugged their shoulders and told us, "Hey, we're not about to kidnap the guy. When he wants to go somewhere, give us a call, but we're not dragging someone out of here kicking and screaming."

Two hours later his daughter arrived sobbing uncontrollably to tell the woes of the family and why none of his children could take care of him at their home, nor could any of them go to his home to care for him. "He'll just have to go to a nursing home whether he likes it or not," she said. And Mr. Sills said, "I'm going back to my own place. I lived alone before and I'm not changin' anything now. Leave me alone, all of you. Quit clutterin' up my life."

It's easy to place someone in a nursing home if they aren't playing "with a full deck," but when an alert adult chooses where to go next, that's his right. The patient-care coordinator

is the one to call on for help. You should know one thing first—
the patient's children are the "first line of defense." The criteria
for placing a patient in a nursing home are just as strict as those
for placing a patient in the hospital. "Unable to care for himself" is not one of the criteria if the insurance company is to pay
the bill.

The stigma attached to the old-fashioned asylum or poorhouse
that was the dread of everyone fifty years ago has transferred
itself now to the "nursing home." It is doubtful that there is one
of us who has not said, "They'll never put me in one of those
nursing homes."

Old folks are not considered to be people any longer. "Undesirable" is the word or "long-term patient," "unmanageable,"
"heavy care" or "senile," cold as the steel that surrounds the
bank vault's heart. These are the patients the wealthiest society
in the entire world somehow cannot afford; a sad commentary
on an urban civilization that sinks millions into performing-arts
centers, mass-transit systems, enormous convention centers,
and sports stadiums. We have not yet found a suitable means of
caring for our aged. Volumes could be written about the social
issues surrounding "nursing home," but in the meantime there
are a few things you should know so you can differentiate one
"nursing home" from another.

The bottom line is your pocketbook. Whether or not insurance
will foot the bill depends upon your coverage, the facility you select, and the criteria under which you are admitted. The first
thing you should do is ask the discharge planner about your options. If you need just slightly less care than that offered in a
hospital, a skilled nursing facility is indicated; extended care facilities (sometimes called convalescent homes) are for those who
need minimal care; and intermediate care facilities are for those
in between. The skilled and intermediate offer medical care on
a twenty-four-hour basis.

The discharge planner totes around the volumes of information that determine what level of care you require after hospitalization. Once that's established, then she can tell you which
facilities accept patients with your type of insurance. Some facilities are "approved" by your insurance carrier and some are
not, while some accept Medicare patients and others do not.

Once that's settled, there are a few other things to consider. Your physician usually won't travel very far to visit you, so if you choose a facility out of his area, you must be transferred into the care of another one contacted by your doctor. Timing is also important, since the one bed available in a good facility may be occupied by tomorrow. This is where your discharge planner can be invaluable. She gives the patient's advocate a list of likely facilities, those she thinks would suit the patient's needs, and asks the family members to go take a look and see what they think. When they come back to her with a decision, she often "pulls strings" to reserve a bed. In fact, she might reserve beds in more than one facility just in case plans go awry.

The "Right" One

How do you choose the right facility once you've a list of possibilities in hand? Well, there's one basic fact to keep in mind: for the aged, there is no "right" facility. Unless you can give them their favorite old rocker that looks out at the lavender wisteria vine they planted years and years ago; unless you can give them the old porcelain wall clock with the little Dutch girl printed in blue and the hands that imitate a windmill, hanging on the same wall above the stove; unless you can give them the sturdy, wide windowsill on which they've always braced themselves while climbing out of the bathtub; unless you give them the same little children running home from school in front of their porch every day; and unless you can give them a mailbox to shuffle to every morning, you really can give them nothing.

You may choose the facility that has "a very progressive activities program," but don't be surprised if Grandma is not the least bit interested in the latest craft projects or bingo games. You may choose the facility with the bright, flowered wallpaper in the dining room, but there is no wallpaper to substitute for the walls at home, however drab they might be.

It is not "the place" that matters to the aged, it is the loss of the familiar, the loss of control over their environment, the loss of dignity, the loss of cherished solitude on occasion, the loss of the feel of their own towels, their own furniture. You cannot choose the "right" place.

There is probably something more depressing than looking for a facility in which to place a relative, but I'm not sure what it is. You simply have to pull yourself together and do it. What should be your criteria? Choose the place that *feels right* to you. Then don't try to talk Grandma into liking it and don't drown in guilt when she begs to be taken away. You've done the best you can.

When you've found the right place, you'll know it, you'll feel it in the pit of your stomach, and that's all it takes. Once Grandma's safely stowed away, you'll have the urge to go out and buy her perky nightgowns, fluffy slippers, boxes of candy, and soft ruffled brunch coats. But you cannot buy Grandma happiness. Bring her the ragged old robe she has worn for years, the slippers that now look disreputable, and the pink gown that lost its perky look many years ago. Bring her the old faded quilt that's frayed along the edges and the old china jar that holds her hairpins, postage stamps, hairnet, and cotton balls. Bring her all the identity and security blankets you can fit into her small space and she'll have everything that you can possibly give her. Then shake the guilt from your shoulders—you can do no more.

HOSPICE

For all of us there comes a time when curative treatment is no longer possible. It is for this situation that the hospice has been designed to meet the patient's physical, psychological, and spiritual needs. At some point, doctors must step back from technology and allow nature to take its course.

Says Dr. John Lee, director of a California hospice, "It's a matter of switching hats, of balancing your scientific mind against the more humanitarian aspect. You use all the tools of medicine—drugs, radiation, surgery—and when you reach the point where prolonging life is futile, you must put on another hat to help the patient die a good death. It's hard to know when to change hats, but easier when you have the hospice to back you up."

Historically, the hospice movement began with the famous St. Christopher Hospice in London, the acknowledged prototype of hospice care. The approach is now sweeping this country and is increasingly fostered and funded by the federal government, the National Cancer Institute, Medicare, Medicaid, Blue Cross, private insurers, corporations, foundations, and scores of individuals.

The hospice may be a special building or home where the terminally ill may go to die in peace, but in most cases it is quite simply an approach, an attitude toward death, a specialized health-care program backed up by trained support teams that can work in one's home or in a special section of a hospital or nursing home. Focus is on the management of pain and other symptoms associated with terminal illness, as well as on total care for the patient and family to minimize the impact of the two greatest fears of dying: pain and isolation at the very end.

Doctors traditionally have been directed toward curing the patient and the dying aspect has largely been ignored. "Cure" is the physician's raison d'être, after all, and death is but a manifestation of failure.

Surrounded by life-sustaining machinery, isolated from the mainstream of life, and regimented by the bureaucracy of modern hospitals, our terminally ill are denied the right to a "good" death, a painfree death, a peaceful death. We are a society focused on the start of life, with only fleeting thoughts of "the end."

We are also a sophisticated society with the technological means to prolong dying long after sustaining life has ceased to be a remote possibility. We have the machinery to play God, though we have not quite reached a consensus on whether God would prolong dying in the name of sustaining life, and we feel legally bound to use the machines we have created, at least in the acute-care hospitals.

And we are an hysterical society, phobic about drugs, violently opposed to the routine use of narcotic pain medications even in terminal-cancer patients. Heroin, indisputably useful in handling terminal pain, is an emotionally charged social issue, legally classified as a "Schedule 1" drug, one with "no medical usefulness" and high potential for abuse. In Britain they are using an elixir called Brompton's Mixture for the control of terminal pain, containing heroin or cocaine, alcohol, and a phenothiazine such as Compazine or Thorazine—"a satisfactory method of relieving pain, nausea, vomiting, depressed moods and other unpleasant side effects of terminal illness when given every four hours around the clock while the patient is awake. It is taken by mouth."

In the beginning, the terminally ill patient is accepted into a hospice program at his/her own request, upon referral by a physician—on an outpatient basis, with the patient remaining at home. Home support is provided by a team of nurses, social workers, physicians, psychologists, physical therapists, and pastoral counselors. The goal is to enable the patient to carry on an alert and pain-free existence and provide a constant flow of information, assistance, and support for the family. Pain is controlled with a carefully calculated dose of a morphine-based elixir similar to Brompton's Mixture and every effort is made to keep the entire family as comfortable as possible.

FOR ADVOCATES

Long-term terminal illness is usually cancer. If you think of cancer as "eating away" at your patient, you're like most people, but wrong. The body contains billions of cells, all with a structure and function, that depend on oxygen and nutrients. Malignant cells behave abnormally, multiply too fast, and consume too much of the body's store of oxygen and nutrients. If these cells are in a mass, the mass may grow to encroach upon vital organs. Cancer is not a "bug" that "eats." It is a condition in which cells have gone awry.

"Metastasis," or "metastatic," or "metastasizing" all refer to the spreading of malignant cells. For instance, if the doctor says, "The primary site was the lungs, but it has metastasized to the brain," he means the malignant-cell production began in the lungs and then one or more cells traveled to the brain and began reproducing there as well.

Toward the end, when families feel they can no longer handle the burden, the patient is transferred to a room at the hospice which is intended to resemble a hospital room as little as possible. Visiting hours are unlimited, family members may sleep in the same room (at no extra charge) to dispel the loneliness that every dying person fears, children and pets are encouraged to visit, patients can eat whatever they want, whenever they want, and pain is controlled so well that no patient has to ask for relief. Above all else, there is no life-sustaining (death-prolonging) equipment standing by, ready to be used to reverse the situation in the final moments.

The final approach in the hospice concept is the care of the family, which continues through the period of bereavement. Over one hundred hospice programs are in various stages of planning and development in thirty-four states. If you would like information regarding those available in your area, contact the National Hospice Organization, New Haven, Connecticut 06511.

HOME CARE

To be ill is to experience the most profound vulnerability and deep loneliness, to fear the known and the unknown, to dread the coming of night with its relentless vortex of memories, to be proven incapable of controlling life, to reveal one's lack of courage and to realize that there is no protective other within the dark corners of the mind. To be ill is to rearrange life's priorities into alien perspectives, to endure that which once seemed intolerable, to find tears where none were before, and to wait, and wait, and wait—wait for someone to come, someone to hear, someone to care, someone to understand, someone to bring pain relief, someone to speak reassuring words, someone to smile, someone to do for us all that we so easily took for granted in the past. To be ill in a hospital is to feel alone on a deserted island.

"I cannot care for him at home," she sobbed. "Look at me, I'm ill myself. This past year has taken a terrible toll on me. My sister told me I can't take care of him at home. I simply can't do it," and she crumpled deeper into the bench by the window. Eventually she admitted fear. "What if something happens that I can't handle?" she asked. The something she referred to was death.

"Will he choke?" Her eyes were wide with terror. "I could stand anything, but not choking. I've never seen anyone die," and she began a fresh round of weeping. Each day the guilt weighed more heavily as Mac begged her to take him home and each day she pleaded with us, in roundabout ways, to tell her what death looked like. On the third day she capitulated to his pleadings, "I'll take him home if you'll teach me how to take care of him."

We began teaching her the most difficult first, how to give his injections of pain relievers. She practiced first on oranges: the *feel* is similar, but the *thought* bears no resemblance. Courage is what she needed, and Mac provided that. Knowing he was going home had given him hope, false hope, but hope and the high that goes with it. He teased her, "Shoot me, baby, anywhere you want. You can't hurt me." She finally did, wincing until her eyes were so tightly shut she might as well have been blind. If it hurt, Mac would never have said so.

We arranged for the rental of oxygen and suction devices, showed her how to use them, and taught her how to perform his tube feedings. On the sixth day Mac went home. We barely waited for the ambulance to arrive there before we were on the phone. This was a first for us and a first for Mac and his wife; success seemed imperative.

We called her every morning, but on the eighth day she called us before we got a chance. Mac had died. He had simply slipped away. No huge traumatic final-moment drama, no terrible guttural sounds, no horrible, twisted clutching at life—simply a peaceful slipping away.

And that's what death looks like. I've never seen it any other way. I don't think it happens any other way. Time passes between each breath until finally there are no more. That's all.

Death is dramatized in stories and on tv much the same way love is dramatized and neither is consistent with reality. The horror in dying, if indeed there is horror, is the psychological trauma of facing one's vulnerability and the physical trauma of adjusting dosages until the right pain reliever in the right amount is found—and all that takes place long before actual death.

If you're considering home care, whether the patient is terminally ill or not, there are dozens of resources to help you such as clever lifting devices, Visiting Nurses, and all the other aids mentioned earlier in this chapter. You have only to see one long-term patient being cared for at home to become convinced that the rewards are incalculable.

More often than not, learning to give injections is not a problem, since pain-relieving elixirs are becoming more popular and are given by mouth. Anyone can learn how to work oxygen and suction—in fact, it has been contended that one could teach a monkey the technical aspects of nursing. You don't need a sophisticated education to learn how to care for one patient, but you do need courage, which is easier to come by if you realize there really is no great mystery to the act of dying.

Death at home is not the norm in our society, unfortunately, but it is becoming far more common each year, and as it does the legal details are becoming more manageable. A physician must pronounce the patient dead before a mortuary can proceed, then the county coroner must be notified that the physician has so complied. The first thing you must do then in an at-home death is phone the physician and then the mortuary.

To suffer a loved one's fatal illness—perhaps that is the greatest suffering there is. To help them to a peaceful end is some small assuagement. You *can* do it. You'll be forever happy that you did.

FOR ADVOCATES

There's something unsettling and frightening about being in a room alone with a patient who is dying. Nurses feel it no matter how often they are exposed to it. You might feel that way also, in which case it's a good idea to have someone with you in the final hours. It doesn't have to be someone close to you—just someone stable so you won't lose touch with reality and allow fear to get a tight grip on you.

In the hospital or a hospice, one of the nurses will make every effort to be with you, but it's very often difficult for her to leave other patients alone for extended periods of time.

If you have no other option, you can always arrange to have

a private-duty nurse stay in the room at all times. Call the nursing supervisor (there's one on duty around the clock) and ask her to assist you with this. She has access to nursing registries and perhaps can choose among them to find the best nurse to fit the situation.

Private-duty nurses are rarely covered by the patient's medical insurance, but check with the insurance carrier to see if there might be certain conditions under which they will pay the bill. Sometimes a doctor's order is all that's necessary, in which case you simply phone the doctor and tell him what you want and why.

If you're caring for the patient at home and need a private-duty nurse, first phone the Visiting Nurses Association. If that doesn't work out, look in the Yellow Pages of the phone book under Nursing Registries and hire one yourself. The cost is about $100 for each eight-hour shift.

CHAPTER

15
Ultimate Crisis

THE CODE

"Dr. Stat, Four West, Dr. Stat, Four West," the Mayday urgency of the intercom freezes forks in midair and slices a swath of silence through the cafeteria, straightening every spine. As though on command, forks drop, chairs tumble, and members of the code team race for the door.

In all other areas of the hospital, syringes are held suspended, conversation stops in midsentence, and the phones are menacingly silent—total immobility follows a "Dr. Stat" call while each staff member runs through in his head the litany of potential victims to determine if he is about to lose a patient, a friend. To staff members, there is no hospital drama to equal a "Dr. Stat" call.

Whether it's "Code Blue," "Dr. Heart Stat," "Dr. Blue," "Code Ninety-nine," or "Dr. Stat," the staff response is the same; code physicians in the hospital are expected to take the fastest route to the scene specified to collide with three nurses, two respiratory therapists, an electrocardiogram technician, the house supervisor, a central-services clerk, and a nurse with a rolling "crash cart."

While there are various terms used to indicate impending crisis (a "code"), you will instantly recognize the urgency of the situation just by the voice on the intercom and the sudden silence. If you should miss that, you'll know something has happened because staff members invariably move about like figures in a slow-motion movie for the first few minutes following a code.

Only the code team moves with lightning speed; they are the stars in the drama, the staff members who have been assigned to retrieve life on the brink of expiration.

And what of you, the terrified patient who recognizes the gasp of crisis or the visitor who is caught in the flying feet of the code team? This is one time your best bet is to stand clear, pretend you don't notice the pandemonium, rearrange the flowers on the bedside table, discuss the weather, and be tickled pink that you are nothing more than a hospital number or a pedestrian at the scene of an accident.

If you involuntarily say, "Thank God, it's not me," that's okay. God probably gets more messages during a code than at any other time. While the uninvolved thank God, the involved plead with God. Even those who claim no God clamor to involve God during a code, for these are matters of life and death.

Technically, a code means a patient has ceased breathing or lost a palpable pulse and blood is not carrying oxygen to the vital organs. Death is about four minutes away. The first person to find the patient in distress has pushed the code button and begun cardiopulmonary resuscitation (CPR), which is mouth-to-mouth breathing for the patient, in conjunction with compressions of the chest to keep the heart pumping blood through the body. While almost all hospital employees are trained in the techniques of CPR as a condition of employment, the code team is generally a group specifically designated to respond to codes with a vast array of lifesaving equipment and medications.

THE DILEMMA

In days gone by, the results of the code were clear-cut: either the patient responded to the efforts of the code team and survived the sudden cessation of respirations and/or pulse or the efforts of the team were futile and the patient expired. No human decision was required.

Today, however, technological advances have brought us the respirator, which causes the definition of "death" to be almost as obscure as the definition of "life." Is the fetus a "life" at the moment of conception, or not until the brain begins to function, or not until the infant begins breathing automatically in response to the delivering physician's first pat on the back? Is a person "dead" when the heart stops beating, or when the brain ceases functioning, or when breathing is no longer independent and automatic? The case of Karen Ann Quinlan is legendary, brought about by the ability of the medical community to sustain breathing through use of the respirator (ventilator), even after the brain has ceased its normal functioning capacity and the patient might otherwise have been termed "dead."

"Mechanical maintenance of life . . . a tribute to our wizards of technology . . . a miraculous advance in medicine," say some. Others pronounce the respirators "the work of a mad sadist, a curse, an inhuman prolongation of death."

Such moral, ethical and legal dilemmas as those precipitated by the respirators fill volumes of pages in medical and nursing journals, since all of us in the profession play a part when crisis calls and each of us has our own perception of "what's right." This is the crux of the problem! *Who* should "pull the plug"? How much of God's work are we tinkering with?

You may not be able to answer such questions but there's a very good chance that you, sometime in your life, will be either the patient or the patient's advocate and be faced with the decisions that surround a crisis. You should have enough information to at least approach the choices so that the outcome is acceptable.

THE PROBLEM

Tim was standing in four feet of water when he was swept out into the ocean by a wave. His friend found him floating face down, dragged him to shore and resuscitated him. When he arrived at the hospital he was promptly placed on mechanical ventilation.

Some days later I asked his intensive care nurse what her expectations were for his recovery. She replied, sadly shaking her head, "No chance, anoxia [lack of oxygen] is definite."

The next day I asked a physician the same question. "No response," he said. "He'll go soon ... hasn't a chance, but the parents don't believe that."

The next day I asked Lynne, another nurse. "Looks good," she said. "He came off the respirator today ... breathing on his own. Hey, I'm a neuro nurse ... I've seen lots of these wake up."

"He didn't have a head injury, Lynne, it's the head injuries that wake up." I wanted to believe her but didn't.

"All I want is a chance," she said. "Look how much better he looks today. I called his mother and told her he needed high-top tennis shoes to keep him from getting foot-drop and she was here with them in half an hour. His whole family works with him every day to keep his muscles from going. The least we can do is give him a chance. Let me work with him ... give me a couple of weeks."

Today he sits up in a chair. He blinks on command. He opens his eyes when he is called by name. Next week or next month or next year, he may speak, but there's not one single soul on this earth who can predict if that will ever happen. Tim is twenty-four.

THE OTHER SIDE OF THE COIN

Karen Ann Quinlan, near Tim's age, and also a victim of anoxia, was given "no chance" unanimously and taken off the respirator. She still lies in a coma several years later. She lives only because she was put on the respirator in the beginning as was Tim.

One nurse has told me that she has seen a patient, whose life was retrieved by a ventilator, recover and walk out of the hospital. I have never seen such a case, but I have seen patients still maintained on a respirator a year after they were first resuscitated.

There are no statistics available on successful resuscitations, and if there were I'm not sure they would be of any value to you. How many chances are enough? If we can "save" one life in a hundred, is it worth resuscitating everyone "just in case" their life is that one? What if it's one in five hundred, or one in a thousand, or one in five thousand? Now to the nitty-gritty—what if it's your wife or husband?

PULLING THE PLUG

There was a patient on a ventilator for whom all the experts, nurses, physicians, and family agreed there was "no chance." There was a chance, however, for two other people awaiting transplants if Sandy's kidneys and heart could be donated, which is what her family wanted.

For technical reasons, the organs would have to be removed *before* the respirator was disconnected. I wondered who then would pull the plug. The question was redundant, of course, since a body will not go on living when kidney and heart function has ceased, despite the respirator. The answers I got when polling the nurses were interesting. All but one said, "I'm sorry, I just can't do it. The doctor will have to do it."

And we wonder about the deification of the physician! We all think it our right to ask him to play God when life is down to the very short strokes. Each physician handles this dilemma in his own way. Dr. Acton was sharp. He told me, "If the family does not want Gene resuscitated, then they can write that in his chart."

"But Dr. Acton," I protested, "he's nothing more than a sliver of what he was, his whole body is riddled with cancer, there's no way of saving him. Why should we call a code on someone, send them to ICU, resuscitate them several times, only to prolong their dying? Is there some remote chance that you will save him?"

He sighed, a heavy sigh of frustration. "Look, it ought to be obvious that there is no way we are going to save him, but if we don't resuscitate him until it simply stops working, here's what'll happen. Three years from now his family will open the morning newspaper and read that some scientists have found cancer can be cured if the patient drinks a mixture of boiled eel and the spleen of a toad. Then the family will sue me because I let Gene die without trying everything there was to try. No, I won't write 'No code,' but the family can if they want to."

I approached Gene's family, who had been pleading with me to get Dr. Acton to write "No code" on Gene's chart, and told them that Dr. Acton felt he could not take that responsibility, that he was aware that there was no chance for Gene, but that he was obligated to call the rescue team if Gene should stop breathing. The family could not bring themselves to write the order. They agonized for days, phoned distant relatives, gathered all the closest of kin, arrived at a consensus—but there wasn't one of them who would take the responsibility of writing the order on Gene's chart. If they all could have held the pen at the same time and written it, then no one person would have felt the impact of "playing God," though some would say we are taking away God's options if we *do* resuscitate.

Some physicians would have written the order and some nurses would pull the plug if the physician so instructs. There are several variations on the theme. If you happen to know exactly what you want in your final hours, you need to know your alternatives and the best way to accomplish them. But first be aware of this: it is policy in most hospitals, if not all, to resuscitate *any* patient who has a cardiac or respiratory arrest and to place the patient on a ventilator if that assistance is needed. If that is what you want read no further.

On the other hand, if you have definitely concluded that you do not want to be resuscitated or kept alive by a respirator, the only sure way to avoid it is to stay out of the hospital because in a crisis situation the first person at the scene flies into action without stopping to ask if the patient or family has requested resuscitation.

THE RIGHT TO DIE

In late 1976, California passed the first right-to-die law and one hundred thousand forms were placed in doctors' offices for patients who wanted to exercise this right. Only a handful have used the forms. Since that time, most other states have passed some sort of legislation, much of it based on California's Natural Death Act.

The act is difficult to read, first because the whole topic is so emotion-laden and second because it is a legal document. Let me sift through it for you and point out the salient features:

1. There are three parts to executing the act:
   Directive to Physicians

Verification of Patient's Directive
Certification of Terminal Condition

2. Directive to the physician must be signed by the patient and witnessed by two people who are not related, not heirs, not creditors, not employees of the hospital or physician, and not the physician. The form is valid for five years.
3. If the patient has been diagnosed as pregnant, the directive has no effect.
4. The directive may be revoked at any time by the patient.
5. The physician is *obligated* to honor the document only if fourteen days have passed since the time he diagnosed the patient as "terminal" and the time the patient signed the document. That is, there is a fourteen-day waiting period after one is diagnosed; you do not have the "right to die" during that time, at least by California law, unless the physician *chooses* to honor your directive.
6. The person who accepts the directive completes a verification form which simply acknowledges receipt.
7. Two physicians must sign the Certification of Terminal Condition. Without that, the patient's directive is invalid.

What does it mean to you? Nothing! Really, nothing! As you can see, there are too many constraints on it. To illustrate how useless it is: Karen Ann Quinlan would never have been covered under this act because she never signed a directive. In fact, fourteen days after two physicians sign the Certification of Terminal Condition form, it's doubtful that the patient would be able to communicate his or her wishes.

Furthermore, you already have more power than this law allows you, just by virtue of the fact that you can refuse medical care at any time. To administer treatment that the patient does not want is to commit assault and battery.

If the law in your state is as useless as the one in California, then you still have two options: (1) Write to the Euthanasia Education Council, 250 West Fifty-seventh Street, New York, New York 10019, ask for a Living Will, and file it with your doctor, with copies to your lawyer, a close family member, and your wallet. On each of these copies, be sure to write the location of the original. (2) Your physician has the authority to make the decision that you will not be resuscitated or kept alive by mechanical means. You can request *in writing* on your medical record that he exercise that authority. He has the right to refuse, in which case you have a right to find a physician who will not refuse.

HEMLOCK

Those who are deeply committed to the rights of the terminally ill are forming societies supporting active voluntary euthanasia throughout the world. One such group, Hemlock, was organized in mid-August 1980 for the United States.

"Self-deliverance" is the term such societies use, and their principle is that the final decision to terminate life is ultimately one's own. Early in 1981 Hemlock expects to make available their book of informational material in order to help members decide the manner and means of their own death.

For more information on this concept, write Hemlock, 2803 Ocean Park Boulevard, Santa Monica, California 90405, or call (213) 391-1871. While you may not agree with the objectives of these groups, active euthanasia is bound to be a big topic during the next few years, both in the news and in the courts, and you'll want to be able to make responsible and knowledgeable judgments and decisions.

THE WORDS YOU USE MAKE A DIFFERENCE

"Heroics" cover a lot of territory, most of it subject to opinion. That which is "heroic" to me might be ordinary procedure to you, which is why you must specify exactly what you *don't* want in the way of treatment.

Natural death can be prevented by drugs, resuscitation, and/or mechanical ventilation, in varying situations and conditions. *Resuscitation* (CPR), a "crisis call," is what the paramedics do "reviving" one whose heart or breathing stops. *Mechanical maintenance of life* refers to ventilators, which keep forcing oxygen into your lungs. These are the machines referred to in "pull the plug" decisions. *Drugs* to sustain life are usually used in conjunction with resuscitation and/or mechanical maintenance, but natural death is more likely to occur without them since there is a point at which the body defies any sort of treatment.

You must choose just how much effort you want expended and specify your wishes by using any or all of the underlined words, preceded by the word "no."

One thing more—it is much easier morally and legally to "do nothing" than to "pull the plug." What is done is very difficult to undo, if respirators are the issue.

CANCER

If you've read this far, then it's likely you're made of strong stuff and can tolerate a discussion of such an ominous subject. You probably hate to even read the word "cancer." We're all looking for euphemisms for it, so you're not alone.

You get up in the morning and shower, put on your deodorant that may contain a carcinogenic substance, then sprinkle on some talc that is carcinogenic, dry your hair with one of those hair dryers containing a carcinogenic substance, take your daily birth-control pill which may be carcinogenic, get dressed, and drink a cup of coffee which will harm your heart eventually. Hop in your car that emits carcinogenic fumes and drive to work behind all those other spewers of carcinogens, work all morning in your office that is located in an area the Environmental Protection Agency has identified as carcinogenic. Brush your hair at noon and spray on some hair spray to keep it in place—this also sprays carcinogens around. Go to Joe's Place and eat a barbecued hamburger (watch out, the charcoal is carcinogenic), and drink a diet soda with a warning label on it because it may also be carcinogenic. Then work four more hours and hope none of your co-workers are puffing out their carcinogenic cigarette smoke in your direction. Drive home in a sea of carcinogenic exhaust fumes, and drop into your easy chair with a drink—which is what you've been looking forward to since noon. But watch it! That cherry in your Manhattan, which is really the best part of the whole drink, has red dye in it that is thought to be carcinogenic too.

Settle down to a peaceful dinner now, if you don't mind clogging up your arteries with cholesterol from eating steak and you don't mind the radiation from the microwave oven where you baked your potato. Do watch out for the pesticides on the lettuce and tomatoes in your salad. Then you could watch tv, but remember there is a certain amount of radiation emitted by tv sets.

Enough said about how you can get cancer or how you can avoid it. . . .

If You Have It

There are over a hundred different types of the disease commonly called cancer. Not all of them indicate an automatic death sentence—the cure rate varies from 0 percent to 100 percent.

Be sure to find a doctor who specializes in cancer, an oncologist, and be sure your hospital offers a cancer program, since such a program will help you and your family through these days of crisis. The "unknown" will probably be the basis of all your fears and the professionals engaged in cancer programs are experts in stamping out those unknowns. Be sure you telephone the American Cancer Society and take advantage of the tremendous services they have to offer.

After diagnosis, you're likely to have the multiple options of surgery, radiation, and chemotherapy, or any combination of the three. Whatever the treatment, the reactions to it might vary from none to debilitating. There are side effects that are so devastating as to make one think the end is quite near, but that is *often* not the case, so don't give up. You might not have any reaction at all.

FOR ADVOCATES

The two overwhelming fears related to dying are fear of pain and fear of isolation. "I don't care how I die, I just don't want to suffer," say most people. They probably are remembering stories of relatives or friends who have died painfully. Unfortunately, there are such things as "agonizing deaths," ones where the patient is begging to be released from pain, but they are becoming less and less frequent as patient advocacy increases.

The typical "agonizing" situation is one in which the physician has ordered pain medication that simply is not effective. The nurse contacts the physician, asks him to increase the dosage, and he replies, "He's already getting a maximum dose," or "His tolerance has built up. Do you want him to become an addict? If you give him any more, you're likely to overdose him."

Such situations are devastating for the patient, the family, and the nurses. The physician does not want to be charged with overdosing or addicting the patient. However, you must keep in mind that there is no reason to allow a patient to suffer in the last stages of life. You, the patient's advocate, are the one who holds the power in this situation. If 10 milligrams of morphine won't control the pain, 20 might, or if 150 milligrams of Demerol doesn't work, 250 might. We have been known to give 50 milligrams of morphine directly into the vein, hourly, for several days, to control the pain of a dying patient. Yes, that's a huge amount of narcotic and, yes, that much morphine would probably bury you or me, but terminally ill patients can build narcotic tolerance levels that are astounding. There is no moral or legal limitation on the amount of narcotic that can be administered to a terminally ill patient. That being the case you would expect a humane approach by *all* physicians. That doesn't always happen, for whatever reason, and here's how to handle it:

1. Call the physician and ask him why your patient is not painfree. No matter what reason he gives you, tell him you want him to change the medication orders. If he changes them your patient should be comfortable within a half hour. If he doesn't change them, regardless of his reason, go on to step two.
2. Go to the nursing station and ask for the supervisor. Tell her of the patient's plight and ask her to intercede. She has two choices: placate you or persuade the physician to change the order. If she attempts to placate you, go on to step three.
3. Ask the supervisor for the name of the chief of staff. She

may call him or you may call him yourself and outline the problem. If he decides to intercede, he will call the patient's physician and attempt to get a change in orders, or he may decide to write new orders himself. If he chooses to stay uninvolved, which is his right, go on to step four.

4. Keep calm and rational while you tell the supervisor you have exhausted all your resources for obtaining pain control and that you wish to advise her that you intend to file a malpractice suit against the physician, the nurses, the chief of staff, and the hospital. This is tantamount to saying to the security person checking you in at the airport, "Today would be a good day to hijack a 747 over Denver." Mention malpractice in a hospital and you can expect rapid responses from some very important people. But just in case you couldn't keep the hysteria out of your voice and you are not being taken seriously, consider step five as your last resort.

5. Ask the nurses for the names of some physicians they know who have a "humane approach to dying" (use those words so they'll know exactly what you mean). You can count on the nurses being eager to supply you with names because few situations evoke as much sympathy in them as the one in which you are now involved. Now call the patient's physician and tell him you would like Dr. Whatever to consult on the case immediately. If he protests, tell him you either want a consultation or a new physician. Legally, he must withdraw from the case. Be sure some other doctor is called in if you indeed have chosen to "fire" him.

While you are learning how to play the patient's advocate, nurses too are learning that they also have the right and the moral obligation to press for death with dignity for their patients. While in the past they may have simply huddled in groups discussing the unsympathetic approaches some physicians have to dying, more often they are using problem-solving techniques and confronting the physician straight on. In fact, the really progressive nurse will go through the first three steps for you without your even knowing anything's happening. Many nurses, though, were trained in the days when a nurse simply followed the physician's orders despite the consequences for the patient, and it might be a few years before they become comfortable confronting doctors.

Also, if you're the advocate of a dying patient, please read *Death and Dying*, by Elizabeth Kübler-Ross, so that you are well acquainted with the stages you can expect to see manifested in some devastating emotions toward you. You may well be the target of the dying patient's anger and he may well be the target of your anger. Anger is the heart's way of crying out, "How could you abandon me like this?" You may be rejected or you may reject the patient, which is a rationalization that prepares you for separation. "I'm not going to miss you. I never loved you anyway. All you've ever done is clutter up my life."

Expect to see a regression to childlike behavior too, in which the patient is so self-absorbed as to appear to exclude you and everyone else from his thoughts. He's retreating, "climbing into the safety of infancy."

The mind is full of coping mechanisms and you're likely to see them all in the patient as well as in yourself. We've all been socialized to cling to life. Living is the thing we do best. We pull out all the stops when confronted with the end of life. Somehow we must cope.

If You Think You Have Cancer But Don't

The five stages of death and dying have been written about enough, so that everyone knows what the experts think you should go through when you've been told your number is up— and one does go through all those stages. One area they don't cover is what happens when you've been told you probably have a terminal illness and it turns out you don't have one at all.

The experts expect the average, normal human being to rejoice wildly and pick up the threads of life where they were dropped when the death sentence was first handed down, but that is not really the way it happens.

In reality, you reach a stage in the process where you shed all responsibility and convince yourself that the advantages of shedding that responsibility come very close to equaling the advantages of staying alive—so close that each problem in life becomes very simplified. "Well, I won't have to worry about *that* anymore." "How nice, that's someone else's problem now." The "should do this" and "must do that" of life become meaningless.

This shedding of responsibility is subconscious, of course, which is why you may feel overwhelmed when your terminal diagnosis turns out to be an error, especially if it's taken several weeks or more to find out you are not doomed after all. The doctor pronounces your condition "benign." Right away you think about the bills that have to be paid, the work that's piling up on your desk, the social obligations you've neglected, the relationships that need repair, and the lawn that needs mowing. It's depressing, but normal.

IN CONCLUSION

"We Americans must learn how to look at death," say the experts. "We don't know how to face it squarely and consider it just another step in the journey through life." I submit that one cannot expect human beings, who have spent their entire lives fighting for survival, to give in gracefully. We install fire alarms, safety belts, and bomb shelters to protect us. We carry assault whistles in our pockets, we get a five-minute spiel on how to bail out safely when we start a plane flight, we have government agencies policing other agencies to see that we come to no harm. We wear life jackets in boats, spend millions to clean up the air, devote the major portion of our lives to working so we can keep food on the table and a roof over our heads. Where are we supposed to get the mental set that says, "Okay, now you can give up the fight for survival"?

It is difficult. The most difficult thing we'll ever do. We are all clingers at heart.

EPILOGUE

It is important to acknowledge once again that the patient is the decision-maker when the topics in this book seem to reflect alternatives that are not promoted by the medical community. Some topics are more controversial than others, which simply means the patient will have more difficulty arriving at a decision.

Indeed, even those who practice medicine often disagree on such topics as cardiac catheterization, coronary bypass surgery, estrogen-replacement therapy, and aggressive treatment of terminal disease. The quality of life is at stake in these matters, and only you can define what "quality" means to you.

Appendix

A PATIENT'S BILL OF RIGHTS

1. The patient has the right to considerate and respectful care.
2. The patient has the right to obtain from his physician complete current information concerning his diagnosis, treatment, and prognosis in terms the patient can be reasonably expected to understand.
3. The patient has the right to receive from his physician information necessary to give informed consent prior to the start of any procedure and/or treatment. Except in emergencies, such information for informed consent should include but not necessarily be limited to the specific procedure and/or treatment, the medically significant risks involved, and the probable duration of incapacitation.
4. The patient has the right to refuse treatment to the extent permitted by law, and to be informed of the medical consequences of his action.
5. The patient has the right to every consideration of his privacy concerning his own medical care program. Case discussion, consultation, examination, and treatment are confidential and should be conducted discreetly. Those not directly involved in his care must have the permission of the patient to be present.
6. The patient has the right to expect that all communications and records pertaining to his care should be treated as confidential.
7. The patient has the right to expect that within its capacity a hospital must make reasonable response to the request of a patient for service.... When medically permissible a patient may be transferred to another facility only after he has received complete information and explanation concerning the needs for and alternatives to such a transfer.
8. The patient has the right to obtain information as to any relationship of his hospital to other health care and educational institutions insofar as his care is concerned.
9. The patient has the right to be advised if the hospital proposes to engage in or perform human experimentation af-

fecting his care or treatment. The patient has the right to refuse to participate in such research projects.

10. The patient has the right to expect reasonable continuity of care. He has the right to know in advance what appointment times and physicians are available and when. The patient has the right to expect that the hospital will provide a mechanism whereby he is informed by his physician or a delegate of the physician of the patient's continuing health.

—American Hospital Association

A MENTAL PATIENT'S RIGHTS

1. To wear his own clothes; to keep and use his own personal possessions.
2. To have access to individual storage space for his private use.
3. To see visitors each day.
4. To have reasonable access to telephones, both to make and receive confidential calls.
5. To have ready access to letter-writing materials.
6. To refuse shock treatment.
7. To refuse psychosurgery.
8. Other rights, as specified by regulation.

A GUIDE TO CUTTING MEDICAL BILLS

- Hospital "shop"—rates do vary.
- Join a health-maintenance organization.
- Reduce your checkups if you're healthy.
- If you're to be hospitalized, have the admitting physical completed in the physician's office.

- Laws are moving toward abolishing "routine" lab tests demanded for hospitalization; watch for this and refuse any lab tests that are done just for routine purposes.
- Studies indicate the five-hour glucose tolerance test is a waste of time and money; refuse it and ask for a fasting blood sugar test instead.
- Find out the *latest* you can appear at the hospital before surgery; you might save a whole day's charge.
- Have surgery done on an outpatient basis when at all possible.
- Keep a list of medications that have been effective for you so that money isn't wasted on trial and error.
- Don't make long-distance calls—they're charged at "operator-assisted" rates and are very expensive.
- Take home any item that has been charged to you—it will only be trashed if you don't.
- Don't use the emergency room for anything but a real emergency.
- If you decide to leave against medical advice, check with your insurance company to be sure they will still cover your bill.
- Check the cardiac rehabilitation and kidney dialysis units; some profiteering has been known to take place in these specialties.
- For alcoholic rehabilitation programs, "shop" for one based on Alcoholics Anonymous.
- Get a second opinion before surgery; one out of five operations can be avoided.
- Get up and moving after surgery to save money and prevent illness.
- *Never* have diagnostic testing done in the hospital that you can arrange to have done on an outpatient basis.
- "Shop" outpatient labs for the best price.
- Insist that all noninvasive tests be tried first before you submit to invasive tests.
- Tell your doctor you want your prescriptions labeled and write on the label the reason you are taking the medication. You may be able to use it again for the same thing.
- Keep a list of what you have in your own drug box and show it to the doctor when he is writing you more prescriptions—you may have something on hand that will work just as well.
- "Shop" for your prescriptions—prices vary considerably.

- Buy in bulk, e.g., a six-month supply of birth-control pills.
- Insist that your physician order medications for you by generic name; there's a 15 to 45 percent difference in price.
- Never buy from a hospital pharmacy unless it is an HMO pharmacy.
- If you think you've been wronged by a physician, try to negotiate with him first. If that doesn't work, ignore your bill; don't be intimidated by collection agencies.
- County hospital charges are based on financial ability; you might have to pay more than at a private hospital.
- If your disease or surgery is complex, spare no expense to get the finest physician in the hospital that specializes in your problem.
- Refuse the services of anyone who comes as a consultant without your prior approval.
- Do *not* attempt to save money by rejecting your right to "shop" for physicians; it may be the most important task of your life.
- Check your hospital bill to be sure:
    Your stay was the same length as you are charged for
    You used the amount of blood you are charged for
    The length of time the doctor says you were in surgery matches the time listed on the bill and the same for anesthesiology
- Question your charges in advance; ask the professionals how much you will be charged.
- "Shop" prudently for health insurance, but don't ever be without it—the average bill for a "final" illness is $22,000.
- Consider alternatives to traditional medical care: meditation, yoga, do-it-yourself diagnostics, or a two-week wait to see if your symptoms disappear.
- Hospice care is worth whatever it costs and usually costs less than a hospital.
- Home care is the least expensive and most satisfactory of all.
- When there is no hope of altering the terminal nature of an illness, the cost of anything other than custodial care for palliative purposes is the biggest waste of money in the health-care industry.
- Refuse treatment in an ICU or CCU unless there is absolutely no alternative.

TRANSLATION OF DOCTOR'S ORDERS

Bedside Signs

Diet

Clear liquid	Jell-O, clear broth, tea, water only
Na	Low salt, usually followed by no. of grams
_____ cal ADA	Diabetic diet preceded by calorie limit
Push fluids	Encourage juices, water, tea, etc.
Restricted fluids	Limit what you drink to a certain amount
Feeder	Someone must help you eat
I&O	Measure all fluids in and out of the body
NPO	Nothing by mouth
Mechanical soft	Diet for patients with poor ability to chew
VMA	Diet of certain foods three days before lab test

Activity

BRP	Bathroom privileges only
BSC	Bedside commode only
OOB	Out of bed, means you must get moving
ROM	Range of motion, exercises for the bedridden
WC	Wheelchair
Ambulate ad lib	Walk around as often as you like
Bedrest	You may not get out of bed for anything
Chair	You must be up in a chair at certain intervals
Lobby privileges	You may go to the lobby to visit
Turn q 2 h	Turn every two hours, usually on the even hours
Up ad lib	Same as Ambulate
HOB up (or down)	Head of bed, usually specified angle follows

Diagnostics

BP stand, sit, lie	Record standing, sitting, and lying blood pressures
Vitals	Temp, pulse, respirations, followed by times
Apical pulse	Taken with a stethoscope placed on your chest
FBS	Fasting blood sugar, a before-meal blood test
Hourly urines	Urine output will be measured every hour
24 h urine	All urine will be collected for a test, twenty-four hours
S&A	Urine test for diabetics (Diastix, Clinitest, etc.); means sugar and acetone.
Clean catch	Cleanse yourself, urinate a bit, catch some urine in specimen jar
Sterile specimen	A catheterized urine specimen
Guaiac, hematest, stool specimen	Guaiac, hematest, and stool are all collections of stool to send to lab for analysis
O₂ _____	Oxygen, followed by number of liters

SAMPLE PRESCRIPTION
Translation appears in parentheses:

James Smith, M.D.
Medical Arts Center of Osho
301 Valley Ave.
Osho, California
(518) 123-4567

Name_____ Date_____

Address_____

Rx: (prescription)
Pro-Banthine Tabs (form) 7.5 mg (strength) #70 (amount)
Sig: (Write on the label)
Tabs ī tid c̄ meals & īī hs
(take 1 tablet three times a day with meals and 2 at bedtime)
LAS (write the name and amount of drug on the label)
Refills__2__ (you can have 210 pills)   DEA#*_____

*The physician's DEA# is his identification number and must accompany his narcotic or controlled-substance prescriptions: stands for Drug Enforcement Administration.

PRESCRIPTION TERMS

āā or a	of each
ad lib	at pleasure
agit	shake, stir
AC	before meals
bid	twice daily
bib	drink
c̄	with
cap	a capsule
comp	compounded of
cont rem	continue the medicine
d	give
dd in d	from day to day
dec	pour off
dexter	the right
dil	dilute, diluted
div	divide
dos	dose
dur dolor	while pain lasts
emp	as directed
febris	fever
garg	gargle
grad	by degrees
gtt	a drop, drops
h	an hour
hs	bedtime
ind	daily
liq	liquid
M	mix
m et n	morning and night
mor dict	in the manner directed
no	number
non rep, nr	not to be repeated

OD	right eye
OL	left eye
pc	after meals
pil	a pill
prn	as necessary
qh	every hour
qid	four times daily
qs	quantity sufficient
qod	every other day
rep	to be repeated
rub	red
sig	write
sing	of each
sol	solution
solv	dissolve
ss	a half
stat	immediately
suppos	suppository
tab	a tablet
tere	rub
tid	three times daily
tinct	tincture
ung	an ointment
ut dict	as directed

CLINICAL RECORD

	N			D			E			N			D			E			N			D			E	

Date

P.O. Day

Temperature

	N			D			E		N			D			E		N			D			E	
	12	4	8	12	4	8	12	4	8	12	4	8	12	4	8	12	4	8	12	4	8	12	4	8

103°
102°
101°
100°
99°
98°
97°
96°

Pulse
140
130
120
110
100
90
80
70
60

Respiration

Blood Pressure

Weight

Lab Work Done

X Rays Taken

Activity

Slept

Stool

Voided

Diet

Appetite G / F / P

MD Visit

Bath — BA SH TU   BA SH TU   BA SH TU

Care — A.M. P.M.   A.M. P.M.   A.M. P.M.

Rails

Nurse's Signature

NURSING ADMISSION ASSESSMENT RECORD

DATE	TIME
ADMITTED TO ROOM	FROM

PER
☐ Ambulatory   ☐ Wheelchair   ☐ Guerney

IMPRINT AREA

Tpr	BP	WT	HT

Prothesis	Yes	No	Comments
Dentures	☐	☐	
Bridges	☐	☐	
Glasses	☐	☐	
Contact lens	☐	☐	
Hearing Aid	☐	☐	
Hair piece	☐	☐	
Artificial limbs	☐	☐	
Other	☐	☐	

ORIENTATION TO NURSING UNIT

☐ Call light   ☐ Side rails
☐ Visiting hours   ☐ Telephone
☐ Overbed lights   ☐ Tray time
☐ Overbed table   ☐ Bathroom
☐ Bed control   ☐ T.V.
☐ Valuables   ☐ Electric. Appl.

DISPOSITION OF VALUABLES

NA LVN OR RN SIGNATURE

RNs ONLY TO COMPLETE SECTIONS BELOW

ALLERGIES   FOOD   DRUG   OTHER

Limitations	Yes	No	Comments	Limitations	Yes	No	Comments
Sight	☐	☐		Orientation	☐	☐	
Hearing	☐	☐		Speech	☐	☐	
Skin sensation	☐	☐		Language	☐	☐	
Mobility	☐	☐		Other	☐	☐	

1. Reason for admission and expectations

2. Duration of present illness

3. Previous hospitalizations, other illnesses

4. Medications

5. Diet preference

6. Hygiene

7. Sleep

8. Bowel and bladder

MEDICAL CENTER

DATE
ROOM NO.

IMPRINT AREA

HOUR INTAKE AND OUTPUT RECORD

TIME	INTAKE					TIME	OUTPUT						
	ORAL	I.V.'s					URINE		OTHER				
	AMT	BTL. #	AMT	Blood	Other		Voided	Cath	N/G	Emesis	Drain	Irrig	
8⁰ Tot													
8⁰ Tot													
8⁰ Tot													
24⁰ Tot													
24⁰ INTAKE =						24⁰ OUTPUT =							

8 (5-78)

CONDITIONS OF ADMISSION TO_____HOSPITAL

1. NURSING CARE

This hospital provides only general duty nursing care unless upon orders of the patient's physician the patient is provid
more intensive nursing care. If the patient's condition is such as to need the service of a special duty nurse, it is agre
that such must be arranged by the patient or his/her legal representative. The hospital shall in no way be responsible f
failure to provide the same and is hereby released from any and all liability arising from the fact that said patient is r
provided with such additional care.

2. MEDICAL AND SURGICAL CONSENT

The patient is under the care and supervision of his/her attending physician and it is the responsibility of the hospital a
its nursing staff to carry out the instructions of such physician; the undersigned recognizes that all physicians and surgec
furnishing services to the patient, including the radiologist, pathologist, anesthesiologist and the like, are independe
contractors and are not employees or agents of the hospital. The undersigned consents to X-ray examination, laboratc
procedures, anesthesia, medical or surgical treatment, or hospital services rendered the patient under the general a
special instructions of the physician.

3. RELEASE OF INFORMATION

To the extent necessary to determine liability for payment and to obtain reimbursement, the hospital may disclose portic
of the patient's record, including his/her medical records, to any person or corporation which is or may be liable, for all
any portion of the hospital's charge, including but not limited to insurance companies, health care service plans or worke
compensation carriers.

4. PERSONAL VALUABLES

It is understood and agreed that the hospital maintains a safe for the safekeeping of money and valuables, and the hospi
shall not be liable for the loss or damage to any money, jewelry, documents, furs, fur coats and fur garments or oth
articles of unusual value and small compass, unless placed therein, and shall not be liable for loss or damage to a
other personal property, unless deposited with the hospital for safekeeping.

5. FINANCIAL AGREEMENT

The undersigned agrees, whether he/she signs as agent or as patient, that in consideration of the services to be render
to the patient, he/she hereby individually obligates himself/herself to pay the account of the hospital in accordance with t
regular rates and terms of the hospital. Should the account be referred to an attorney for collection, the undersigned sh
pay actual attorney's fees and collection expense. All delinquent accounts shall bear interest at the legal rate.

6. ASSIGNMENT OF INSURANCE BENEFITS

The undersigned authorizes, whether he/she signs as agent or as patient, direct payment to the hospital of any insuran
benefits otherwise payable to the undersigned for this hospitalization at a rate not to exceed the hospital's regular charges. It
agreed that payment to the hospital, pursuant to this authorization, by an insurance company shall discharge said insuran
company of any and all obligations under a policy to the extent of such payment. It is understood by the undersigned that h
she is financially responsible for charges not covered by this assignment.

7. HEALTH CARE SERVICE PLANS

This hospital maintains a list of the health care service plans with which it has contracted. A list of such plans is availat
upon request from the financial office. The hospital has no contract, express or implied, with any plan that does not appe
on the list. The undersigned agrees that he/she is individually obligated to pay the full cost of all services rendered
him/her by the hospital if he/she belongs to a plan which does not appear on the above-mentioned list.

* * *

The undersigned certifies that he/she has read the foregoing, receiving a copy thereof, and is the patient, or is du
authorized by the patient as patient's general agent to execute the above and accept its terms.

Date	_Patient/Parent/Guardian_
Time	*(If other than patient, indicate relationship: _____*
	For purposes of Financial Agreement, Assignment of Insurance Benefi
Health Care Service Plan, if financial responsibility assumed by other th
patient, parent or legal guardian:
Date	
Witness	

A COPY OF THIS DOCUMENT IS TO BE DELIVERED TO THE PATIENT

CONSENT TO OPERATION, ADMINISTRATION OF
ANESTHETICS, AND THE RENDERING OF OTHER
MEDICAL SERVICES

Date_____

Hour_____ ____M.   _____
                                    Name of Patient

1. I authorize and direct_____M.D.

any surgeon and/or associates or assistants of his choice to perform the following operation upon me_____
_____

and/or to do any other therapeutic procedure that (his) (their) judgment may dictate to be advisable for the patient's well-being. The nature of the operation has been explained to me and no warranty or guarantee has been made as to the result or cure.

2. I hereby authorize and direct the above named surgeon and/or his associates or assistants to provide such additional services for me as he or they may deem reasonable and necessary, including, but not limited to, the administration and maintenance of the anesthesia, and the performance of services involving pathology and radiology, and I hereby consent thereto.

3. I understand that the above named surgeon and his associates or assistants will be occupied solely with performing such operation, and the persons in attendance at such operation for the purpose of administering anesthesia, and the person or persons performing services involving pathology and radiology, are not the agents, servants or employees of the above named hospital nor of any surgeon, but are independent contractors and as such are the agents, servants, or employees of myself.

4. I hereby authorize the hospital pathologist to use his discretion in the disposal of any severed tissue or member, except_____

                        Patient's Signature_____

                                Witness_____

(If patient is a minor or unable to sign, complete the following:)

Patient is a minor_____, or is unable to sign, because_____

_____   _____
          Father   Guardian

_____   _____
          Mother   Other Person and Relationship

_____
          Witness

LEAVING HOSPITAL AGAINST MEDICAL ADVICE

Name of Hospital_____

This is to certify that _____,
a patient in the above-named hospital, is leaving the hospital against the advice of the attending physician and the hospital administration. I acknowledge that I have been informed of the risk involved and hereby release the attending physician, and the hospital, from all responsibility and any ill effects which may result from this action.

_____   _____
Date   *Patient/Parent/Guardian*

If signed by other than patient, indicate relationship:

_____   _____
Witness

PERMISSION FOR DISPOSAL OF
SEVERED MEMBER

TO WHOM IT MAY CONCERN:

I do hereby authorize and direct the pathologist of the above named hospital to use his discretion in the disposal of the member,

_____, severed from my body at
(specify)

the time of the operation performed upon me _____
(date)

Witness: Signed:_____
(full name)

_____ Date _____ Hour _____

CONTRIBUTION OF ANATOMICAL GIFT

Donor _____ Date _____

Recipient _____ Time _____

1. In the hope and with the expectation that this contribution will inure to the advancement of medical science and education and/or will benefit the above-shown recipient by preservation or prolongation of his or her life and well being, I, a person authorized by the   Anatomical Gift Act to make this contribution, do hereby authorize the retention, preservation, donation and/or transplantation of the following anatomical gifts: _____

_____

_____

2. I hereby acknowledge that this authorization is volunteered without obligation of any kind on the part of the recipient, this hospital, or any individual or organization authorized by law to receive this contribution and that this authorization is motivated exclusively by humanitarian instincts without hope or expectation of reward or compensation of any kind. I therefore release and surrender any and all claims which may now have or which may be acquired by my legal representatives or me against my physician, his associates, this hospital, its agents or employees, any recipient or authorized individual or organization.

3. This contribution and authorization is subject to and expressly conditional upon the following conditions:

_____

_____

Signed: _____

Relationship, if signed for or on behalf of donor:

_____

Witness: _____

Witness: _____

Patient's Copy
PATIENT-PHYSICIAN ARBITRATION AGREEMENT

1.   It is understood that any dispute as to medical malpractice, that is as to whether any medical services rendered under this contract were unnecessary or unauthorized or were improperly, negligently or incompetently rendered, will be determined by submission to arbitration as provided by California law, and not by a lawsuit or resort to court process except as California law provides for judicial review of arbitration proceedings. Both parties to this contract, by entering into it, are giving up their constitutional right to have any such dispute decided in a court of law before a jury, and instead are accepting the use of arbitration.

2.   I voluntarily agree to submit to arbitration any and all claims involving persons bound by this agreement (as set forth in Article 3) whether those claims are brought in tort, contract or otherwise. This includes, but is not limited to, suits for personal injury, actions to collect debts, or **any kind of civil action.**

3.   I understand and agree that this Patient-Physician Arbitration Agreement binds me, my heirs, assigns, or personal representative and the undersigned physician, his/her professional corporation or partnership, if any, his/her employees, partners, heirs, assigns, or personal representative, and any consenting substitute physician. I also hereby consent to the intervention or joinder in the arbitration proceeding of all parties relevant to a full and complete settlement of any dispute arbitrated under this agreement, as set forth in the Medical Arbitration Rules included in this booklet.

4.   I agree to accept medical services from the undersigned physician and to pay therefor. I UNDERSTAND THAT I DO **NOT** HAVE TO SIGN THIS AGREEMENT TO RECEIVE THE PHYSICIAN'S SERVICES, AND THAT IF I DO SIGN THE AGREEMENT AND CHANGE MY MIND WITHIN 30 DAYS OF TODAY, THEN I MAY REVOKE THIS AGREEMENT BY GIVING WRITTEN NOTICE TO THE UNDERSIGNED PHYSICIAN WITHIN THAT TIME STATING THAT I WANT TO WITHDRAW FROM THIS ARBITRATION AGREEMENT. After those 30 days, this agreement may be changed or revoked only by a written revocation signed by both parties.

5.   I agree to be bound by the Medical Arbitration Rules of the California Hospital Association and California Medical Association and the CHA-CMA Rules for the Arbitration of Hospital and Medical Fee Disputes hereby incorporated into this Agreement.

6.   I have read and understood the attached explanation of the Patient-Physician Arbitration Agreement and I have read and understood this Agreement, including the Rules, and this writing makes up the entire arbitration agreement between me and the undersigned physician.

NOTICE: BY SIGNING THIS CONTRACT YOU ARE AGREEING TO HAVE ANY ISSUE OF MEDICAL MALPRACTICE DECIDED BY NEUTRAL ARBITRATION AND YOU ARE GIVING UP YOUR RIGHT TO A JURY OR COURT TRIAL. SEE ARTICLE 1 OF THIS CONTRACT.

DATED: _____, 19____

_____
(PATIENT)

Physician's Agreement to Arbitrate
    In consideration of the above-named patient's promise to be bound by this Patient-Physician Arbitration Agreement, I likewise agree to be similarly bound by its terms, as set forth in this Agreement and in the Rules specified in paragraph 5 above.

DATED: _____, 19____

_____
(PHYSICIAN)

_____
(TITLE—e.g. PARTNER,
PRESIDENT, ETC.)

_____
(NAME OF PARTNERSHIP OR
PROFESSIONAL CORPORATION)

Index

Abdominal surgery, 111, 118
Activity (exercise), 49–50, 116–17,
    118; in cardiac rehabilitation, 89;
    stress test, 140–41; translation of
    doctor's orders re, 281
Acupressure, 245
Acupuncture, 245
"Acute" hospitals, 8
Addiction, drug, 67–68
Adhesions, 111
Admissions, hospital, 15–23, 24–26ff.,
    163–64; Conditions of Admission,
    171–72, 288; emergency room,
    78–79; what to bring, 17–19
Against medical advice (AMA), leav-
    ing, 79, 178, 181, 224, 290
Aides, 211, 216; nurse's, 208, 212
Al-Anon, 94
Alcoholic rehabilitation, 93–95
Alcoholics Anonymous, 93
Allergies, 21
Alternative birth centers, 246–47
Ambulances, 74, 76–77
American Arbitration Association,
    190
American Cancer Society, 248
American Heart Association, 76
American Hospital Association,
    166
American Medical Association,
    191–92
American Red Cross, 75
Amputated members, 174, 290
Anatomical gifts, 177–78, 263, 291
Anesthesia (and anesthesiology),
    111–12ff., 216 (See also Surgery);
    and bladder function, 56; charges
    for, 223; and empty stomach, 48;

general, 111–12, 114–15; and IVs,
    51; local and spinal, 114–15
Anesthesiologist, 216. See also Anes-
    thesia
Anesthetist, 216
Angiography, 133, 137
Anoxia, 261–62
Anxiety, surgery and, 120–23
Antabuse, 93
Antibiotics, myths re, 66, 68
Antiembolism stockings, 87
Antineoplastic drugs, 66
Appendix, 107
Arteries, 108. See also Cardiac cath-
    eterization
Aspirin, 66
Assertive behavior, 28
Augmentation mammaplasty, 167–69
Autopsies, 174–75, 176–77

Back pain, low, 111
Backward incentive, 13, 228–31
Barbiturates, myth re, 68
Barium enema, 131
Barium swallow, 131
Bathing, 50
Bathrooms, emergency button in, 29
Bed, buttons to control, 30
"Bed crunch," 16
Belly button, surgery and, 125
Bernstein test, 133
Bile, 122
Bills, 11, 220–25 (See also Insurance);
    ambulances and, 76–77; cutting,
    278–80; and malpractice, 188–89
Birth centers, alternative, 246–47
Bladder catheters, 55–57
Blankets, 18